THE URBAN PLANTATION

THE URBAN PLANTATION

Racism & Colonialism in the Post Civil Rights Era

Robert Staples, Ph. D.

THE **BLACK**SCHOLAR PRESS ■ Box 2869 ■ Oakland, CA 94609

Acknowledgements

Chapter 7 of this book originally appeared in *Mental Health: A Challenge to the Black Community*, Lawrence Gary, ed., Philadelphia: Dorrance and Company, 1978, pp. 73-94. Copyright 1978 by the Institute for Urban Affairs and Research. Reprinted by permission.

Chapters 3 and 5 originally appeared in the *Western Journal of Black Studies* (Spring 1983 and Summer 1984). Reprinted by permission of the *Western Journal of Black Studies* and Washington State University Press.

First Printing 1987

LC #85-73439

ISBN #   0-933296-13-4 (paper)
          0-933296-12-6 (cloth)

Printed in the United States of America

Published by:
The Black Scholar Press
P.O. Box 2869
Oakland, CA 94609

Dedication

To Robert Chrisman,
a foe of the urban plantation,
and
My Brothers,
John and Melvin,
two of its victims.

CONTENTS

INTRODUCTION

Some years ago Marx stated that the class struggle is the paramount conflict between the human species. While that may be the ultimate and decisive battle, the interim clashes between religions, genders and races have taken front stage in some capitalistic societies, especially the United States. The U.S. is a nation founded on the displacement of the non-white aboriginals, and race has occupied a central role in its social organization. Unlike the racial homogeneity of its European homelands, the United States fought a brutal civil war over the status of its black denizens, and 100 years later, had its social fabric torn apart by a civil rights movement and race riots in its major cities. With ostensible racial harmony prevailing in the 1980's, proclamations have been issued that the U.S. has become a color blind society. What has happened is that race and racism have taken a different form in the post-civil rights era. It is the purpose of this collection of critical essays to examine the changing forms of racial oppression in the context of larger changes in U.S. society in the 1970's.

The civil rights movement of the 1960's was originally based on attaining the narrowly defined goals of equal rights of citizenship. From that point it expanded into an evolving ideology of black power, which was generally defined as self-determination for black communities. As the movement against white racism took on violent forms, the ruling elites responded with both concessions and the brutal suppression of the most militant leaders and organizations. By the mid-1970's the black movements had spawned a host of imitators among women, gays, ecologists, other racial minorities and the disabled. While all of these other groups had legitimate grievances against the ruling order, their combined struggles against the political-economic hegemony strained the capacity of capitalism to maintain itself and democratize the social order. Waging an unsuccessful neo-colonial war in Vietnam, besieged by political scandals and buffeted by the increase of third world nations' revolts against imperialism, the U.S. fell into an economic decline in the 1980's.

Meanwhile, black Americans were largely bereft of a central leader or ideology in the 1970's. Three ideological tendencies evolved during that period. One that was encouraged, even forced upon blacks, by the society was assimilation and acculturation. In one sense blacks were already more acculturated than most white Americans, having lived on the American continent for 400 years. Added to the old acculturation was the sharing of white America's interests and a denial that blacks had any special interests as a racial group apart from the goals defined by the white rulers.

A second tendency that developed was that of parallel institutions. Using white-oriented institutions as models, blacks developed or expanded their own institutions, with black leaders, to meet their needs. This ideology was implemented by electing blacks to political office, creating the concept of black capitalism and striving to improve predominantly black schools and colleges. While this ideology ran counter to the assimilation tendency, it enjoyed limited success because, even in the new color blind society, blacks were still physically and socially segregated from most of white America.

The third ideological force, rather minor in impact, was the separatist, nativist tendency. This group defined its relationship to the Euro-American majority as an internal colony subject to all the dynamics of classical colonialism in Africa, Asia and Latin America. Separatists related ideologically to other third world countries, particularly the revolutionary politics of Cuba, Grenada and Tanzania. A pride in black culture was combined with radical political ideologies in tune with the evolution of the black community in the 1970's. Nativists formed organizations such as the National Black Political Assembly, published magazines like *The Black Scholar* and made alliances with radical third world countries.

The three ideological tendencies are not mutually exclusive nor the only ones that exist in the black community. However, they were the dominant responses to black minority status in the 1970's and 1980's. Undergirding my own analysis is the internal colonialism model, which views blacks as an exploited class and racial group, two inseparable units of analysis. The tenets of that model are explained in the first chapter. I have chosen the title *The Urban Plantation* because it illustrates the race and labor problems of modern cities in the United States. Industrial capitalism has replaced the plantation owner, and mayors, often black, have supplanted the overseer. Capitalist exploitation still prevails although labor is theoretically free to sell itself to the highest bidder. This exploitation retains the goals of securing a cheap and disciplined labor supply by maintaining the racially based system of labor selection and dividing the working class by its racial caste organization.

These essays trace changes in the black condition since the civil rights marches and establishment of national legislation to effect equal opportunity for all Americans. Beginning with the theoretical perspective that blacks in the U.S. are an internal colony, I attempt to dissect and examine changes in black life during the last two decades. My major conclusion is that fundamental changes have not occurred that alter the basic relationship of blacks to whites in a racially stratified society. The substance of that relationship remains white superiority and black subordination as the dominant racial motif in U.S. social structure.

The urban plantation is an extension and refinement of antebellum plantation life, where the slave quarters have been supplanted by urban ghettos. Cities are nothing more than plantations controlled by whites who dictate order to the black overseers. Schools have become holding prisons for black youth. Rebels are consigned to prisons, and others are infused with alcohol and drugs. The colors of the rulers have changed as blacks take over the reins of the political and educational systems in large cities. However, the dynamics of internal colonialism leave the control of economic power firmly in the hands of whites.

Through the employment of an international perspective, I examine the status of non-white peoples in areas colonized by white settlers. Finding an amazing similarity in the status of non-whites in white settler societies led me to the development of a Theory of the Fourth World. This world consists of those non-white peoples who have fallen under the influence and domination of Europe's displaced peoples in various parts of the world. My studies of Aboriginals in Australia and Mauri in New Zealand indicate that the outcome of European penetration in non-white occupied territory has been the disruption of native culture and institutional subordination of indigenous peoples.

Among the subjects I explore are the relationship between race and crime, the role of blacks in politics, how internal colonialism has impacted upon the black family, the depiction of blacks in the media, how racial ideology shapes the educational system, and an analysis of the constituent elements in the urban plantation.

Much of this material has been published before, primarily in *The Black Scholar*. With the exceptions of Chapters 1, 8 and 9, all of the essays were written after 1983. All of them have been revised and where possible, studies and statistical data have been updated. The revisions have been extensive enough that the majority of the book's material is new. I have arranged the essays in such a way to give the book a unity and continuity. Part One consists of my own conceptual model for analyzing black life in the United States, a critique of the Pan-Africanist model and the emergence of a Theory of the Fourth World. Part Two deals with the mechanism of institutional racism used by the dominant group in the forms of higher education, the criminal justice system and the mass media. The last part describes neo-colonialism in the black community as it impacts on the family and political structures. My final chapter on "The Urban Plantation" describes the plight of blacks in urban locales.

Since these essays were written over a period of time, I cannot thank all the people involved in their production. Among the people I would like to thank are Sally Maeth, who typed both the original chapters and the revisions. JoNina Abron worked most closely with me in editing, typesetting and promotion and has my gratitude. Larry Loebig urged publication of the book and played a very instrumental role in its final creation. I am grateful to Terry Jones, who co-authored the chapter on black media images and made critical comments on the book's organization. Last, but certainly not least, I am indebted to my publisher, editor and companero, Robert Chrisman, who spent the equivalent of a month working with me on the book's thematic sturcture, ideas and content and arranged for its publication. As he has been throughout my career, Robert Chrisman was a source of inspiration intellectually, spiritually and emotionally. While the book is the product of a group effort, I am responsible for its final form and any shortcomings.

Robert Staples
San Francisco

Part I:
Theory and Ideology

CHAPTER ONE

Race and Colonialism: Theory and Praxis

In the post-slavery years various theoretical perspectives have competed as an explanation of the status of Afro-Americans in the United States. Until the last 20 years those theories were all in the range of biological determinism to racial equality through assimilation. While Pan-Africanism took hold as a social movement during certain early periods, it never fitted into the mainstream of scholarly thought about the condition or fate of Afro-Americans until recent years. After assimilation concepts were put to a reality test by the civil rights movement during the 1960's and found wanting, a more nationalist orientation emerged among black intellectuals in the late '60's. Along with a renaissance of Marxist theory, the theoretical perspective that began to dominate the scholarly interpretation of black life was internal colonialism.[1]

This transformation in theory and ideology arose because blacks began to define the nature of their situation, to write their own books and publish through black-controlled media. Members of the liberal sociological establishment either retained their faith in assimilation as a solution to the race problem, retreated from the study of race relations or in a few cases became part of an intellectual neo-conservative white backlash. As conceptual models Pan-Africanism and Marxism seemed more relevant to the black reality. Pan-Africanism filled the need to link up the cultural unity and common struggle of peoples of African descent while Marxism stressed the class exploitation of the black population. Both models, however, have limited visions of black life. As William Strickland has noted, "The Pan-Africanists seemed to want to substitute the African reality for the American while the Marxists appeared to feel that only the Russian and Chinese experiences were meaningful."[2] Although still in the embryonic stage, the internal colonialism model promises to combine the elements of Pan-Africanism and Marxism into a syncretic theoretical framework. This model arose in response to the deficits of conventional race relations theory.

THE COLONIAL MODEL

Colonialism is a social system traditionally characterized by a state's establishment of political control over a foreign territory and a settlement of members of the home state to that territory for purposes of exploitation and political hegemony. It has existed for many centuries and was practiced by the ancient nations of China, Greece and others. During the 19th century the demarcation of the color line became important in colonization efforts as European peoples established control over the third world continents of Asia and Africa. In those countries that came under colonial domination, the administration of their social and economic life was in the hands of Europeans. Non-white natives became wards of the white community or politically subordinated.[3]

Within the period of non-white colonization the practice took on a number of different forms. The prominent feature of this system is the control of the institutions of a native people by foreigners and predominantly by Europeans. The United States never had much of a formal colonial empire in the classical sense although some consider the situation of Mexican-Americans, Native Americans and Puerto Ricans examples of pure colonialism.[4] Historical records also reveal that the founding fathers considered colonization as the favorite solution to the race problem. Numerous proposals were put forth from Jefferson to Lincoln to establish free blacks as a separate colony in some foreign land where they would eventually gain their independence. Such efforts failed because of the refusal of free blacks to emigrate to a foreign land, although Liberia and Sierra Leone were colonized by American blacks.[5]

When the question of colonialism began to be of scholarly interest in the United States, it was paradoxically after the system of European domination over peoples of color was ostensibly in a declining state. By far the most influential writer on the colonial situation was the late psychiatrist and activist from Martinique, Frantz Fanon. As was true of other black intellectuals, he was initially an advocate of assimilation of colonial blacks to French culture,[6] but later developed a theory of colonialism and race which emphasized the necessity of violence, cultural and national autonomy among those he called the wretched of the earth.[7] It is on the basis of his writings that many of the internal colonialism works are dependent for their analysis of colonialism as a domestic form in the United States.

The concept of internal colonialism is not all that recent. One of the first discussions of oppressed minorities as a colony came from V.I. Lenin who raised the issue of self-determination for oppressed minorities within a nation.[8] While the issue was raised, it was never joined by Lenin, Trotsky, Stalin or other Marxists who have continued to conceive of black Americans as super-oppressed members of the working class. In the last 25 years there have been numerous references to Afro-Americans as a colonial people by students of race relations. One of the earliest statements came from writer Harold Cruse who wrote in 1962 that, "The only factor which differentiates the Negro's status from that of a pure colonial status is that his position is maintained in the home country in close proximity to the dominant racial group."[9] Another work which echoed the internal colony theme was published in 1965 by Kenneth Clark who charged that "The dark ghettos are social, political, educational, and—above all—economic colonies. Their inhabitants are subject peoples, victims of the greed, cruelty, insensitivity, guilt and fear of their masters.."[10]

These and other references to Afro-Americans as colonial subjects began to appear more frequently in the black literature of the '60's. Probably the most sophisticated sociological exposition of the internal colonialism model derived initially from the works of a white sociologist, Robert Blauner.[11] In describing the characteristics of internal (or domestic) colonialism, he equates the situation of Afro-Americans as being similar to classical colonial societies because of the coercion involved in the relationship between the colonizer (Euro-Americans) and the colonized (Afro-Americans), the involuntary modification of native values and the presence of racism which ranks racial groups into superior-inferior categories. He also acknowledges the limitation of this perspective in that classical colonialism has a different ratio of colonized to colonizer, a more developed culture among native inhabitants and a less intense ghettoization of natives. Moreover, a major theoretical deficiency he admits to is the failure of this model to account for more than the effects of racism and the exploitation based on it.

In the 1970's the concepts of Fanon and Blauner were expanded upon and empirically tested by a number of social scientists. As we pass the halfway mark of the '80's, the concepts have clearly gained ascendancy as the explanatory model for the contemporary black condition. It is a theory which has developed out of the movement for black liberation. As Marx had noted, "Theory becomes a material force as soon as it has gripped the masses." A new generation of radical—and predominantly third world—behavioral scientists has emerged to question the traditional assumptions that America is a society bound together by a basic consensus on values and that assimilation into mainstream culture, as it presently stands, is the most fruitful path to social parity for racial minorities.[12] However, there are problems in the definition and measurement of internal colonialism that must still be resolved.

FOCUSES OF STUDY

The main concern of the internal colonialism model is the structural inequality between racial groups and the dynamics of social institutions and practices that maintain racial differentials in access to social values and participation in the society. It focuses on structural variables instead of exploring individual motivations. The consequences of colonialism can be brought about without conscious intent. Blauner has noted that the processes involved in majority group domination may frequently be unintentional in contrast to individual racism which is inclined to be more direct and volitional. Hence, there may be advantages to all Euro-Americans from a colonial system, whether they wish or take them, because racism is built into institutions which inherently discriminate against racial minorities and from which tangible benefits accrue to racial majorities. As an example, the systematic exclusion of blacks from major institutions such as the economy, education, law and the polity opens up opportunities to Euro-Americans who might otherwise occupy a lesser position in a society that it is also stratified by class.[13]

A major point of departure from traditional theories of race relations is the study of the system of racial domination itself, especially the mechanisms whereby the ruling elites in the majority group maintain their hegemony. The process by which they manage to maintain, adapt or modify the existing system of domestic colonialism comes under scrutiny. For instance, a decline in overt racism such as segregated schools and total exclusion from other institutions is replaced by racial tokenism and the emergence of a symbolic racism, which is characterized by negative public reaction to symbols like affirmative action, welfare, and crime—phenomena that may be non-racial in denotative meaning but that are associated primarily with blacks. These are the social processes which reveal the ways in which racial domination is maintained and the specter of race kept alive in the public consciousness. A politician's appeal to the body politic on these issues is simply a covert way of exhorting the majority group to consolidate its racial gains.[14]

Culture and the values it produces also come under investigation. Colonial society constructs hierarchies of culture with the Euro-American values occupying a domineering position. Perforce, the culturally distinct racial minority finds itself being judged by how close it conforms to Ango-Saxon cultural norms. At the same time the colonized groups are the victim of an historical and social process which served to destroy much of their culture in its original form and substitute the American cultural values and goals without the means with which to achieve them. Culture then becomes an element in colonial rule by its attempt to stereotype groups which are culturally different and to use this as the raison d'etre of racial exclusion. On the other hand indigenous cultural forms may be assets in the colonized group's struggle for survival. The consequence of its acculturation while the essential features of racial colonialism remain unchanged may be to render it more vulnerable to certain social forces.[15] For instance, abandoning the black value of communalism for individual expression means subordinating collective needs to personal desires, a practice which undermines the group's ability to effectively resist the vicissitudes of colonialism.

Historical epochs should also be a matter of concern. Colonialism is not a static system and can take on different forms in various periods. The colonization that existed during slavery is qualitatively different from the system that prevails in contemporary urban America. Racial oppression as well as the ideology that sustains it have changed as the imperatives of political and economic conditions require modifications in its character. Only through an historically oriented model can we begin to understand the colonization of Afro-Americans as a series of links in a chain of events which have as their basic commonality a structure of white superordination and black subordination. Historical analysis also allows us to extract the distinctive black cultural forms which comprise its heritage, that reflect the struggles it waged under conditions and circumstances it was forced to face.

Status ordering systems should also be a subject of concern to adherents of the colonial model. To the extent that racial membership is associated with status, we would expect to find some kind of prestige ranking by race-linked phenomena. The standards of a colonial society will automatically confer a higher value on traits and values associated with the Euro-American majority. Thus, their language, food habits, sexual behavior, standards of beauty and other characteristics will be considered superior to those customs which are different. Occupations may be race-linked with the higher paying, high status jobs reserved for members of the majority group with the colonized minority being relegated to the low-paying, low status positions. Even with no differentials in income, certain jobs which are considered dirty or servile may be eschewed by Euro-Americans because they are regarded as being unbecoming to members of their racial group. An excellent example of this racial status connection was the almost absolute concentration of Southern blacks in jobs such as garbage collectors and domestic servants.[16]

The basic focuses of study in the internal colonialism model are racial inequality and the social processes which create and maintain it. Racial differentials in status and income are rarely seen as an accidental outcome of random causes but rather as the calculated effect of a social system which manages to place non-white minorities consistently under the control of Euro-American majorities. Within this context exploitation takes place as a result of a system which rationalizes it as the natural order of things. The entire society is structured to produce this effect since the gains from it outweigh the loses to those in power. Those who benefit from such a system tend to look at it benignly. That includes those Euro-Americans who study race relations from the standpoint of the conqueror analyzing the vanquished. Consequently, the research relationship itself often is a function of the position individuals hold in the racial hierarchy.[17]

DEFINITION OF CONCEPTS

Concepts are distinctive terms which delineate the aspect of reality with which a conceptual model deals. These terms, generally speaking, specify the arena of investigation and the underlying assumptions that are the focuses of study. Thus, it is instructive to describe and classify some of the major or distinctive concepts in the internal colonialism model.

Alienation is a feeling of psychological deprivation arising from the belief that one does not feel a part of society, that the values of a nation are not congruent with the individual's own orientation. In the case of colonized Afro-Americans, it is best illustrated by the saying that the oppressor has no rights which the oppressed must respect. Alienation may also take the form of estrangement from one's traditional community and her or his very being as a black person. This state of mind differs from traditional Marxian definitions because colonialism is a process which not only exploits but dehumanizes the oppressed as well.[18]

Assimilation is the process by which selected members of the colonized group are brought into the institutions and world of the ruling group. Almost always this is a unilateral transaction since the values and culture of the colonized are not accorded any legitimacy under a colonial system. Often assimilation means acquiring the values of the dominant group but not being permitted entry into any of its social, economic or political life. Generally, assimilation is not permitted to the masses of an oppressed group but only to individual members selected to play important roles in the colonial order. When colonialism is transformed into a neo-colonial form, the highly assimilated members of the oppressed group will be selected to take over leadership roles because they most highly identify with the values and institutions of the colonizer.

Decolonization is the process by which the oppressed group begins to determine its own destiny and run its own affairs. Not all official efforts at granting freedom to the colonized should be considered decolonization since neo-colonialism is often the social system which supersedes colonialism. A genuine decolonization effort is breaking the psychological, cultural, political and economic shackles of the old order. It is the emergence of a new system or revitalization of traditional ways prior to the introduction of colonial rule. Former colonial nations have been known to retain the language, educational system, legal codes and other institutions of their former colonial masters. Moreover, the substance of their economic relationship with the colonizer remains fundamentally the same: The mode of production is geared to meeting foreign rather than indigenous needs.

Dependency is a feature of all colonized societies which is both economic and psychological in form. The dependency takes economic form when the trade or economic organization of the colonized group structures itself internally to meet the needs of the dominant group. In internal ghettos businesses tend to be service-oriented and inextricably linked to organizations controlled by Euro-Americans. With few exceptions, e.g., churches, funeral parlors, small restaurants and barber shops, most of the businesses in internal colonies are owned by the colonizer.[19] Racial colonialism is also believed to have a psychological effect on those subjected to domination by an alien group. It creates feelings of inferiority and fosters bonds of dependency by the colonized people upon the colonizers.[20]

Neo-Colonialism. A post-emancipation form of colonialism, it replaces members of the dominating group with selected members of the colonized nation as leaders and authority figures. Theoretically, the colonized people are granted self-determination, but they are indirectly ruled by their former colonial masters. Under internal colonialism this is manifested by the election of blacks to impressive but often powerless political offices and the establishment of black capitalism programs as a solution to black poverty. The native politicians elected will frequently cater to white values and institutions while using rhetoric of racial solidarity to get elected by the black masses. Black capitalism, whether effectively implemented or not, will only enrich a minority of the colonized population while the masses will continue to exist slightly above the misery level.[21] Neo-colonialism, however, does elevate the black consciousness to a higher level where the problem is interpreted as a function of class as well as racial oppression.

Privilege is considered by Memmi to be at the heart of the colonial relationship.[22] According to Blauner all white Americans gain privilege and advantage from the colonization of black communities. His definition of privilege is "an unfair advantage, a preferential situation or systematic headstart in the pursuit of social values."[23] While privilege is not unique to racist societies, the concept of racial privilege is unique to the dynamics of internal colonialism. In a classical colonial nation such as Rhodesia (before its revolution), composed of 278,000 whites and six million blacks, there were no visible poor whites, no whites in menial jobs and not a single white who had a black as his working superior.[24] A similar racial disparity existed in the United States of a decade ago. While the caste structure is no longer as rigid, there are still economic, political and psychological advantages that accrue to Euro-Americans on the basis of race alone. The fact that the median black family income is only 58 percent of similar white income is but one indicator of white privilege. Given the existence of a finite number of high status jobs, the underrepresentation of blacks in certain occupations redounds to the Euro-American majority.

Racism refers not to individual attitudes but to the pattern of domination in a society. In Blauner's conceptualization of the internal colonialism model, racism is but one element in the colonization process by which a group is seen as inferior or different in alleged biological characteristics is exploited, controlled and oppressed socially and psychically by a superordinate group.[25] In a similar vein Memmi regards racism as one of the best justifications of and symbols for oppression. Specifically, he defines racism as "the generalized and final assigning of values to real or imaginary differences, to the accuser's benefit and at the victim's expense, in order to justify the former's own privileges or aggression."[26] It is the congealment of individual racist attitudes into practices and institutions that brings about a society in which one racial group is dominant and the other(s) excluded or restricted in its participation in the social and economic life of the nation.

The *colonizer* defines those members of the dominant racial group who benefit from the colonization of non-whites. In an operational sense, the system is run by a small elite of this entire group who are mostly white, Anglo-Saxon and male. Although important decisions are made by this small group, there are numerous instances in which the Euro-American majority express their desire to retain their racial privileges. These instances include their votes for racist politicians, excluding non-whites from labor unions and certain neighborhoods, and their votes on state initiatives to legalize racial discrimination.[27]

The *colonized* are classified as members of those racial groups who are without power or status in their own communities. In the United States these are primarily Afro-Americans, Chicanos and Native Americans. While other groups have recently claimed minority status, e.g., women and homosexuals, their situation is qualitatively different from the former groups. The colonized (sometimes referred to as natives or fellahs) obviously differ from their counterparts in classical colonial societies in that they are a numerical minority but their essential relationship to the colonized society, and the subjugated group is powerless to effect changes in its own community. An essential commonality of classical and internal colonialism is that a high class position does not remove members of the colonized group from the vicissitudes of colonialism.[28]

RELATION TO OTHER THEORIES

As I mentioned earlier, the two competing theoretical perspectives with internal colonialism are Pan-Africanism and Marxism. Both are older theories with their own camp of followers. However, some theorists have shifted from one perspective to the other, and a few claim membership in two or three frameworks and see them as complimentary, not competitive. To deal, first, with Pan-Africanism, it is generally regarded as a political program rather than a conceptual model. Although a very old ideology, it has yet to produce a work containing a systematic analysis of its assumptions or methodologies. A working definition of Pan-Africanism is the Chrisman view that its basic premise is that people of African descent throughout the globe constitute a common cultural and political community by virtue of their origin in Africa and a common racial, social and economic oppression.[29]

Because of this model's amorphous nature, it has attracted a number of different ideologies whose common denominator is their opposition to the oppression of a group because of its race. A certain segment of the black intellectual community whose numbers are unknown, claim that revolutionary Pan-Africanism recognizes the class nature of black oppression. Some would even assert that people of African descent must define the class character of their oppression and the measures to eliminate it for themselves.[30] However, through the emphasis on racial factors conveyed via the literature and other public forums, many advocates of a black capitalism program or apolitical afficionados of a racial consciousness and personality feel quite comfortable in the Pan-Africanist movement.[31]

It is this writer's opinion that the internal colonialism perspective can accommodate many of the elements in Pan-Africanism. Up to this point it has not clearly demonstrated its potential for doing so. Most of the colonial literature has concentrated on the oppressive and exploitative character of colonialism. A significant exception and fruitful beginning is the Blauner work on black culture that accepts the authentic cultural reality of Afro-Americans while delineating the impact of racism and colonization on their cultural development.[32] Fanon also discusses the struggle of the colonized to retain and to reclaim their national culture in the face of colonialism's efforts to destroy it.[33] Perhaps a significant difference in the two models' perspectives of native culture is the Pan-Africanists' tendency to accept it as a given and use it as the basis of group unity while the colonial model views it as a dynamic element in colonized societies, constantly being attacked by racist forces and being refashioned and modified as circumstances require.

While Pan-Africanism has been criticized for not always opposing the material conditions which produce racism, some Marxists have leveled the same charge against the internal colonialism model. One such Marxist has asserted that the colony theory has appeal for radicals on the left and black capitalism proponents on the right. Furthermore, he charges that focus on the idea of underdeveloped ghetto communities distracts from the struggle against racism, war and poverty which stems from and is controlled by capitalism.[34] In part his concern is valid because the concept of blacks as a colonized people has been employed by conservative writers who are believers in capitalism as a viable system.[35] However, these same writers have never expanded upon the meaning nor significance of internal colonialism. For the most part they used the colonial analogy to dramatize the powerlessness of Afro-Americans or to draw support for the program of black capitalism.

In fact the users of the colonial model have been ideologically closer to Marxism than capitalism.[36] Some even consider themselves basically Marxists when looking beyond the question of racial exploitation. Fanon himself was a Marxist who believed socialism to be the system which will allow the colonized people to go forward more quickly and harmoniously. As he noted in his book, *The Wretched of the Earth*, "Capitalist exploitation is the enemy of underdeveloped countries."[37] On the other hand, he and many other black intellectuals saw the exclusive class perspective of Marxism as insufficient in a world where class and racial conflict are presently of equal import. Marx had focused primarily on the relationship between the workers and capitalists in Western Europe and the economic exploitation therein. The internal colonialism model addresses itself to a process and situation where racial minorities are not only economically exploited but are subjected to attacks on their cultural integrity and dehumanized as well.[38]

As the colonial model now exists, with some degree of imprecision and inconsistency, there are some salient differences between it and Marxism. In the Marxist framework, institutions are not analyzed apart from their larger setting. Its basic unit of analysis is economics and history. Hence, the concentration of blacks in certain jobs is seen, not as the *causes* of racism but the *consequences* of racism caused by a combination of economic and political factors in earlier forms of class society.[39] These factors are generally regarded as a sufficient explanation of the continued existence of racism in a capitalist society. Thus, the hope for black liberation can be found in a struggle against capitalism, not racism. As the black Marxist, Henry Winston, has declared, "Black liberation can develop only as part of a wider struggle for national control over the economic and political life of the entire country."[40]

Not all Marxists are so parochial in their view of the black strategy for liberation. Some years ago even Trotsky conceded that he saw no reason why blacks should not advance the demand for self-determination.[41] The group of Marxists known as Trotskyites have proclaimed that black demands for community control can lay the basis for broader future struggles.[42] This view is based on the premise that revolutionaries must develop those intermediary forms which will raise the political consciousness of the people. Ultimately the class and racial struggles must be joined when the material conditions and state of subjective readiness coincide. Until that time the issue of racial oppression will have to be dealt with in a nationalist framework in order to prepare for the inevitable transformation of class relations.

With that in mind the users of the colonial model have departed from or expanded upon Marxist theory. The geographical frame of Marx's analysis was Western Europe while the colonial model focuses on the non-Western world. Marx saw the bourgeoisie as playing a valuable role in developing the material forces of the capitalist world and the proletariat as the agents of revolutionary change. Fanon categorized the native bourgeoisie in colonial countries as essentially worthless and believed the

rural peasants and lumpen proletariat to be the true revolutionary force. The Marxist perspective of violence was that it was
inevitable, but Fanon insisted that it was an absolute necessity
and a critical tool in the psychological liberation of the colonized individual. Moreover, while Marx believed the
superstructure (laws, culture, politics, etc.) to be a mere appen-
dage of the economic infra-structure, the colonial model sees it
as being a pre-eminent force in colonial relationships.[43]

Notwithstanding these salient differences between the Marxist
and colonial model, most users of the colonial perspective would
acknowledge its limitations as a comprehensive explanation of
the multiple inequities that exist between classes, sexes and
races. Despite no explicit recognition in the colonial literature,
it is primarily a middle-range theory which does not satisfac-
torily link racial oppression to capitalist structure and
dynamics. But as long as racism exists and Marxism persists in
its straight economic determinist interpretation, the internal
colonialism model most adequately deals best with both exploitation and racial oppression. Blauner reminds us that America
is clearly a mixed society, both capitalist and colonial. And
neither the Marxist nor colonial model has adequately delineated
the complex interaction of class and race in such a society.[44]

CONTRIBUTIONS TO THEORY, RESEARCH AND PRACTICE

Among the major contributions of the colonial model is its
theoretical innovations. It has managed to shift the focus of
study from the victims of racial oppression to the oppressor and
his exploitative system. In turn that has created black pride,
fostered unity and militancy and pinpointed the nature of the
remedy that is required, at least for racist oppression. It lends
itself to interdisciplinary efforts because racial colonialism is a
complex of economic, psychological and sociological factors. At
the same time it has expanded upon Marxism by its incorporation of race in the vortex of oppressive modes occurring in
capitalist societies.

Research implications have been slow in emerging because of
the problem of operationalizing the concept of internal colo-

nialism with the kind of data readily available to social scientists. Jones claims that "one need only look for gross racial inequities in the outcomes of institutional operations to level charges of institutional racism."[45] Such a facile approach to the problem of linking theory to data can mean subordinating the concept to methodological convenience. At this point in time most of the works using this model have been theoretical essays or research which have used the colonial analogy in a serendipitous and unsystematic manner.[46]

To date, the most serious application of the colonial analogy has been the use of economic models in analyzing racial inequities in the marketplace. Other studies have focused on the educational system and how it penalizes racial minorities by its adherence to policies and practices which require adherence to middle-class Anglo-Saxon norms.[47] A few studies have concentrated on the criminal justice system as a function of colonial rule. The obvious racial disparities in arrests, police practices, prison sentences and related factors, make the area of crime a fertile subject for the colonial model.[48] Although psychology, history, anthropology and political science can also be generative of concepts using the colonial framework, few members of this discipline have delved into its implications so far.[49] However, this model is just beginning to gain credibility, and we may look forward to more productive research as soon as some of the problems in conceptualization are worked out.

On a practical level the model has had some effect. Throughout black and other communities, struggles have been waged to gain control over specific agencies and institutions. Among the efforts in this direction have been demands to establish a community controlled police force composed of residents of the community; efforts to exercise community control over local school districts, health centers, day care centers; promotion of a black political assembly with its own candidates and platforms; and the creation of community councils to make policy decisions and administer the affairs of the black community.

INADEQUACIES AND CONTRADICTIONS

The internal colonialism school is not without its share of critics. As might be expected many of them are members of the assimilationist tradition or biological determinism camp. They have vested interests because the colonial model calls into question their own culture and institutional loyalties. Yet, the challenges to the colonial model serve a purpose in that they sensitize us to the variations between the domestic situation and the international case. It serves to inspire further development and refinement of this perspective in order to make it a valuable tool of social analysis. However, we should not lose sight of the racial reality which brought forth the colonial model. It arose out of the conditions of black life that revealed that previous theories had failed to adequately assess this stage of a racial group's struggle for its humanity as well as freedom from economic exploitation.

Some advocates of the colonial model are in agreement with many of the critiques of their framework, particularly those that relate to the somewhat weak parallels between internal and classical colonialism. While classical colonialism itself did not take on the same form in every nation, the distinctions between it and and the domestic case should be drawn. This is particularly significant when one considers the effectiveness of the remedies prescribed for the colonized situation. At any rate the common objections raised to the colonial analogy are:

1. Colonialism is based on a spatial as well as racial relationship. Afro-Americans and Euro-Americans share the same geographic space. Moreover, whites were here first and cannot be said to have colonized an indigenous majority of blacks who had settled here prior to their arrival.[50]

2. The colonized minorities in the United States differ quantitatively from colonized people in other parts of the world. They are more concentrated within the colonial nation, have greater material advantages than their international counterparts (in part because of their country's neo-colonialism abroad) and form less of a culturally distinct group because of their partial acculturation of Anglo-Saxon values.[51]

3. The black ghettos of America are not as involuntary or powerless as has been charged by proponents of the colonial model. Although the pace is slower, they are proceeding along the same path as earlier immigrant groups who also faced

economic and political discrimination. While there are differences in the character and scale of the experiences of white ethnics, they are not sufficient to warrant the characterization of blacks as a colonized people.[52]

4. Decolonization as a solution to racial oppression is impractical and possibly harmful. In a classical colony, decolonization means establishing an autonomous economy in its territory. The black ghetto community is symbiotically linked to the nation's total economy and has no resources of its own to found a separate, viable economy. Moreover, specifying such a remedy for colonization lends itself to the neo-colonial bourgeoisie's attempt to administer the affairs of the black community in the interests of monopoly capitalism.[53] Even if a more radical organization of the colonized community was initiated, it is utopian to believe that a socialist sub-society could exist within a capitalist nation.[54]

5. Much of the colonial model is still conceptually imprecise and ambiguous. This makes it less susceptible to measurement and subsequent validation. Inequities in the outcome of institutionalized operations may be easily verified, but this alone will not distinguish blacks from certain segments of the racial majority such as white women. The other elements of colonial oppression are more elusive to operational definitions. Psychological effects or cultural repression are difficult to empirically test, particularly when they may be unevenly distributed among the black population. Because the focus is on racial oppression rather than class exploitation, it becomes conceptually problematic to distinguish between the two factors in determining causal relationships. Since the colonial model has institutional racism as its basic unit of analysis, it is still a flawed construct.

Some of these criticisms of the colonial model are being addressed by its proponents. Others may be shared by them. At this point in time none of the critiques are serious enough or strongly undergirded by alternative explanations to dissuade those of us who have placed our faith in it. As Stavenhagen has noted, "In the long run any theory will be validated by its utility as an instrument of action in the hands of organized social groups."[55] The utility of a productive conceptual model is not validated by its adaptability to statistical verification but by the practical day-to-day problem solving of real life issues. As we stand on the threshold of a society where class interests have been subordinated to racial privilege, we need a theory which will explain the relationship between races. As the struggle against oppression of all kinds ascends to a higher level, our theoretical orientation will coincide with the revolutionary efforts that break out against that ultimate source of all our ills.

SUMMARY

At this juncture in history the internal colony theory seems most relevant for understanding the complexities of race and class in a society which is both racist and capitalist. Methodological and theoretical imperfections do not diminish its explanatory power. As for the basic criticism of the discontinuity between classical colonialism and the domestic situation, the case can be made that the essential connection remains between a society whose institutional mechanisms are structured in order to achieve Euro-American domination over what are deemed to be inferior cultures and people. As one observer has noted, "Territory is merely the stage upon which these historically developed mechanisms of super-exploitation are organized into a system of oppression."[56]

As a process oriented model, the colony theory helps to explain the function of race in a society based on class and sexual exploitation. It is instructive to note, for instance, that in a period of economic decline that we witness the resurgence of public antipathy toward such race-linked phenomena as affirmative action, welfare, social programs and the plight of the cities. Even such a respected member of the establishment as the late Hubert Humphrey labeled the criticism of social programs and big government as a form of racism. An esteemed labor leader, the late George Meany, once declared that the high unemployment rate and competition for jobs could result in racial warfare. While such statements could easily be construed to be self-serving, they also illustrate how a race-ordered nation can make a powerless racial minority the scapegoat for its economic ills.

Several other trends are noticeable in the evolution of racial colonialism. Among the most pronounced ones are the accelerating pace of ghetto colonization and the erection of a neo-colonial system to deal with the natives. Almost 81 percent of the Afro-American population is situated in urban enclaves while fewer than 30 percent of the white citizenry lives in the inner city.[57] The increasing gap between the powerless and poor peoples of color in the city and affluent whites in the suburbs once led a government commission to predict that the United States would be divided into two societies: a poor black one in the central cities and an affluent white one in the suburbs.[58] What was not emphasized in that report was how involuntary this concentration of blacks into small urban land spaces is and the role of white economic institutions in creating and maintaining racial ghettos.[59]

At the same time a small but declining number of blacks is moving into the middle class and out into the suburbs. It is this same group from which bureaucrats will be selected to administer and control the black community. They will be small in number but very visible in appearance. Many of them will have acquired the credentials, values and behavior patterns of the colonizer. They will be used to promote the interests of the dominant racial group. One cannot help but note the very visible presentation of blacks in high positions as the conditions of the black masses worsens. Hence, we can expect to see more and more blacks elected or appointed to administer the decaying cities that will be primarily composed of racial minorities.

Placing these events into the internal colonial perspective helps us to understand the pace and nature of social change. Ultimately these events have to be linked to a more global theory that can connect them to wider cultural and economic causes. Moreover, the colonial analogy can be heuristic in understanding the internal functioning of the black colony, particularly for delineating class cleavages within the black community. Other internal problems of the ghetto inhabitants are best explained by the colonial perspective, particularly such phenomena as black on black crime, deteriorating marital and family relationships and psychological dislocation. Marxism does not touch on them at all, and Pan-Africanism has tended to focus on the positive features of black life while ignoring some hard realities of ghetto disorganization. In the internal colonial model is contained the promise of a fruitful tool of social analysis. It will stand or fall only as we look at it in historical perspective.

CHAPTER TWO

Pan-Africanism As Ideology and Utopia

IDEOLOGY AND UTOPIA

Most social movements have ideologies that serve to orient and justify their actions. Sociologists define an ideology as a relatively authoritative, closed and explicit belief system that commands obedience from adherents, covers a wide range of situations and is organized around one or a few pre-eminent values.[1] Black social movements have been conspicuous for the lack of an ideology or the prostitution of ideologies to serve a multiplicity of different and conflicting goals. Under the banner of nationalist ideology there are groups advocating socialism and capitalism, violent revolution and cooperation with the system. These same movements have been more heavily reliant on the charisma of a leader than an ideology. Whatever the leader said was the ideology, not a guiding set of principles that were binding upon all members of a particular group.

We also have to distinguish between ideologies and a social movement. The ideology is an articulation of ideals that set goals and guidelines for aspirations and policies. A social movement is the dynamic implementation of actions designed to reach those objectives. In some cases we have ideologies but not social movements. The ideology of black separatism is a good example. While there are a number of black separatist organizations, few are engaged in the active process of securing separation from whites for their members or the masses of black Americans. Similarly, many of the advocates of a black capitalist philosophy are themselves not private entrepreneurs but salaried employees. While there may be extenuating reasons for this seeming contradiction, it does illustrate that ideologies are statements of ideals and not necessarily related to ongoing social movements.

Within the black community over a period of time there have been a number of ideologies proposed and followed. For the most part only a small minority of Afro-Americans have been adherents of a particular ideology. It seems reasonable to assume that most blacks have simply desired liberation from the restraints of racial oppression rather than an ideological struggle over the nature of the society in which they live. This has probably been true of most groups throughout the history of the world. Revolutions have usually been carried out by a small minority with the tacit support of the majority. It is an ideology, however, that inspires that minority in a social movement to take the risks that participation in an act of resistance usually entails. It is an ideology that motivates them to pursue a course on behalf of their cause, which they would not ordinarily undertake.

Among the most distinct ideologies followed by Afro-Americans is racial separatism. Black separatism as an ideology refers to total withdrawal from white America. Where to relocate differs according to the philosophy of the particular separatist organization. Some advocate withdrawal to Africa while others designate parts of the United States as a separate black territory. In some cases the United States has been asked to grant a certain amount of land anywhere to be used to establish a black nation. The demand for land that would enable blacks to physically separate themselves from whites is a consistent goal of this ideology. Otherwise, black separatist organizations may have entirely different orientations and programs. The Nation of Islam, for instance, seems to only give token lip service to the idea of black withdrawal from white society while pursuing mostly a proselytizing and economic program. Meanwhile, the Republic of New Africa had set about trying to take over certain Southern states where it wanted to establish a black republic.

Black separatism is an ideology that specifies means instead of ends. The means is physical separation of blacks from whites because a racist society is incapable of reforming itself. Separatists are a little vague or sometimes unrealistic about the nature of the black nation. The Nation of Islam does not really describe what kind of separate territory it will create unless one is to assume that it will be modeled after the Nation of Islam. Unless the separatists can offer a radically different and infinitely more meaningful form of economic life, they cannot hope to attract the black masses away from black capitalism. However, one of the characteristics of an ideology is that it contains myths that are attractive to its followers. Promising blacks their own homeland where they will be free and enjoy prosperity is but one myth of the separatist philosophy.

One black scholar advances the thesis that the ideology of black separatism serves a useful purpose. According to Forsythe, separatism increases the options open to black people. By so doing it could speed up the realization of a harmonious pluralistic America. Moreover, due to the ever looming possibility of racial genocide, he says, separatism may be the only viable way to insure black survival. Forsythe argues that movements with a separatist orientation are tremendously important in terms of their mobilizing and therapeutic effects. These movements unleash a creative mental energy that is not found among those striving for assimilation. Moreover, he asserts, black separatist ideology decreases psychological feelings of marginality and inferiority while an integration orientation increases psychological deprivations because it has historically meant broken dreams, frustrations and exploitation. On the other hand, a separatist ideology means pride, unity, independence and power.[2]

While that may be the function of separatist ideology, it is quite clear that it has the support of few blacks. Securing land from the ruling powers of America to establish a black nation is quite unlikely. The return of Afro-Americans en masse to Africa is also improbable. No African nation is prepared or willing to accept 30 million Afro-American refugees into its midst. Bennett makes the point that the choice of either integration or separation is a false one and leaves blacks in an ideological void. Neither ideology confronts the real problem: racism cannot be dealt with in a climate of economic inequality because it is a function of labor, productive relations, money and power. Neither separation nor integration deal with that reality but only with the question of whether blacks are better off in the presence or absence of white people.[3]

One of the most distinct and durable of black ideologies was Pan-Africanism, one of the oldest and most comprehensive black belief systems. Chrisman cites as its basic premise the belief that people of African descent throughout the world form a common cultural and political community because of their origin in Africa and a similar racial, social and economic oppression.[4] Pan-Africanism contends that political, economic and cultural unity is critical to people of African descent in order to bring about an effective effort for the freedom and progress of the African peoples and nations. It has evolved into this ideology, which is not universally accepted, as a result of several movements and conferences that have occurred over a number of years. Afro-Americans largely dominated the Pan-African movement until 1945. The origin of the term Pan-Africanism is traced to the first Pan-American conference held in London in 1900 and attended by 32 delegates, primarily Afro-Americans. A larger and more significant conference was held in 1919. Both these conferences stressed the African heritage of New World blacks and protested European colonial policies in African and Caribbean nations. As the representative vehicle of Pan-Africanist ideology, the five Pan-African conferences did not go beyond stressing the need for an international community of Africans and the diaspora and protesting white colonialism in Africa.[5]

There is a need to evaluate the ideology of Pan-Africanism. First, the ideology is nebulously defined and has a different meaning for different people. Marcus Garvey, for instance, saw Pan-Africanism as the resettlement of Afro-Americans on African soil.[6] In the view of W.E.B. DuBois, we should learn about our African past and coordinate our struggle against our white oppressors. How this was to be done is unclear, and DuBois did not proceed beyond the intellectual nexus between Africans and Afro-Americans before his death.[7]

One of the better known proponents of Pan-Africanism was the ex-president of Ghana, the late Kwame Nkrumah. He saw Pan-Africanism as the fusion of African nation-states into a centralized national federation. According to Nkrumah:

I do not believe that the economic development of Africa can reach an effective stage until Africa's human and material resources have been mobilized under a Continental Union Government of Africa. But I do believe (and nothing that has happened or can happen, will swerve me from my belief), that the emergence of a continental Government of Africa will immediately make the independent states of Africa a Mighty World Influence. We shall then be in a far better position to liberate our brothers in colonial bondage and rule, to drive out imperialism and neo-colonialism from our continent, to make us a powerful ally of the Asian peoples in their own struggles against imperialism, and to make us an effective force for World peace.[8]

A revolutionary Pan-African ideology views the problems of African people on three levels: political, cultural and economic. It sees the need for developing independent black controlled political tools and institutions to bring about self-determination for the African continent and the diaspora. These tools and institutions will be employed to educate African people to a level of political consciousness that will mobilize them for a struggle against racism and imperialism and achieve their libera-tion. Culturally, Pan-Africanism seeks to free Africans and the diaspora from the cultural domination of Euro-American values and institutions. An African culture and personality must be recreated and maintained that will stabilize African-American institutions and form the guidelines for a value system that is revolutionary and humanistic. The economic aspects of Pan-Africanism reflect the traditional African values of coopera-tion and communalism. In an industrialized African nation and among the diaspora this means following the principles of scientific socialism. Economic organization is geared toward meeting the needs of its people and not the profit motives of a small elite class of the owners of the means of production.

A common and often studied theme of Pan-Africanism is its African cultural orientation. By psychological identification with Africa, Afro-Americans gain a language, a history, iden-tification and a total humanity. By emphasizing the cultural unity of people of African descent, Pan-Africanism ignores the crucial question of what kind of political and economic strategies black people need in specific geo-political contexts. This has led to the charge by some black scholars that Pan-Africanism is an all-inclusive ideology that accommodates all black people of various and conflicting tendencies into its fold. It has been asserted that its apolitical character permits it to be used by enemies of the African revolution. The culturalization of Pan-African ideology is perceived as a cheap substitute for a revolutionary struggle based on a scientific, political belief system. As a result, cynical, hustling elements manipulate the symbols of the ideology to exploit the black masses.[9]

Stokeley Carmichael (also known as Kwame Toure) has declared himself a Pan-Africanist. He states that we are first of all and finally Africans. Our fight, he agrees, is clearly a fight against both capitalism and racism. One cannot eliminate capitalism without struggling against racism. An identification with Africa will serve two purposes: to give us a language, a history, identification and a total humanity; and to provide a land base for black liberation, a land that we can say belongs to us.[10]

While this writer understands the need for a revolutionary culture, a culture that can be used to liberate the minds and bodies of black people everywhere, the need for a land base in Africa is not quite clear. As an oppressed group of colonials in white America, black Americans live in the heart of the most industrialized country in the world. Of what important use is a land base when liberation can only be achieved through the takeover of factories, businesses, the communication media and military establishment? America is not the peasant societies of Russia, Cuba and Africa. The black American's goal should not be a redistribution of land to agricultural peasants but control over the means of production.

Secondly, the question must be asked: What is the practical relationship between Pan-Africanism and black liberation in the United States? While it is certainly important to relate to an African identity and request moral support from Africans for the black struggle in the United States, what else can be realistically expected from the African peoples? If we think in terms of concrete support in the event of an armed struggle, Afro-Americans confront the reality that in order for our African comrades to even get into the United States, they must first purchase a ticket on Pan-American Airlines and apply for a visa from the American government.

THE THEORY OF AFRICAN CULTURAL SURVIVALS

The cultural nexus between black Americans and Africans, however, is an important one. In part, the dilemma of black Americans on the American continent flows from the societal definition of them as a group lacking a distinct culture of its own, yet set apart from other Americans of a lighter skin pigmentation. This denial of a black cultural ethos must be examined and rejected. No group exists without a culture. Only by defining culture in very ethnocentric or restricted terms can black Americans be said to lack a culture. As Mandel observed, "Being Jewish in the days of Nazism was in some ways similar to being black in America today. Black people can take on all sorts of pale colorations, even live identical to their white countrymen, but whenever others look at them, they are, above everything else, black, which is why many black people years ago stopped trying to disappear and decided, instead, to make the most of their indelible marking, to take pride in things they share with non-blacks and in the one special thing they share with each other."[11]

THE CULTURAL CONNECTION

For those who believe in the existence of a distinctive black culture, the question inevitably arises as what the source of that culture is. The most reasonable answer is that black culture derives from a number of diverse forces and it would be difficult to trace it to one source. Surely, a history of over 300 years of slavery and oppression has left its mark on black behavior. The socialization process is an important mechanism for transmitting the content of a culture to its youth. Within the socialization process the imitation and modeling effects of role models and behavior tend to subtly convey cultural content. The other source of Afro-American culture is the African heritage that has been retained in part over time and space.

African survival is a controversial theory that states that blacks in the diaspora have retained many of the cultural traits they brought over from the African continent. Primarily associated with the late anthropologist, Melville Herskovits, it begs the question of how they were maintained and in what form. The Herskovits answer was that some Africanisms were retained by New World blacks because they were practiced in secret, traits such as voodoo. As to the form in which they are exhibited, he claimed they were often disguised as a combination of cultural elements that had been integrated to form one cultural complex. This is the process of syncretism and is expressed in Afro-American music, language, customs, food and religion. In the case of Afro-American social organization, many characteristics regarded as European were actually African in origin. The prevalence of female-headed households, common-law marriages and respect shown to elders are but a few examples.[12]

We will discuss some of the possible African survivals in Afro-American cultural traits later. However, no matter how convenient it may be to believe that Afro-Americans are an African people in their cultural behavior, there is not sufficient evidence to reach such a conclusion. The retention of African features has a stronger case in some Caribbean and South American societies for reasons that are peculiar to them. But a group rarely is totally stripped of all its cultural heritage, especially when it lives the kind of segregated existence of American blacks. Blassingame provides us with a good evaluative yardstick for assessing Africanism in Afro-American culture with his statement that, "Whenever the elements of black culture are more closely similar to African than European traits, we can be reasonably certain that we have identified African survivals."[13]

With the exception of those who are proponents of the African survival theory, slavery would be regarded as the original source of black cultural forms that were developed in the United States. Since the Africans brought to this country represented different tribal cultures, the more uniform Afro-American culture had to evolve from a variety of cultural forms during the slavery era. Hence, the culture of the slaves combined features of their African heritage along with some elements of American culture. This process of cultural reorganization was facilitated through the social organization of the slave community. The slave's primary environment was the slave quarters where he or she interacted with fellow slaves. In that setting slaves created their own religion, songs, dances and superstitions.[14] Out of this slave culture came a unique form of language, customs, beliefs and ceremonies that serve as the basis of a distinct Afro-American cultural system. This cultural form is a blend of African traits, elements formed out of the slave experience and American patterns.

Among contemporary Afro-Americans, customs and rituals are an expected mode of behavior that meets with group disapproval if not performed in the appropriate context. In the black community, especially in Southern and rural areas, it is expected that most people will visit close friends and relatives. On these occasions the sharing of food is a normative part of the visiting routine.[15] Church going is another cultural value in Southern black communities since the church may be the center of the community's social life. Most rituals peculiar to blacks are carried out in this institutional setting. Black church services are seldom the same as in the white church (even in the same denomination). Funeral services maintain some similarity to African customs. After the deceased is buried, the mourners celebrate his journey home by dancing, singing and drinking. The body remains open to the view of others in rural Baptist churches. A collection is often taken as a form of mutual aid as the mourners file by the corpse. A prayer band and the all-night prayer meeting constitute another form of unique religious worship.[16]

Among the various fine arts that embody black culture, music is one form most related to its African origin. As in African societies, music plays a central role in Afro-American life. For blacks, music is not an event but is integrated into their daily existence. Afro-Americans rarely respond to music in a passive manner. Levine notes that unlike any other group in the United States, blacks consider music a participant activity rather than primarily a performer-audience phenomenon.[17] Afro-American music is also transmitted in the oral tradition of African societies rather than by notation as among Euro-Americans. As is true of most Afro-American culture, music is basically social and comes out of black gatherings at church, work and in the community.

There appears to be little dispute over the African origin of much of Afro-American music. There are similarities in the approach to playing the notes or tones, a relationship between the verse form in both idioms and the call-and-response pattern found in the blues and spirituals. Keil[18] claims that falsetto singing stems directly from Africa where it is regarded as the very essence of masculine expression. The singing styles of Ray Charles or B.B. King are very similar to the falsetto techniques of a West African cabaret singer.[19] Whatever its origin, Afro-American music reflects the experiences and culture of blacks in the United States. As Donald Byrd expresses it, "It is expressionism, emotionalism, spiritualism and imagery. It is form, content and the imposition of black feeling on an Aryan culture."[20]

African parallels are also found in certain forms of black dancing patterns. This is particularly true of the black church and in some forms of jazz dance. In the church, African survivals can be seen in the practice of hand clapping, foot tapping and in the ritualistic leaps during church services.[21] As typical of other black cultural forms, dance is a part of the expression of black people in social settings. The sensual nature of African dances is often reflected in Afro-American dances where body movements are not restricted as was common of Euro-Americans. Kinney has called attention to the responsorial form of dancing found in West Africa where the men interrupt the movement of their women in a call-and-response manner. She also observes a similar pattern among mainland blacks where the women interrupt the basic movements of their partners.[22]

Flamboyancy and improvisation in clothing are not recent black practices, but they seem to be pronounced cultural traits in the Afro-American community. Few blacks ever adopted the somewhat casual and sloppy dress of many white youth. Black women have been admitted for the way in which their clothing is embellished and worn. Although the reason for this cultural trait is unclear, Murray does remind us that African culture places emphasis on design and stylization. He cites the example of masklike makeup, flamboyant tribal headwear and other inventiveness found among Africans as indications that black dress styles are a possible extension of an African tradition.[23]

One of the essential ingredients in a cultural system is a distinct language and communication pattern. It is in this area that some research has been done, and there is a general consensus on the existence of a separate black language code. Disagreements do arise over its origin and value. As a form of communication, language is the medium through which culture is organized. People who have a unique language also have a separate world view. Language is the primary conveyor of cultural attitudes toward people and events. Since the shared experiences of blacks differ from whites, the language they speak forms and reflects their cultural values. As Fanon points out, "A man who has a language consequently possesses the world expressed and implied by that language."[24]

The origin and nature of what is called black English remains in dispute. Some linguists have contended that it is nothing more than a direct descent from British dialect, which the newly arrived slaves mastered in order to communicate with their masters and fellow bondsmen.[25] Contrary to this opinion is the view of others that the slaves created their own language according to the basic syntax of their West African languages. Since the slaveholders would not permit them to speak in their native tongues, they borrowed from the English language and integrated its words to the rules of their own languages.[26] Even today, linguists have noted parallels in African and Afro-American usage. There are similarities in the vowel sounds where the vowels are generally shorter and more stable, the use of the habitual tense, expression of plural nouns and multiple negatives and employment of one-gender pronouns. Seymour comments that only the legacy of West African languages can explain the regularity of such language habits among black people in various parts of the Western Hemisphere.[27]

Other racial differences exist in communication patterns. La France and Mayo found that blacks tend to look at a person when speaking to him and away when spoken to. With whites it is just the reverse pattern.[28] It has been noted that the custom of avoiding eye contact when others are speaking is typical of West Africans. Although not unique to blacks, touching is another form of communication not found among white Anglo-Saxon types. Touching is a way of establishing trust and confidence in individuals. Among many white Americans it is indicative of a sexual approach and often leads to feelings of distrust.

Afro-Americans are among the few ethnic groups in the United States to maintain a storytelling tradition that forms a part of their cultural complex. This practice of storytelling stems from the oral tradition of blacks and serves to validate cultural rituals and institutions and maintains conformity to the expected patterns of behavior. Again, we find that the folk tale was an important cultural form in West Africa. Storytelling was a normal practice that involved acting, singing and gestures. Animal stories were a particular favorite because Africans humanize animals, whom they perceive as human beings in disguise.[29] The folk tales of Southern slaves also included African animals such as lions, monkeys and elephants. Among the freedmen, the rabbit and tortoise figured prominently in their folklore. A common theme to these animal stories was the ability of the weaker animal to outwit and defeat his stronger opponent.[30] Although Brer Rabbit is no longer a prominent figure in black stories, particularly in the urban North, Hannerz has noted that black stories of today still emphasize the ability of their characters to overcome their weaknesses and triumph.[31]

Another characteristic black myth is a belief in folk cures and magic. In certain areas of the rural South, there is still a strong belief in folk remedies for illnesses. Instead of going to doctors many people use herbs to cure certain illnesses. For some illnesses, the "root man" uses magic to cast off the spell that brought about the illness. These practices are found mostly in the area of "baffling diseases, mental states and love or sex problems."[32] In urban black communities there is a strong belief in signs of the Zodiac as a guide to certain kinds of behavior. While astrology is of current interest to many Americans, this writer's observation has been that blacks have a much stronger faith in it than white Americans. Even class differences among blacks do not seem to vary the strength of their belief that there is a correlation between the signs of the moon and human behavior.

While the source of Afro-American culture may be Africa, the significance of that cultural unity may be irrelevant to the ongoing struggle of black Americans for justice and dignity in the

United States. Still, the struggle should be viewed as more than a political or economic matter. A group viewed as having no culture to defend or protect is subject to the devaluation of self in a society that has not always been hospitable to its aspirations. Pride in its ancestral homeland and awareness of its cultural source can be instrumental in mobilizing a group for political struggle. Besides the role of cultural forebear to millions of Afro-Americans, what is the significance of Africa to most of Black America?

A JOURNEY TO AFRICA

In the summer of 1984 I revisited the countries of Senegal, Nigeria and added Kenya to my itinerary. Armed with a greater knowledge of the first two countries because of my previous trips plus considerable reading on the African continent, I was a more acute observer this time. After leaving the United States, Senegal was the first country I entered. The first thing I noticed was the proliferative growth of new hotels. Senegal had become a popular tourist spot for vacationing Europeans. The hotel rates were as high as $95 a day for a single room. Not surprisingly, there were few black Africans staying in these hotels. In a country with a per capita annual income of less than $500, it was obvious that the prices were designed for Europeans and North Americans. The strength of the American dollar could not be seen in Senegal since the prices of most items in the stores were similar to prices in the United States. Most of the visible hotel staff were black Africans. When the doors of the offices were occasionally left open, there was a sea of white faces at the desks. The American or British influence was exhibited in the large numbers of Senegalese who spoke English.

During my stay in Senegal, I was constantly warned to be careful where I went. It seems the crime rate was quite high in Dakar, the major city in the country. Nobody in an official position could supply me with reliable figures on unemployment. One informant told me that about 10 percent of the native Senegalese were gainfully employed. Only 10 percent of Senegal's population is literate. While the tourist trade had increased since my last visit, the country seemed to be in worse economic condition. Part of the reason was the famine, which had produced abnormal food shortages. The lack of food in the countryside had driven many Senegalese into the cities where there was no housing or jobs for them.

Senghor had stepped down as president, and the new leader had adopted an "Africanization" policy. Thus, there were many black faces in the major businesses. The French presence was still evident. In fact, one informant claimed there were three times more French in Senegal now than before independence. Every time I asked about who lived in a magnificent house, I was told it was a Frenchman. Other than dealings necessary for conducting business, there seemed to be little social interaction between the native Senegalese and the French. The French have even managed to develop their own school system. Reminiscent of the Southern caste system in the United States, black Africans may serve you in stores and restaurants, but a Frenchman or his wife handles the money. When asked about the continued French influence in Senegal's affairs, one government official states: "Eventually the French will have to leave and be replaced by Africans, but that day is a long way off."

On to Lagos, Nigeria, where I saw a slightly different picture. Nigeria has less European influence than most African countries. It produces more than two million barrels of oil a day and ranks tenth among the world's oil exporters. However, its oil revenues of 20 billion dollars a year has to be spread among 80 million people.[33] During the heyday when oil money was flowing in, the country embarked on a massive construction of offices, hotels and housing, which could be seen in the skyline of Lagos. The increased purchase and use of automobiles has created traffic jams of unimagined proportions to most Americans.

When I noticed the heavy military presence in Lagos, I had a sense of deja vu. After a period of civilian government rule, the military regained power in January 1984. Much of the oil money never reached the masses. At least 500 former officials faced corruption charges for amassing billions of dollars. In one case alone, a group of officials was reported to have embezzled five billion dollars, which they deposited in a Swiss bank. Most of the country's development plans were in limbo as the military government tried to sort out the country's entangled financial affairs. The precipitous drop in oil prices only compounded the country's economic problems. Having experienced previous military governments, few Nigerians expressed much optimism for their country's future under military rule. Their only consolation was that they appeared to be relatively better off than other African countries.

My next visit, for the first time, was to Nairobi, Kenya, the crown jewel of the continent. Certainly, it looks much in appearance like many American cities. The tall buildings, variety of stores and restaurants and Western dress mark Kenya as the most Westernized of all African nations. It was impossible to distinguish many Kenyan women from black American women. Most wore Western clothes, had their hair straightened (or wore wigs) and often spoke in American slang. This was the only African country where I encountered any significant number of single or divorced women. Most of the men were married, and some had several wives. One deterrent to the traditional practice of polygamy was the bride price a man's family had to pay for his wife. In the large cities a wife could cost as much as 40 thousand dollars.

Kenya's reputation as the showplace of Africa is based on its stable government, thriving commerce and sizable African middle class. The underside of those characteristics is the neocolonialism that pervades Kenyan society. The stable government is a one-party state, once ruled with an iron hand by the late, former radical, Jomo Kenyatta. It is a government that has allowed deep penetration of international capital if native Kenyans were given a share. Hence, the major businesses are owned by Europeans with Kenyan minor partners, many of them government officials or members of a well-connected family. Despite the flourishing tourist trade, coffee exports and other commerce, the largest employer of native Kenyans is the government. One reason may be the large number of foreigners who reside in Kenya, more than I saw in any West African country. The merchant class is composed of Indians, who once numbered 190,000 in Kenya until native prejudice and government regulations reduced their numbers to 85,000.[34]

The Kenyan middle-class is running a system inherited from

its British colonizers, retaining the currency, language, dress and values from the days of their subjugation. Moreover, the middle class represents only a small minority of all Kenyans. The massive poverty of the country is visible on the edge of downtown Nairobi. Most housing is without indoor plumbing or electricity. The annual per capita income is $340 for those who earn wages. Most Kenyans operate outside a money economy. There is only one doctor for every 25,600 people in Kenya compared to ratio of 1:580 in Europe. Even government employees earn less than $200 a month.[35] The fear of crime is everywhere. It is not uncommon to see private security guards patrolling the homes of the elite class.

In a sense, Kenya differs from other African countries in the magnitude of neo-colonialist practices. Much of the present difficulties facing African nations are directly traceable to their colonial past. One of them is tribalism. The Africa of pre-colonial days consisted of several hundred independent states, which the Europeans condensed into about 40 pieces of territory. Consequently, very different and often antagonistic tribes were placed together in the same national boundaries. To my surprise, tribal identity operates much the same as racial identity in the United States. Members of different tribes may grow up in close proximity to each other, yet speak unrelated languages, eat different foods, wear completely different clothes and have a different cultural orientation altogether. The strength of tribalism is such that one sociologist speculated that there may be more cases of racial intermarriage in Africa than intertribal unions. A Kikuyu friend escorted me around Nairobi, and every person he introduced me to was Kikuyu. Each business we frequented was owned by a Kikuyu. His comment was, "In the U.S. you say buy black—in Kenya we say buy tribe." Tribalism pervades every aspect of Kenyan society and embraces language, religion, land ownership, marriage and education.

Kenya, like most African countries, faces a multitude of problems: inflation, crime and overcrowding plagues its cities. Most Kenyans who can afford it return to their villages where their parents still till the land. Colonialism drove many of Africa's young men out of the countryside, leaving fewer people to produce food for the cities. As a result, most African nations have become net food importers. Meanwhile, the cities cannot provide jobs for the unskilled and uneducated people who come to them, thereby creating a subterranean economy based on selling cookies, trinkets and bodies. Alongside the direct problems caused by the colonial past is the drought in Kenya, which as created food shortages. Kenya also has the highest birth rate in the world, four percent.[36] Women bear an average of eight children, something that little is done about because large families are part of the country's traditional culture; they increase a tribe's power base and represent a form of social security for the elderly.

This view of Africa represents observations filtered through the prism of a Westernized black American. Much of African life is vibrant and, despite its overwhelming poverty, the continent still has a lower rate of mental illness, drug addiction, divorce and other social problems than plague the West. Many of the native Kenyans rationalize one-party rule with the argument that an embryonic nation cannot afford the luxury of multiparty systems that would divert energies away from development and into fractious squabbling among divided tribes. This argument would have more validity if these one-party leaders were not elitists who have accumulated immense individual fortunes, disregarded human liberties and solidified their power at the expense of national well being. One graphic example of African leaders' failure to embark on a new direction, other than neo-colonialism, is the statistic that reveals that in the 1970's spending on arms increased four times faster than the continent's gross domestic product.[37] Still, it must be remembered that the African continent is only 25 years free of the shackles of colonialism. It has had to overcome the rape and pillage of its people, resources and cultures by foreigners who corrupted its borders, religions, languages and ways of life. For them the future has just begun.

RELEVANCY OF PAN-AFRICANISM

Although the cultural element in Pan-Africanist ideology has been much discussed and served as the impetus for most of the Pan-African congresses, contemporary Pan-Africanists are focusing on ways and means of improving the socio-economic conditions of Africans and blacks in the diaspora. While Pan-Africanism has been much more than a search for cultural survivals in the diaspora, it has lacked a systematic theoretical body of knowledge on which to base a unified black struggle. There is also the question of how relevant the ideology of Pan-Africanism is to achieving black liberation in the United States. Whereas one might hardly question the necessity of Afro-American pride in and identification with Africa, the problems confronting Afro-Americans must be solved in the context of the American form of oppression. Hence, Pan-Africanism must be viewed as only an interim movement in this stage of the black struggle against colonialism and racism.

AFRICAN LIBERATION MOVEMENTS AND SOCIAL CHANGE

The most salient characteristic of African liberation movements is that there are very few of them. In the last 25 years some 40 African nations have received formal political independence from their colonial rulers. With five exceptions, Zimbabwe, Angola, Mozambique, Algeria and Guinea, this independence was granted through peaceful negotiations with their European masters. As a result, native Africans took over the political machinery that had been formerly manned by Europeans, but the basic value orientation, social and political institutions and philosophy of government and education remained the same. Hence, what we find on the African continent today are three primary political segments: those areas where the imperialists and racists still endure, the regions characterized by neo-colonial control and the Africa where revolutionary transformations are taking place. Colonial Africa consists of one country, South Africa. The neo-colonial sector is composed of Zaire, Nigeria, Senegal, Kenya and others. Revolutionary Africa is very small and is primarily limited to Tanzania, Guinea, Zimbabwe, Angola, Mozambique and Ethiopia.

In colonial Africa a white minority remains in obvious control of South Africa. There are 3.5 million white settlers who are economically exploiting 16 million native Africans. With a massive infusion of foreign capital and arms, the white rulers of these countries have managed to maintain a strong control over their African subjects. The United States, for example, sends 34 percent of its African exports and 60 percent of its capital investments to South Africa. Although the upholders of apartheid maintain that the blacks are not prepared to accept equality with whites, it is a simple fact of economics. Over 87 percent of the South African land area is occupied by the 19 percent of the population that is white.[38] The low salaries paid native African workers allow almost all white settlers to lead lives of comparative affluence.

The neo-colonial political structure of most of African society results from a combination of geo-political and social factors. Instead of directly controlling African politics and economics, the European capitalists have installed educated elites to staff and operate the government. The consequence of Africans with commitment to European values and interests being in leadership roles has been a hopeless cycle of economic dependence on foreign capital in industry, finance and agriculture. As a result, there is no country in Africa with an independent economy. Those that are not in heavy debt to the Western capitalists must rely upon either the Soviet Union or China. With this control over the African economy, foreign interests continue to manipulate and dominate the African continent. African nations find themselves in the peculiar position of having formal political independence but unable to depart too radically from the policies and interests of the former colonial powers.

Revolutionary Africa has adopted progressive, anti-imperialist and even anti-capitalist measures. The non-capitalist sector of the various economies have experienced a dynamic growth, and the political leaders have worked for the progressive erosion of the positions of international capital. In the country of Tanzania, for instance, non-capitalists have tried to recreate and adapt traditional African society, based on rural socialism and self-reliance, rather than imitate capitalist Western society based on industry, urbanization and outside aid. However, these African countries are still weak in terms of economic growth and military strength, and the survival of their respective nations has been threatened in the recent past.

The direction of change in black Africa has been toward a neo-colonial structure that has become even more unresponsive to the needs of the masses. Members of the African elite class have chosen to travel paths that are to their advantage rather than give expression to the mass of grievances against the control of African natural resources by the rulers of international capitalism. One result of the native African bourgeoisie class' limitations in restructuring African society has been declining agricultural production, a decrease in their share of world trade and an increasing dependency on foreign capital. In 1981 only four African countries had an annual growth rate of five percent or more, and a dozen other countries reported a negative growth rate in the same year.[39] Changing the situation through normal political channels has become even more difficult in the last decade. There have been over 70 coups in the 27 years since independence began in Africa, which has left military rulers in charge of the affairs of most of the major African states.[40] Most of these military coups involved installing men who were more committed to the interests of foreign capitalists than their predecessors. Subsequent increases in the military budgets, the political power of the military and widespread corruption all attest to the fact that those changes in governments did not represent any progress for the African peoples. Because the struggle of the African peoples had been for national liberation, the strategy of the former colonialists to substitute native black faces for white ones has left the masses without an ideology or movement to fight against the neo-colonial regime. Africans will have to be educated to the reality that they will also have to fight Africans before they win their freedom.

It is in the colonial sector that we find the most dynamic social movements occurring on the African continent. Although African protest is in an incipient stage in South Africa, it is beginning to emerge in mild forms such as strikes and demonstrations. Guerrilla activity has spurred the exodus of many whites from South Africa, and the white youth are becoming draft resisters. Throughout the world, blacks and whites are protesting the existence of apartheid and their countries' support of that oppressive structure. Revolutionary groups have been fighting since 1961 against the last vestige of colonialism still on the African continent. Even with the aid of the United States government, South Africa is having difficulty maintaining apartheid without resistance. It has the support of the U.S. power structure, which fears that the leaders of the revolutionary movement cannot be relied upon to set up a neo-colonial structure that will maintain and protect American investments in that area.

The debate over the nature of Pan-Africanism continues. It was again joined at the Sixth Pan-African Congress, the first gathering of its kind in almost 30 years, which took place at the University of Dar es Salaam in Tanzania in June 1974. As its objectives, the Congress sought to: (1) increase understanding of the issues involved in the struggle in South Africa (2) discuss how to end economic dependency and exploitation and (3) dialogue about the fulfillment of the potential of political independence.[41] Because the Congress invited most members of the diaspora, with a variety of ideologies, it was inconclusive and bogged down in the participants' existential definitions of the nature and goals of Pan-Africanism. Some equated Pan-Africanism with socialism and a united front against imperialism while others saw black control of the African continent as the ultimate goal. The extreme cultural nationalist position was expressed by Madhubuti's comment that "we are being manipulated and duped by the Arab-Marxist clique."[42] Conversely, the left's position was represented by Baraka's observation that "basically it is the struggle between reactionary nationalism, which pulls finally for black skin privilege as opposed to white and objectively seeks to cover the oppression of the black neo-colonialists under the banner of race..."[43]

Hence, there seems to be no consensus as to the state of Pan-Africanism as a viable ideology. It also appears that Pan-Africanism as a social movement has certain millennial qualities. While its impact is minimal in the daily lives and deeds of most Afro-Americans in contemporary life, the success of Marcus Garvey and his back to Africa movement shows that Pan-Africanism can grasp the loyalty of a group brutalized by racial oppression. Black Zionism, however, can have the same negative consequences of Jewish Zionism. Instead of liberating

Jews, Zionism has used Jews as colonizing imperialist forces in the Middle East. The one example of Black Zionism was the colonization of Liberia by black Americans who oppressed the indigenous peoples and established an Afro-American surrogate for American imperialism in Liberia during the nineteenth century.[44]

African liberation is still an ideal for most of the continent. The dream of a United States of Africa is far from a reality as the artificial boundaries created by the colonialists in the form of nation-states have diverted the African struggle into intense ethnic and national rivalries. The incapacity of the African rulers to deal with the plaguing problems of drought, famine and poverty are related to the socio-economic structures of neo-colonial Africa and to the manner in which the wealth of that area is used and distributed. It seems quite clear that what is required for African liberation is a disengagement from international monopoly capital, and this goal can be accomplished only through struggle against the native African elites who remain committed to colonial values and interests.

CHAPTER THREE

Towards A Theory of the Fourth World

In the history of homo sapiens a world was generally confined to their immediate environment. As members of racial groups began to migrate to various parts of the world and cultural contact was established, worlds lost any mono-racial significance. Members of different racial groups inhabited the same continent and lived in relative harmony.

During the 20th century, worlds have been divided by ideology and color. The first world was conceptualized as North America, Western Europe, Australia and New Zealand, ostensibly political democracies with a capitalist ideology. The second world consisted of Eastern European nations with a communist ideology and a collectivized economy. The third world comprised underdeveloped nations inhabited largely by peoples of color in Africa, Asia and Latin America, who had mixed economies and were nonaligned with either first or second world nations, particularly the United States and the Soviet Union. Third world nations were largely underdeveloped.[1]

The precise criteria for categorizing nations were rarely consistent, especially those nations that belonged to the third world. Japan, for instance, is a non-white nation that is the third most industrialized country in the world while Ireland, a white country in Europe, is one of the most underdeveloped nations. During the 1960's, racial minorities in the United States began to refer to themselves as third world people because most were descended from Latin America, Asia and Africa. They saw themselves as suffering from a variation of colonialism that had beset their ancestral homelands and tried to forge an identity with those countries. While the commonality with the oppression and subjugation by white colonizers existed, it was never clear how the linkage would produce any visible changes in the condition of non-white peoples inhabiting first world nations.

During the 1970's, the term "fourth world" was introduced in a variety of forms. Horowitz applied it to tribal societies that were underdeveloped socially and culturally in addition to lacking economic and technical resources. This kind of underdevelopment was in contrast to third world nations that had mature peoples but backward economies.[2] The use of the term fourth world to denote non-white minorities in first world nations seems to appear in the work of Manuel.[3] He defined the fourth world as pre-colonial inhabitants of countries dominated by other groups. These minorities were dispersed throughout the first, second and third worlds and were characterized by a lack of autonomy, political independence, and most were tribal in nature. This definition encompasses a number of diverse groups, ranging from the Orang Asli in Malaysia, the Bedouins in Egypt, to the Miskitos in Nicaragua and Indians in North America.[4]

My own definition of the fourth world is a concept emerging. It is not a fully developed theory and may be altered as my perception and the development of this world unfolds. I diverge from other fourth world theorists by including only non-white minorities in four first world nations, Australia, Canada, New Zealand and the United States. Moreover, within those countries I designate only the Aboriginies in Australia, Maori in New Zealand, Indians and Eskimos in Canada and Indians and blacks in the United States.

My reasoning for confining the fourth world to these four nations is their common history as white settler colonies emanating from the British Isles and their present status as the most advanced and affluent capitalist countries in the first world. The inclusion of black Americans may provoke the most controversy since a common definition of the fourth world has been an indigenous group with some attachment to the land.[5] I argue that the longevity of blacks in the United States places them much in the same position to their colonizers as do the indigenous groups. Moreover, like the natives, blacks are in their first world nation involuntarily, having come to the United States as slaves while other non-white minorities came as voluntary immigrants.

The attachment to the land characteristic is a tenuous one. Only the Aboriginals and Eskimos could be said to maintain an almost exclusive relationship to the land in the sense that most of them still live off it. Most Maoris and Indians have been uprooted and urbanized and, increasingly, Aboriginals and Eskimos are moving to the cities. While the struggle of those groups is often rooted in land-based issues, the reality is one of urbanization and proletarianization. Black Americans, then, represent a vanguard and a future projection. From these unfolding social transformations we can ultimately expect ethnic identity to be replaced by a class identity. For the interim, the fourth world consists of those people who have a conscious recognition of a common identity in struggle, of common values and of common opposition to forces which oppress them not as workers but as ethnic inferiors.

Furthermore, as Stea and Wisner suggest, fourth world people are not simply enclaved minorities within large dominant societies but share a number of characteristics beyond their current situation.[6] They are all the victims of the structural unemployment and wars created by capitalism in Europe which caused the dumping of millions of whites on continents inhabited by non-whites. Not only did Europeans expropriate the land but in the process, destroyed the economic organization of the indigenous groups. The Europeans structured a society in which their culture was defined not only as superior but as the only form in which success and mobility could take place. Schools were designed to destroy native culture, language and economy in addition to socializing natives into colonial values.

What indigenous groups have in common with black Americans is the model of the black movement for social change. Due to the massive publicity afforded the civil rights movement in the United States, other fourth world groups developed national organizations to force court decisions regarding their rights and gained substantial cash compensation for past abuses. Another commonality between the fourth world groups is their continued location at the bottom of the social strata while each successive European immigrant group moved ahead of them.

IN THE FOURTH WORLD

The South Pacific is an arc of islands located on the fringe of Asia. Some anthropologists and archaeologists believe the origin of homo sapiens was in Africa and that they eventually dispersed into Europe, Asia, the South Pacific and ultimately North and South America.

Due to the necessity to adapt to their physical environment, early humankind lost some of their African characteristics but retained their pigmentation in other tropical or temperate climates. In the South Pacific there was a tripartite racial division: (1) the Melanesians, prototypically black people (2) Micronesians, a racial hybrid of black and Asian peoples who lived on islands and (3) Polynesians, a group assumed to be black in origin but amalgamated with Asian Mongoloids and white Europeans.[7] As true of other blacks throughout the world who would be classified as black by American criteria of racial membership, many of these groups have taken on a racial identity that fuses their African heritage.

Whatever their racial origins and contemporary appellation, these groups now have an American black strain in their genetic makeup. Around the middle of the 19th century, black Americans came to the South Pacific as whalers from ports in Rhode Island and Massachusetts. These black sailors were welcomed by the Pacific Islanders, who valued them for their knowledge of Western customs and their skills with munitions. Many of these black Americans mated with the native women and produced offspring that were assimilated into the Pacific Island community. Unlike the rigid American system of racial classification, the Pacific Islanders accept multiple racial identities without any invidious evaluation. Those part-black Americans are no different from Melanesians and Polynesians in physical appearance, dress, manners, language or self-identification. Hence, they are absorbed and accepted by natives of the South Pacific.[8]

Probably the greatest influx of black Americans in the Pacific Islands occurred during World War II. Many were stationed in those islands and mingled, without discrimination, among the native islanders. Some met and mated with native women, the children of such unions often being absorbed in the Pacific Island community. Others, where possible, married and brought the women to the United States.

In the white settler nations, Australia and New Zealand, Afro-Americans were not as welcome. During World War II, planes carrying black soldiers were not permitted to land in Australia. Later this policy was changed to allow black soldiers into some northern Australian territories that were affected by the war or likely areas of conflict. However, black soldiers were confined to the more squalid areas and forbidden to venture into other parts of town. Folklore has it that when black soldiers attempted to venture beyond their designated areas, white American soldiers lined up and killed them.[9]

When black Americans go on vacations or scholarly expeditions, they generally choose Europe, Africa and the Caribbean. In recent years more of them have gone to Latin American and Asian countries. A neglected area of the world has been the South Pacific. With the exception of Hawaii, an American state, few blacks know much about the South Pacific region. This is an area of the world that contains a number of blacks and Polynesians hold black Americans in high esteem and share a similar political and economic situation.

Among those countries in the South Pacific with a substantial or interesting black/Polynesian population are Australia, New Zealand, Tahiti, Papua-New Guinea, the Solomons, New Caledonia, Samoa and the Fiji Islands. Many of the groups in these a countries identify with the minority status of black Americans but do not regard themselves as members of the African diaspora. While they would be defined as black by American standards, their racial identity is often based on their geographical location, language, hair texture and religion. Africans and even some black Americans came to that part of the world years ago.

The most prominent country in the area is Australia, a nation of 14 million European immigrants and about 500,000 blacks who are indigenous to the country. Having lived in Australia for six months, this author can speak from a personal perspective of its value to black Americans.

First, we must deal with Australia's image as a racist nation.

That image is based on the white Australian immigration policy that existed until 1972. The policy, which forbade citizenship for non-whites, was originally aimed at Asians but just as strongly applied to blacks. Since Australia is surrounded by two and a half billion Asians, it was trying to prevent the loss of white control. Although few blacks applied for citizenship, they, too, were not welcome as citizens or visitors. In 1972 the restrictive immigration policy was dropped, and about a third of the immigrants to Australia in the most recent years have been Asians.

Because the racist image lingers on, the only substantial number of American blacks who visit the country are soldiers, athletes, entertainers and a few scholars. As for Australia's racism, presently it is probably no more racist than the United States. Most Australian states have laws prohibiting racial discrimination, and there is no official racial segregation and discrimination allowed. However, in certain "redneck" states, such as Queensland and the Northern territory, discrimination or poor treatment may be blatant. Most of the harsh racial practices in these areas are reserved for the domestic blacks, known popularly as Aboriginals and Torres Strait Islanders.[10]

Australia is about 8,000 miles away from the western coast of the United States. A visa is required to enter the country and a detailed visa application, with photo, must be completed. Airfare from America to Australia is as low as $1,200 round trip, which may include stopovers in other countries. Including the time spent in airports, it takes almost a full day to get to there. Physically, Australia looks very similar to the United States. While Australia has only about a tenth of the U.S.'s population, the former's land mass is almost as large, with most of the citizenry residing in five large cities. English is the official language.

Generally, American blacks are treated in a cordial manner by white Australians. In some cases the whites will be exceedingly friendly. Since there are very few black Americans who visit Australia, they are regarded as a group who poses no threat to white domination.

If one is interested in the situation of the domestic black population of Australia, one would want to make contact with the Aboriginals. Depending on where one goes in the country, the Aboriginals are not difficult to find. The majority live in the countryside, some on what are called missions or reserves (reservations). Many Aboriginals are living in substandard housing. While some do not use English as their primary language, they still greet American blacks as long lost cousins, and they will share whatever they have. Talking to Aboriginals is a wonderful opportunity to become acquainted with a culture that is many centuries old. Aboriginal music, art, dance and craftmaking are renowned for exquisite beauty.

In the cities, Aboriginals are not as visible although there are certain districts in which large numbers are ghettoized. Many of the government agencies have Aboriginal units, and there are a number of Aboriginal organizations.

The Aboriginals in cities are often more educated, speak English and represent a variety of physical types. Most will relate to some aspect of Aboriginal culture and will welcome other blacks into their community. In addition to their political and educational activities, there are a number of social activities given to benefit Aboriginal causes. Even a simple lunch can turn into a gala occasion as many clans or Aboriginal associates gather for a long afternoon of drinking and eating.

Across the Tasmanian Sea from Australia is the island nation of New Zealand. Similar to Australia in many ways, it is a smaller country of three million people, most of them British immigrants. The country was originally occupied by a Polynesian group known as Maori. There has been sufficient miscegenation in New Zealand to make racial categories meaningless. However, Maori is officially defined as any person who has 50 percent or more of Maori blood. Maoris consider any person Maori who identifies as one. By the latest unofficial count, there are approximately 300,000 Maoris, about 12 percent of the population. Unlike the Aboriginals, Maoris are an urban working class group, more acculturated, have a higher level of education and income, speak English and are more physically integrated into New Zealand.[11]

Even fewer black Americans visit New Zealand although it has much to offer. There is a growing population in Auckland, Wellington and Christchurch of Polynesians, mostly Samoans, Cook Islanders and Fijians. The southern part of the country is breathtakingly beautiful. Auckland, the largest city, is hilly and located between two harbors. Agriculture is the largest source of revenue, and meat and dairy products are plentiful and comparatively inexpensive. Although both Australia and New Zealand were colonized by the British, the British influence is more pronounced in New Zealand. Australians are more friendly, but Maoris have a less downtrodden position in New Zealand society than do the Aboriginals in Australia.

The Maoris were not as totally conquered by the white settlers as were the Aboriginals. Maoris are a more aggressive group and were still fighting the British colonialists as late as the mid-19th century. Consequently, they retained more of their land, culture and language. In the past decade New Zealand has used urbanization as a major agent of assimilation. Rural Maori land has been underdeveloped, and Maoris have been enticed into urban areas where housing and other facilities were available.[12]

Despite their war-like nature, Maoris are a hospitable people. When this author arrived in New Zealand, one Maori whom I contacted, through an Aboriginal friend in Australia, met and accompanied me during my entire stay in the country. A "Marae" visit is necessary to understand Maori culture. The "Marae" is the focal point of Maori culture. It is usually a grassed area and community buildings, of which the meeting house is the most important in a Maori settlement. All important gatherings are held on the Marae, and there one hears Maori spoken and Maori social forms followed. One will find the Maori women beautiful, the food delicious, and arts and cultural life enhancing.

Other predominantly black countries exist in the South Pacific. The Fiji Islands, Samoa and Tahiti* are small islands that are developing their tourist trades. Only in American Samoa is English extensively spoken. Papua-New Guinea is a predominantly black country that is larger than the other predominantly black South Pacific countries (roughly three million inhabitants). Formerly a colony of Australia, Papua-New

---

*American Samoa and Tahiti still have official colonial relationships to the United States and France, respectively.

Guinea is a country of many tribes and over 700 languages. Once outside the larger cities, travel can be rough because of limited roads, but plane travel is plentiful and convenient. Little English is spoken. The island's customs are so unique that it has been a favorite haunt of anthropologists.

Probably the most exploited and brutalized victims of European contact were the Aborigines of Australia. These black people had existed on the Australian continent for 40,000 years before Britain decided to use this beautiful land as a dumping ground for its criminal class. The Europeans brought with them diseases, liquor and firearms that effectively decimated the Aboriginal population. Aborigines were removed from their hunting groups and placed on reservations; the women were raped or turned into the concubines of Europeans; children were taken away from their families and placed in foster homes; and the group was shot like wild animals.[13] After their total subjugation of the Aboriginal population almost two centuries ago, Australian whites enjoyed the highest standard of living in the world after the United States, Canada and New Zealand.[14]

While the Anglo-Saxons progressed from a penal colony to the most affluent residents of the South Pacific in less then 200 years, the Aboriginies were reduced to less than one percent of Australia's population and one of the most downtrodden minority groups in the world. They have a life expectancy of less than 50 years compared to more than 70 years for whites, a higher infant mortality rate and a higher incidence of diseases, particularly eye infections and alcoholism. Few progress beyond the sixth grade in the public schools, and less than 200 graduate from college each year. Only six Aborigines are lawyers, and a couple are doctors and dentists. Many families live in shacks on river banks. The Aboriginal unemployment rate is six times (37 percent) that of the general workforce and ranges as high as 90 percent in some towns. Aborigines are 13 times more likely to be in prison than whites.[15]

As a group, Aborigines are a racial anomaly. There is a great deal of uncertainty about their racial origins, even their current racial identity. Some anthropologists have classified them separately as Australoids. Others have defined them as archaic Caucasoids and some as Mongoloids. They may be the only group regarded as belonging to all three major racial groups. Conventional scholarship in Australia views them as descendants of the Southeast Asian region.

Whatever the case, physically, Aborigines have Negroid traits, except for their curly hair, and white Australians regard them as blacks, with all the disadvantages and social deprivations attached thereto. Until 1972, for administrative and divide-and-conquer purposes, Aborigines were classified by their quotient of European ancestry: full-bloods, half-caste or one-fourth caste. In some states, anyone other than a full-blooded Aborigines was classified as white. Only if an Aborigine was fair enough to pass as European and willing to forsake his kinsmen was the legal definition as white meaningful. Today, an Aborigine is any person who identifies as one and is accepted in that community.[16]

(The term Aboriginal means original inhabitant of a territory. It does not denote race. Many tribal Aboriginals identify themselves by their tribal affiliation. Because of their dispersion, many Aboriginals do not have a tribal identity. In certain parts of Australia they call themselves Koories. Aboriginal is the only term that nationally identifies the group. Some Aboriginals do not wish to be called black, and the other identifying terms are peculiar to regions.)

A PERSONAL ODYSSEY

Australia is an unfamiliar land to most Americans, whether they are black or white. To most of us it is a small island whose location is generally unknown, inhabited by kangaroos, koala bears, a few white settlers and Aborigines. As is true of those same Americans, I knew little about it. My knowledge of Aborigines was limited to the fact that they were the original black inhabitants of Australia whose numbers had been decimated by European settlers. Black Americans have tended to regard Aborigines as part of the black diaspora although few of us have ever had any contact with them. Evonne Goolagong's exploits on the tennis courts were always featured in black magazines. *Ebony* magazine did a feature story on Aborigines.

With that background I was pleased to receive a telephone call from Ms. Jeanne Roberts, a white faculty member of the Aboriginal Task Force at the South Australian Institute of Technology. Since I had written many books and articles on black Americans, she wanted to talk to me about my work. As it turned out, I obtained much more information on Aborigines than she received on black Americans. When Ms. Roberts revealed the history and contemporary conditions of the Aboriginal people, I was shocked. While black Americans have experienced their own travail in the United States, there were no comparable experiences in our recent history. These atrocities were being committed against Aboriginal people in the 1960's. After hearing of their plight, I suggested that their situation was more analogous to the American Indian. However, Ms. Roberts informed me that Aborigines identify more closely with black Americans.

Although Aborigines are called blacks, their colonial history, depressed status and small numbers do make their situation similar to Native Americans. Aborigines who come to the United States on study programs tend to study Native American institutions and programs. However, they are generally more familiar with black Americans because of their larger presence in the American literature, movies and television programs.

It was remarkable coincidence that earlier that day I had received a letter from the director of a research institute in Melbourne expressing an interest in my work on the black family. Australia is not a place many black Americans visit. It has always been strongly associated in the minds of black Americans with South Africa due to its former whites-only immigration policy. Having a six-month sabbatical from my position as a professor of sociology, I decided to go to Melbourne, Australia, for that period.[17] The institute extended me an invitation to be a visiting fellow there. The institute's office was located next door to the Department of Aboriginal Affairs.

When I arrived in Melbourne, I had no idea what to expect. Almost all the whites I encountered were friendly and helpful beyond my expectations. There were more luncheon and dinner invitations than I could handle. Still, my main interest was in making contact with Aboriginal peoples. I had no conception of urban Aborigines. My only knowledge of them came from pictures of tribal Aborigines. I was interested in the urban group because the similarity would be greater between them and black Americans. Since Ms. Roberts was white, I had no Aboriginal contacts in Australia. After getting settled in Melbourne, my first task was to go the Department of Aboriginal Affairs (D.A.A.) and ask to see an Aborigine. The person who chose to see me was a man named Kevin Coombs. After telling him I wanted to meet Aboriginal people and visit their organizations, their generosity and hospitality were exemplified.

Kevin took time off from his valuable duties at the D.A.A., and we made the rounds of Aboriginal organizations. At each place the director and staff took time out to talk to me. I was invited to Aboriginal events, given posters, buttons and other gifts. At a graduation ceremony for Aborigines enrolled in a community welfare course, I met most of the leaders of the Aboriginal community. My initial entry into the Aboriginal community was translated into a total involvement in their affairs. While the whites were friendly, I truly felt at home with the Aborigines. Although my primary purpose in coming to Australia was to do a scholarly analysis of the Aboriginal situation, my involvement with them was a total embrace of their culture and lifestyle. We ate, lived, danced and demonstrated together. There was no aspect of my life or theirs that did not touch. At the end of my six-month visit a group of them gave me a farewell dinner party at which I was presented with an Aboriginal wood carving.

Obviously, our camaraderie was based on our commonalities as a black and oppressed group in white settler societies. While we have that historical affinity, our contemporary situation diverges at critical points. Black Americans, of course, live in one of the most powerful and populous countries in the world. They represent 15 percent of the U.S. population and constitute an ever larger proportion of American cities. As a group, American blacks are probably one of the most educated and affluent non-whites in the world. Their median educational level is 12.0 years. One million Afro-Americans are presently enrolled in college, and there are thousands of doctors, lawyers, dentists and other professionals. In 1985 they earned 202 billion dollars. As a result of their political struggles in the 1960's, black Americans are represented, although not equally, in almost every sphere of American life.[18]

Still, black American empathy for the Aboriginal people is predicated, in part, on the former's vivid memory of the recent past, when they could not go to white schools, eat in white restaurants, live in white neighborhoods, vote in political elections or obtain jobs other than as servants or menial workers. Moreover, racial inequality continues to be a fact of American life and is on the ascendancy under the conservative administration of Ronald Reagan. Out of 15,000 commercial banks in the United States, only 50 are black. There are 47,000 savings and loan associations, but only 42 are black. There is one white doctor for every 546 whites, and one black doctor for every 5,000 blacks. There is one white lawyer for every 482 whites, and one black lawyer for every 4,000 blacks. Today, black family income is less than 56 percent that of white families. Black families are 41 percent of those in the bottom fifth of the income scale while white families make up 95 percent of the highest one-fifth.[19]

Blacks are disadvantages vis-a-vis whites in the United States. Yet, their situation pales in comparison to the harsh conditions under which Aborigines live in Australia. There has been some improvement in the Aboriginal situation since the 1950's when families were herded into reserves, women were raped, men imprisoned or shot, and children kidnapped from their families. Nowadays, there are some services for Aborigines such as study grants, hostels, medical centers, low-interest housing loans and others. The Australian government's current policy toward Aboriginals is one of encouraging "self-determination." In practice, it is colonial rule. The decisions on Aboriginal land rights, funding levels, services and control of Aboriginal affairs remain in the hands of whites.

Moreover, the paucity of the Australian government's efforts in this area is reflected in the fact that its entire budget of 150 million dollars for Aboriginal services is slightly more than the 139 million dollars the United States' government provides to Howard University to educate 12,000 blacks.

With this in mind, I began my odyssey through Aboriginal land. My first stop was the Aboriginal Task Force at the South Australian Institute of Technology in Adelaide. Peter Pinning-

ton, Aboriginal Liaison Officer at Melbourne University and a
graduate of the Aboriginal Task Force, accompanied me. We
stayed at the home of an Aboriginal family. Although the
Aboriginal students had a free day for study, most of them came
in to meet me. I gave a presentation on the black American
situation, and we discussed the plight of Aborigines, especially
in educational institutions. At the end of the day they presented me with a few small gifts.

During our dialogue, a statement was made, which I was to
hear over and over during my stay, to the effect that black
Americans who visited Australia would not associate with
Aborigines. Nothing in my intimate knowledge of black Americans could explain such behavior. It is possible that those Afro-
Americans who travel to predominantly white countries want
to escape any identification with race or racial problems. Some
of them would not associate with other black Americans.

During my six-month stay in Australia, I only met one other
black American, and he was introduced to me by Aborigines.
When I asked him about the black American avoidance of
Aborigines, he had no knowledge or explanation of such behavior. Later, I was to find out that a number of Aboriginal
women had married black Americans. Aborigines had gone to
the United States and lived with black families, performed with
black dance troupes, gone to black schools, and published
poetry in black magazines. If Aborigines lived in the United
States and identified as blacks, they were accepted in the black
community. Certainly, blacks in America would not condone
the behavior of their fellow citizens who refused to associate
with the Aboriginal people.[20]

There have been some tensions between overseas blacks and
Australian Aborigines. In January, 1982, nine Aborigines attacked two black American runners participating in an international track meet in Melbourne. The Aborigines' rationale was
that the black Americans were participating in an event spon-
sored by a company that was insensitive to Aboriginal interests, c.f. Militant Black Activism, *The Toorak Times*, July
**17, 1982: 11. In 1981 an Aboriginal leader branded African
leaders "honorary whites" when Africans refused to publicly
support the Aboriginal boycott of the Commonwealth games**

held in Australia. c.f. "Militant Black Activism Policy One," *The Toorak Times,* July 18, 1982: 11.

However, most Aborigines were very favorably disposed toward black Americans. When I went to Canberra, the national capital, for a one-day visit, one Aboriginal woman in Melbourne made contact with Aborigines in Canberra, and the red carpet was rolled out for me. Here I was, a black American, without portfolio, and the highest ranking Aborigines in the Commonwealth government turned out to meet me. I visited the national headquarters of the Aboriginal government offices and was wined and dined. The day was topped off by a dinner that included Senator Neville Bonner, the only Aboriginal member of Parliament. He made a brief speech that was so moving it brought tears to my eyes. Then he presented me with a set of cufflinks bearing the Australian Senate seal. Subsequently, we went to Parliament where we witnessed Senator Bonner's oratorical skills in a late night session. Later I met several members of Parliament and the Minister of Aboriginal Affairs and Social Security.

As a consequence of my visit to Canberra, I was invited back to give a lecture at the Institute of Aboriginal Studies. By the time of my lecture I had been in Australia for four months and also traveled to New Zealand and met with the Maori people. One conclusion was how similar the struggles of American blacks, Aborigines and Maoris had become. One reason for this similarity was that the Australian and New Zealand governments, following the lead of the United States, had responded to the cultural awakenings and political protests of their black populations in a similar fashion: handing out the carrot while carrying a big stick. My visit to New Zealand provided me with another example of the fourth world.

BROTHERS AND SISTERS OF THE FOURTH WORLD

Whereas I had developed a fraternal bond with the Aborigines and still maintain strong ties to that community, there were great differences between their situation and that of black Americans. Aborigines are a rural, land-based group that comprises less than one percent of Australia's population.[21]

Hence, I journeyed to Auckland, New Zealand, to seek out the Maoris, with whom black Americans share a greater commonality.

Having obtained the names of a few Maoris from my Aboriginal friends, I flew to Auckland for a brief visit. As soon as I called Colin Reeder, an urban planner for the Auckland City Council, he immediately came to get me, and I was introduced to other members of the Maori community. At once I was struck by the degree to which we shared a similar situation in our respective white settler countries. Both the Maori and black American groups constitute 12 percent of the total population of their respective countries, and each group is an urban, working class population.[22] Those salient characteristics, coupled with their existences in countries settled by Anglo-Saxons, has led to an incredibly surprising resemblance between the two groups.

Before pointing out those likenesses, it is incumbent upon me to note some variations. Maoris are the original inhabitants of New Zealand, an indigenous group which has retained much of its language and culture. Black Americans were brought from Africa to the United States as slaves and stripped of their names, languages and cultures. An interesting distinction between Maoris and Afro-Americans is that the former were not allowed to claim Maori membership until recently unless they were of more than half Maori origin. Conversely, black Americans had no choice in their racial membership. Any degree of black ancestry classified them as black.

Because of their native status, the Maoris have a special relationship to their white settler government that black Americans do not. There is a special political role for Maoris and other governmental units devoted entirely to them. While black Americans receive some special governmental assistance, it is generally assistance available to all economically disadvantaged groups in the United States. That assistance targeted toward special groups has to be shared with other racial minorities (Indians and Hispanics) and occasionally with women of European descent.

An interesting similarity between the two groups is the role of women. In my encounters with Maori women I observed that many of them were strong and independent and maintained positive relationships with men. I found out that Maori women held leadership posts in many Maori organizations. Some of them had organized what might be called a Maori feminist movement to deal with women's issues.[23] Those patterns parallel similar tendencies among black American women.

A disparity between the two groups is the sex ratio. The 1981 New Zealand census reported that there were approximately 567 more Maori men than women, a sex ratio of 99.6 females to every 100 males. In the marriageable years, 20-44, there are slightly more Maori women than men.[24] In the United States, there are approximately a million and a half more black women than men, a sex ratio of 87 males to every 100 females. Such an imbalance in the sex ratio makes it difficult for many American black women to form a monogamous family and contributes to the high proportion of female-headed households.[25]

Because Maori and black American men are both physically aggressive groups, they play a dominant role in their nations' athletic teams. While the sports played in the two countries differ (U.S., football, New Zealand, rugby), the two groups bring to their sports a special style of speed and aggressiveness that makes them much sought after for these activities. Maori and black American men are also over-represented in their respective nations' military, partly due to a high unemployment rate among their youth and because they are physically aggressive.

Of course, some of the Maori/black American differences are traceable to diversities in the two countries. New Zealand is a small country of four million people with a gross national product based on agricultural activity, whereas the United States is an industrialized society with more than 235 million people. Hence, persons of Maori descent numbered 385,524 in the 1981 census in comparison to 27 million blacks in America.[26] Nevertheless, the statistical evidence is cogent proof that non-whites do not fare well in white settler societies. While there has been much progress in the last 20 years, it is clear that due to differences in skin color, cultural values and life styles, non-whites do not have equal access to opportunity structures in countries dominated by Anglo-Saxons.[27]

Beginning with the right to earn a living, the United States and New Zealand censuses show an unemployment rate of 21 percent for black Americans and 27 percent for adult Maoris—a rate much higher than that of Anglo-Saxons (eight percent in the U.S. and six percent in New Zealand) in 1983. Similarly, and even worse, are the unemployment rates of black American and Maori youths. The rate of unemployment in 1981 for Maori youth was 49 percent and for black American youth, 53 percent. Both Maori and Afro-American families earn about 55 percent of the income of Anglo-Saxon families. In terms of occupational distribution in 1981, main occupations of Maoris were laborers, food and beverage processors and transportation equipment operators. Black Americans were in three summary occupational groupings: operators, fabricators and laborers. Anglo-Saxons were more heavily concentrated in managerial, farming and technical occupations.[28]

Educational differences between the groups are harder to measure as are the school qualifications for certain occupations. The educational differences between black Americans and Anglo-Saxons have narrowed in the last decade, with Anglos having a median educational attainment of 12.3 years of schooling, compared to 12.0 for black Americans in 1982. In that same year, the percentage of Anglo-Saxons between the ages of 25-34 who had completed at least one year of university training was 46 percent, whereas 36 percent of black Americans had attained the same level.[28] The comparable figures for New Zealand show that in 1981 the highest school qualification held for 18.5 percent of the Anglo-Saxons was university entrance or equivalent, and that of only 3.7 percent of Maoris had reached the same level.[29]

Because black Americans and Maoris have higher rates of unemployment and less income than Anglo-Saxons, they are also over-represented among those arrested and imprisoned for violations of the law. Again, the statistics show the remarkable affinity of the two groups. In 1982, Maoris made up 33.1 percent of all New Zealanders arrested and brought to trial while black Americans composed 36 percent of all arrests—much higher than their percentage in the general population.[30] Another factor contributing to their higher arrest rates is the younger ages of the Maori and black American populations. Chronic offenders are often under the age of 25. The median age for the Maori population in 1982 was 18.3 years compared to a median age of 28.9 years for the Anglo-Saxon population. In 1982, black Americans had a median age of 24.3 years, and Anglo-Saxons had a mid-point age distribution of 30 years.[31]

Because non-whites in white settler societies share a common situation and a shared fate, I have used the following paradigm to conceptualize their commonalities.

Comparisons of White Settler and Fourth World Value Orientations

Value Orientations	White Settlers	The Fourth World
Time	An element in society by which the individual compulsively regulates his life. Punctuality is of highest priority.	Flexible adherence to schedules. What is happening now is important and one must adapt to ranges in time rather than fixed periods.
Emotions	To be under rigid control in order to maintain discipline and not reveal emotional weakness. To be very guarded in public settings and never to be fully released.	Expression of natural feelings in all settings, public and private. Spontaneity in response to events and gestures is common. Be uninhibited and loose in reactions to verbal and physical stimuli. Let your inner feelings show and exude warmth.
Money	To be frugal in its use, saved for future purposes. To be accumulated even when not needed, in order to possess the value it has. Often used to control persons who have little of it and limited access to its acquisition.	Is to be used to further communalism. Money per se is not important, not the measure of human value. Wealth is consumptive rather than exploitative. How money is used is more important than its acquisition. Property is a collective asset, not an individual one.

Value Orientations	White Settlers	The Fourth World
Morals	Strongest ones relate to personal morals such as sexual behavior, belief in God, cleanliness, moderation in use of alcohol, tobacco, etc.	How you treat people is of highest priority. Helping people in need is an important moral. Abstaining from harm to people or groups. A belief in the dignity of your fellow humans.
Status	Based on your income, family background, cultural skills, amount of power over others, race, religion, sex, etc.	Stems from personal qualities, such as courtesy, compassion, friendliness, and naturalness. Innovation and adaptability also admired.
Children	**Are often extensions of the parents. Expected to achieve a status similar to or higher than parents. Will be loved and supported if they conform to parental values. Love is withdrawn if they deviate from certain social norms. Obedience to parental authority highly valued**	**Are seen as a value in themselves, to be nurtured as a dependent being and loved throughout life regardless of their achievements. Creativity and free expression are encouraged. Often regarded as equal members of the family structure.**
Individualism	**In human society each individual must make his own mark through competition for the prestige goals of his culture. The rewards of his victory in the competition are his alone, to be shared only with certain prescribed people (e.g., wife, children) over whom he has control. Those who have not achieved success or are without sufficient resources have only themselves to blame because of their inability to compete.**	The concept of the individual is usually subordinate to a group orientation. It is the group that is important and the self is an incorporated part of the social group. Cooperation through collective efforts is the accepted means of achieving culturally prescribed goals.

THE FOURTH WORLD

As a result of my visit to the South Pacific, I developed the concept of the "fourth world." The concept is not new, only the way I apply it. Earlier, George Manuel had written a book by the same name referring only to indigenous people living in first world nations under third world conditions.[32] My concept is similar except that it includes black Americans and possibly other non-white groups that are not indigenous.

Using the fourth world concept as I do goes against the grain of conventional wisdom in oppressed minority communities. Black Americans, for instance, have generally identified and aligned themselves with Africa and the third world. My feeling is that they have more in common with Aborigines and Maoris in terms of the future issues they must confront. However oppressed and economically dependent third world nations have become, they still have more autonomy than non-white minorities in first world nations. Moreover, contemporary rhetoric notwithstanding, there is the critical question of how non-white minorities are to obtain full self-determination in societies where whites hold all the political and economic power. This question is particularly critical when even the whites in those societies are governed by a ruling capitalistic elite.

My conception of the fourth world is based on an analysis of the current world situation. It appears that the fate of non-white minorities will be determined by what happens in their host countries, not their ancestral homelands. A certain amount of progress in race relations in the United States was made because of this country's concern with its image in third world countries. However, we seem to have reached a point of diminishing returns. Future progress may depend more on the active struggles of non-white groups, domestic political strategies and concerns, and the internal economic situation.

While it goes against some of the contemporary rhetoric of black nationalist groups, there has to be some kind of alliance between non-white minorities and segments of the white majority in order to obtain any significant gains past a certain point. Ultimately being a numerical minority, with little access to a nation's wealth or political power, will be more important than ideological and cultural ties with other third world countries. Hence, my conception of the fourth world is based on that fundamental fact.

Without considering the case of South Africa, which contains the possibility of autonomy for the black majority, the fourth world is similar in many ways. All of its inhabitants are victims of a system of internal colonialism. This means: (1) They are not in the social system voluntarily but have it imposed on them. (2) Their native culture is modified or destroyed. (3) Control is in the hands of people outside their community. (4) Racism prevails, i.e., a group seen as different or inferior in terms of alleged biological traits is exploited, controlled and oppressed socially and psychologically by a group that defines itself as superior.[33]

Internal colonialism manifests itself in the unequal life chances of non-white minorities. In comparison with class privileges, whites maintain racial privileges in racially stratified societies. Black Americans, Aborigines and Maoris are similar in the unequal status they hold based on the sociodynamics of racism. All three groups have a lower level of education, higher rates of unemployment, and lower income than the white majority. Even with class-control, they are more likely to be arrested and imprisoned than whites.

More important are the consequences of internal colonialism for the internal functioning of the minority community. High rates of homicide and lower life expectancy rates due to poor health conditions tend to decimate the able-bodied, young men in minority groups. As a result, women have a much stronger position in the fourth world. One natural consequence of the castration of men has been the destruction or unavailability of monogamous families for the women and an unequal share of the burden of minority groups.

The salient issues that face fourth world groups are internal divisions within their own communities. A divide-and-conquer strategy of the ruling elites exploits differences within fourth world groups. It is instructive to note the division between the grassroots and the bourgeoisie among Aborigines, Maoris and black Americans. Among Aborigines, the division is even extended to tribal Aborigines and those of mixed ancestry.

Another variation of the divide-and-conquer strategy is to pit

Aborigines, Maoris and Afro-Americans against other minorities. In the United States it is blacks versus Hispanics. Australia will eventually pit Aborigines against the new Asian immigrants, and New Zealand already has exacerbated the conflict between Maoris and other Pacific Islanders.

Meanwhile, as Aborigines and Maoris will belatedly find out, economic recessions tend to bring out racial tensions that remain latent in more prosperous times. Already there is manifestation of a new kind of racism in Australia and New Zealand, which has reached its apex in the United States. Increasingly, whites speak out against the special treatment and benefits accorded non-white minorities under the guise of a color-blind meritocracy. Such a philosophy is a thinly veiled attempt to stabilize present racial inequalities and roll back the meager gains of the 1970's. Minorities who seek self-determination and group solidarity are subject to charges of racial separatism and reverse racism.

Probably the greatest danger to fourth world groups is the issue of assimilation. This issue is particularly critical for groups small in number, such as the Maoris and Aborigines. A pertinent matter that must be addressed is how much of an oppressed minority's culture can be maintained in the face of strong pressure to take on Anglo-Saxon lifestyles, values and culture. However, this pressure or invitation to assimilate is generally applied to only a minority within the minority. Can those pressures be resisted when the consequences are continued isolation and the denial of the benefits of an affluent society?

However, the fourth world need not be defined solely by the negative effects of its status. It is also a world community of people that place people above property in their value schemes, possess a spirituality that puts them in touch with nature and their feelings, maintains a world culture that believes in mutual aid and compassion for the downtrodden and where the kinship group is still strong and the elderly receive respect. These are all aspects of tribally organized group life that have not been totally destroyed by European conquest and settlement. And it is this bond that connects us across oceans and epochs.

Part II:
Institutional Racism

CHAPTER FOUR

Racial Ideology and Intellectual Racism

America is a country of immense attraction to millions of people throughout the world. It is known as a land of unfettered opportunity, where fame and wealth awaits any person willing to work hard. This country represents a source of wealth and personal and political freedoms not available in more autocratic and traditional societies. However, the ideology of equal opportunity masks the reality of a country stratified along racial, gender and class lines. Because the decade of the 1970's opened up heretofore unavailable opportunities to formerly excluded groups, such as women and racial minorities, the competition for the values of this society intensified as classes, sexes and races all struggled for a piece of a rapidly dwindling pie. Hence, the decade of the 1980's has been witness to the fragmentation of American society into special interest groups, each one trying to penetrate the white male monopoly of educational and occupational resources.

In the area of education, the battle has been joined. Prior to the 1950's, higher education was a preserve of the upper classes in society. Its standards and values sought engender and perpetuate an elite class whose role would be carved out for the leadership positions of government and industry. For white males, the elitist universities provided the context and means to acquire the personalities, values and social contacts necessary to attain a position among the corporate aristocracy. To white women, matriculation at higher status colleges represented the only opportunity to marry a man of a higher status or one to which they were accustomed. Racial minorities were largely excluded from the elitist, predominantly white male institutions altogether.

The civil rights and black power movements of the 1960's fundamentally altered the character of America's higher educational system. Not only did it bring unprecedented numbers of blacks into the nation's colleges but increasing numbers of Chicanos, Native Americans, Asians and working class white men and women as well. America's ideology of equal opportunity in education had not changed—only the political pressures to make it a reality. Those pressures, initiated by blacks, took the form of violence in urban centers, resulting in manifold deaths, injuries, arrests and fires. Once on the campus, blacks again applied pressure in the form of student sit-ins, threats and violence to secure greater numbers of black students, faculty, services and academic programs. As a result, the numbers of black students and faculty on white college campuses more than doubled in the last decade. In 1981, there were over a million black students enrolled in post-secondary schools, more than 75 percent in predominantly white institutions.[1]

Those figures of educational progress notwithstanding, the era of the 1980's is largely one of black decline in the educational arena. Between 1980-81 the number of entering graduate students declined by one percent overall, but black enrollment decreased by seven percent.[2] The figures on enrollment, while showing the decline in black student enrollment, do not tell the whole story. White-oriented colleges enroll considerably more black students than they graduate. While composing 10.2 percent of the enrollees, blacks receive only 6.5 percent of the degrees granted. In the nation's leading public university, the California system, only 120 of every 1,000 black males graduate, compared with 428 whites. Those dismal survival rates at white colleges explain why historically black colleges continue to produce half of this country's black college graduates, while enrolling only one-fourth of them.[3]

Race is not an insignificant factor in the retention rate of black college students. In part, colleges are a socio-psychological as well as educational environment. According to one study, blacks who attend an historically black college develop higher levels of self-esteem and academic achievement.[4] The problems of black students at white colleges can be traced, in the main, to the origin of their entry into those institutions during the

1960's. America's educators were trying to buy racial tranquility with the mass enrollment of black students while generally devoid of any commitment to educating them for occupational and income parity with white Americans.[5] As the black student movement declined, so did the white university's sensitivity to the needs of racial minorities. As one student sagely observed: "I think the pressure is off. They (blacks) can come to the university on the university's terms. The university is less inclined to adapt itself to the needs of minorities than it was when they first appeared on campus in the 1960's." While there were certainly some provisions in the early 1970's for minority students such as special admissions programs, grants, loans, counseling services, ethnic studies, etc., the curriculum and racial makeup of the faculty did not substantially change after the entry of minority students. Only those who accepted and adopted Anglo-Saxon values were relatively successful. In the 1980's even the willingness to conform to shoe values was insufficient as whites began to feel the pinch of government cutbacks and the economic recession.

Probably a more compelling force in the problems of black college students in the 1980's is the hostile environment of white college campuses and the racial attitudes of their white peers. The dislocations of the American economy have created a massive scramble for the shrinking supply of college level jobs in the 1970's. With more than a million Americans getting college degrees each year, it is estimated that there are three college graduates competing for every "college" job.[6] Two out of three college graduates will be underemployed. Race, then, becomes one of the variable in the competition for scarce resources in the society. While the battle is fought over which special interest group will achieve ascendancy in the struggle for societal goals, the ideology of equal opportunity dictates that the war of racial interest groups be articulated as a question of who is most competent and capable of benefiting from education. It is akin to the social Darwinist argument of the survival of the fittest.

Thus, the debate centers mostly on the issue of reverse discrimination against whites. This issue is repeated and magnified to the extent that it is reified among the white population and internalized as a truth, because it is instrumental in maintaining the privileges of white males, who continue to make the rules and hence dominate the society. The ultimate affirmation of the reverse racism doctrine came from the Supreme Court of the United States when it ruled that one white man's (Alan Bakke's) civil rights had been denied by 16 blacks, Chicanos and Asians who wanted to become physicians. Lost in that court ruling was the fact that 96 percent of America's doctors are white, that 90 percent of them will treat white patients, and this society's minorities will continue to suffer the maleffects of their low representation among medical personnel.[7]

Whereas the Bakke defense was predicated on the basis of his higher score on culturally biased, ofttimes irrelevant, standardized tests, the real issue was that physicians are the most prestigious and highly paid occupational group in the United States. The number of whites who want that prestige and high income is greater than the slots available in medical school. For racial minorities, it is a matter of who will live or die. However, morality is a secondary concern in these conflicts over access to the society's values. Surveys indicate that 70 percent of 1982 college freshmen identified the ability to make more money as a very important reason for attending college.[8] Concomitant with that preoccupation with status and money as the main function of education are hardened racial attitudes. A *Newsweek* poll reveals that 61 percent of white college students were opposed to their university making a stronger effort to recruit minorities, and only 45 percent felt college dormitories should be integrated.[9]

Affirmative action has become the buzz word of the 1980's for whites who identify it as the source of America's troubles. One poll found that a third of white respondents blamed affirmative action as the cause of the decline in the American economy. Among a group of white college students surveyed, only 36 percent thought university affirmative action is a good idea.[10] A large number of whites have convinced themselves that whites as a group are suffering from "reverse discrimination" and, *ipso facto*, racial minorities are the source of their reduced opportunities and general deterioration in their standard of living. Consonant with those attitudes are the re-emergence of the stereotypes of blacks as lazy, morally flawed and intellectually inferior. The image of blacks as intellectually inferior is used to justify their exclusion from colleges and professional schools. According to one poll of graduates from Princeton, Yale and Harvard, a large percentage of that group considers blacks intellectually inferior to whites. Only Harvard graduates had a majority of respondents (57 percent) who answered no to the question of whether blacks were inferior to whites.[11]

THE MYTH OF THE MERITOCRACY

The ideology of a merit-based society is strongly ingrained in American culture. Sociologists have chronicled the transformation of this country's evolution to a society where achievement is derived from ascribed status (i.e., determined at birth) to achieved status (determined by ability). Weber asserted that the bureaucracy gave rise to a rational selection of individuals by merit instead of family and kinship ties.[12] That a great deal of class mobility has occurred in this country lends credence to the ideology of the meritocracy and sustains the individual's belief that his status is based on the fair interplay of ability and opportunity. For racial minorities and women, this ideology has been exemplified more in its breach than its observance. Since it is important to the maintenance of the social order that its members believe the ideology is operative for everyone, the barriers to achievement are hidden in a complex web of informal rules and processes.

First, ideologies are used in the interest of self-preservation, according to one's reference group. Race, depending on the issue at hand, tends to be the primary identity of most people in the United States; for whites because it locates power, privilege and status, and for blacks because it identifies constraints and disadvantages. These racial identities co-exist with the ideology of a universalistic society that is color blind. It is what Dreyfuss calls "the new racism": It denies the existence of racism and accepts no responsibility for inequality.[13] While whites rail against quotas for racial minorities in the school and workplace, they call for quotas on foreign imports that threaten their jobs. They oppose government intervention in enforcing affirmative action and racial discrimination regulations, but accept it on other moral issues and the conscription of young men for military service. While insisting on governmental aid to private schools and increases in the so-called entitlement programs such as social security, veteran benefits and unemployment insurance that benefit the white middle class, they call for reductions in welfare, food stamps and public housing that minorities heavily rely on.

Ideologies and their implementations are shaped to meet the interest group's priorities. As the late Patricia Harris, former U.S. Secretary of Health, Education and Welfare, once noted, "We are still a society in which, for white people, whiteness is very important in which blackness is very threatening."[14] While every statistic available shows blacks to be underrepresented in every positive area of America life and to be losing what gains were achieved in the 1960's and 1970's, the eighties bear witness to the definition of reverse discrimination as a more serious social problem than white racism. Although the mechanical imposition of racial quotas can and has led to incompetent and inefficient individuals in schools and the workplace, there is no conclusive proof that the number of incompetents is any less than produced by the racially based selection system of the past. All that can be demonstrated is that the pool of students and workers is more representative of the population at large. Due to their greater visibility, any black performing incompetently leads to negative group stereotyping of all blacks as incompetent. Blacks are denied the right to have their fair share of incompetent individuals.

In a society in economic decline, the new racism is based on the proposition of a zero-sum equation: that every place in school and every job a racial minority obtains, a white person loses or never gets. Under this increasing perception of many white Americans, strategies are devised to maximize their gains and minimize their losses. In some cases, there is no racist intention, but the social processes produce racist outcomes. It should be noted that the jockeying for position is unevenly distributed in the society. Few, if any, white students have claimed reverse discrimination in being denied admission to a department of history, sociology or anthropology. Those fields offer few job opportunities for their majors in this conservative era. Instead, the competition exists for admission to the medical, law and business schools where job offers and high incomes abound upon graduation.

A similar dichotomy may be detected in the striving for white collar jobs, which carry with them greater prestige than '!¹ e collar jobs that are shrinking in supply. Blue collar jobs also have the distinction of being highly unionized, with retention being determined by seniority and not employer discretion. Rarely are standardized tests required for entry into blue collar jobs, and the demonstration of proficiency is fairly precise. While there are still racial inequalities in the blue collar world, they are not as disparate as in white collar jobs where the opportunities for subjective and hence, arbitrary, recruitment, and evaluation processes lends itself to racial discrimination. A little noted statistic is the fact that as blacks become more educated, the unemployment rate and income differential between them and their white peers is greater. In 1980 the U.S. census revealed the unemployment rate for black male college graduates was 5.5 percent while the rate for similar white males was only 1.6 percent.[15] Data of a black poll showed that nearly 60 percent of black college graduates report having experienced racial discrimination in applying for a job, compared to less than a third of blacks with less than a high school education.[16]

Many white collar jobs involve no specific skills nor require any training or education beyond high school. Employers may demand a college degree as only one of the screening devices to select workers for jobs done quite capably by people without college degrees. Ability to do a job is only coincidental in many employment decisions in a marketplace where capable applicants far exceed the number of available jobs. Time and time again, the courts have concluded that employment outcomes are irrelevant to individual merit or business efficiency. Becker contends that employers are not only prejudiced but have the power to act on their prejudices.[17] Hence, they make employment decisions on the basis of judgments about people's personal lives, physical appearance, personality, race and gender. To defend the ideology of the meritocracy, they require amounts

of education irrelevant to job performance, give tests which cannot be shown to predict performance, and use systems of tests
and promotion rules originally designed to make blacks,
women and other minorities look bad.[18]

While the ideology of universal merit is the cutting edge of
the movement against affirmative action, the key to getting a
job is still a matter of whom you know. At least one study found
that having the right contacts was an important factor in a person's initial job placement.[19] In a period of high unemployment,
especially in the white collar sector, workers have to have some
proximity or some connection just to hear about jobs that are
available. There are visible signs that employers are depending
more on "personality fit" than a candidate's credentials. They
are seeking new applicants who will "fit into the family." As
one employer, who offered bonuses to his employees to recruit
new workers, put it, "We want employees to bring in more
people like themselves."[20] The racial implications of this basic
element in social organization are evident. Almost all employers are white, and the races remain segregated in different social worlds. Ability may determine how well you can do a job,
but social contacts largely shape your ability to secure one. The
fact that many people use contacts derived from kin and social
networks does not mean they are unqualified to do the job. However, most jobs in this society can be performed by as much as
80 percent of the population, with some on the job training.
Hence, all things being equal, it's the use of contacts to secure
the initial job placement that determines one's life chances.

Racial minorities and women have relied on affirmative action
and networking to circumvent the old boy social contacts in attaining jobs monopolized by white males. White females should
be more successful since they are marginally in the same kinship and social network as white males. Moreover, while many
white women regard it as demeaning, sexual enticement can be
an effective tool for limited mobility in the work world. Blacks,
on the other hand, lack such options and must depend more on a
non-threatening personality or superior performance to achieve
the same employment outcomes as white males. As Kenneth
Clark has noted, "Blacks are not held to the same standards of
on-the-job performance–they are either evaluated more severely

or more leniently than others."[21] Nowhere is this statement more accurate than in the world of the intellectual class.

INTELLECTUAL RACISM

Colleges would seem to be a model of race relations for other institutions in the United States. With the academic world's concentration of highly intelligent people and the spirit of scientific inquiry, one would reasonably expect irrational racial prejudices and ethnocentric attitudes to be largely absent from this domain. Yet, racial inequality pervades the educational arena in American society, although its form is peculiar to the knowledge industry. When blacks, for instance, are excluded from politics, churches, neighborhoods or the workplace, it is often assumed, even by whites, that racial discrimination accounts in large part for their absence. However, the conventional rationale for their underrepresentation in colleges, especially the elite ones, is that blacks lack the intellectual capacity to compete for places in the classroom with the intellectually superior white student.

Moreover, to maintain a low ratio of black students, colleges have an arsenal of mechanisms which validate the claim of white intellectual superiority, in the form of I.Q. tests, college entrance examinations and grades. That these mechanisms have no demonstrable relationship to a black student's ability to perform well in an academic setting is irrelevant in a society where a college degree can pay off with million dollar lifetime earnings, 40 percent higher than those of high school graduates.[22] While a college degree no longer guarantees a high paying job, the lack of one does determine who will fall behind and most likely remain unemployed or consigned to do America's dirty work.

Perforce, the competition for college placement is perceived as a struggle for position in the nation's hierarchy. Groups that are in power, mostly white and male, create or maintain rules, mechanisms and barriers which work in their favor and discriminate against interlopers. Moreover, the intellectual class has the command of language and knowledge with which to rationalize their monopoly of the most prestigious and highest paying positions. To wit, the politics of the academic world are no different from those of business or government. It is just shrouded in the lexicon of standards and practices that are not as easily challenged by those outside its orbit. The modern educational complex is no longer the idyllic gathering of dedicated scholars and intellectually gifted students. It is a billion dollar industry and often run as such.

Increasingly, colleges are headed by good managers, not distinguished scholars. They are men hardened in the corporate mold, whose commitment to intellectual ideals is subordinate to the bottom line of a deficit-free financial statement. Instead of turning out a well-rounded student of consummate knowledge, colleges are preparing workers for whatever industry is currently expanding its labor force and paying the highest salaries. Fewer than 10 percent of 1980's freshmen prepared for careers in teaching, scientific research, social work and ethnic studies, while 41 percent planned careers in business, engineering and computer programming.[23] The professors have sold their services to the highest bidder, which at any point in time may include the C.I.A., other government agencies and industry. Those faculty members not supplementing their incomes in these ways have joined labor unions to increase their salaries and benefits. In 1982, more than a third of college faculty members belonged to unions.[24]

Within this vortex of competing groups of administrators, professors and students, the rhetoric is one of academic excellence while the real goals are those of power, money and status. Enter the black student or professor with perhaps no nobler goals, but with considerably less knowledge of how the system works and the disadvantage of being in an institution designed to serve race and class oriented ends. If we start with graduate students, who will ultimately enter the academic world as professors, the specter of intellectual racism can be illustrated.

First, the percentage of black graduate students has been steadily declining since the late 1970's. The number of black graduate students declined from six percent to 5.8 percent between 1977 and 1979. Although representing 15 percent of America's population, black students received only 3.8 percent of the doctorates granted in 1980.[25]

There are a number of factors accounting for the decline in black graduate students, not the least being the lack of commitment to affirmative action programs and a consequent decrease in financial aid and fellowships for black graduate students. Certainly, a significant factor is the lack of counseling and faculty support for black undergraduates. When black undergraduates were admitted to colleges under special admissions standards, white faculty and students began to perceive all black students as unqualified and intellectually inferior. Thus, many white professors failed to identify bright black students and point them in the direction of graduate study. In the past, at least, most black college students were enrolled in historically black colleges and did receive the encouragement to pursue graduate education. Even the rare black student at white colleges received such a stimulus because it was assumed that he or she had met the same academic standards as the white students.

Once a black student enters graduate school, he or she reports often finding a lack of understanding—thus of support—among their peers and the faculty. In the main, it is only a variation of the problems encountered by black undergraduate students. They are generally in separate social worlds than their white cohorts and not privy to backstage information that is more accessible to white students. In classroom situations, black students find that white students concede little credence to their comments unless they specifically involve black issues. Despite the inclusion of ethnic studies in college curricula, such courses are rarely integrated into the core curriculum of any discipline. Hence, most black students will find themselves studying topics of little relevance to their daily lives, experience or history.

On the graduate level, students often develop personal relationships with a graduate professor. This relationship is similar to the apprenticeship system into which the student is socialized for his future role as a scholar. Black students tend to maintain a more formal relationship with white professors, and there are rarely any black faculty members to serve as role models or mentors. In part, this occurs because blacks and whites do not socialize easily because of their different lifestyles, experiences, values and lack of trust.

Moreover, white professors tend to be most interested in students who will adopt, or already share, the professors' research interests. That is rarely true of most graduate black students. In fact, it is most problematic when the time comes to select a dissertation topic. Frequently, black graduate students pick a subject related to their culture and experience, a subject that the white faculty member may know nothing about, care little about and regards as being of little scholarly value. Hence, it is understandable that black graduate students require a longer time to complete their degree than do their white cohorts.

Not having a close personal relationship with their professors or white peers has serious implications for black graduate students' future successes in the professions. The academic world is a small clique of people from the same schools, disciplines, theoretical perspectives and regions of the country. These people speak the same language, live in similar social worlds and communicate to each other through seminars, unpublished papers, and the top professional journals. These modes of communication are facilitated through the social networks that are formed in graduate school. Because black students are outsiders in this social process, they are forced to play by the formal rules while whites rely on the informal process for mobility in the academic structure. The fact that black students maintain formal, sometimes hostile, relationships with their white professors denies the students the benefits of the professors' ties to the network of scholarly colleagues, who can offer beginning jobs, invitations to present papers at conferences, research grants and other assistance.

RECRUITMENT, SELECTION AND PROMOTION OF FACULTY

More than a decade ago, black Ph.D.'s were in great demand a predominantly white colleges. One study of black Ph.D.'s in the academic marketplace between 1969-1971 found that they received an average of 16 offers or inquiries of availability during the 1969-1970 academic year.[26] Other studies found that black Ph.D.'s in the social sciences earned a higher median salary than their white counterparts.[27] Those boom times for black

Ph.D.'s were a function of their former exclusion from white colleges. In a 1950's study of the academic marketplace, Caplow and McGee found, "Discrimination on the basis of race appears to be nearly absolute. No major university in the United States has more than a token representation of Negroes on its faculty, and those tend to be rather specialized persons who are fitted in one way or another for such a role."[28]

Student protests and urban riots served to increase the representation of black professors on white college campuses in a fairly short period of time. As Burstein has noted, "Universities are generally extremely decentralized, with internal decisions relatively little subject to market forces."[29] Hence, when the mood of the country tended to favor the exclusion of blacks, blacks were excluded from the university. When racial ideology shifted, blacks were brought into the university. It is abundantly clear that the 1970's was a decade of retrenchment in efforts to include blacks on the faculty of predominantly white universities. Although the pool of black Ph.D.'s had increased several fold in that decade, the percentage of black faculty declined at predominantly white colleges.

Overall, only four percent of all college teachers are black. The majority of that small number probably teach in historically black colleges. According to a 1976-77 study of the distribution of full-time faculty be race at public colleges in 14 Southern states, eight percent were black, and over 75 percent were concentrated in the black institutions. This figure is well below the 18.5 percent which blacks represented of total population in the region in 1975.[30] In contrast to earlier studies, which indicated that black Ph.D.'s in the social sciences earned higher salaries than their white peers, a survey of sociologists in 1982 revealed that minorities reported lower incomes than their white counterparts.[31] It is clear that the shift in racial ideology has resulted again in the exclusion of blacks from the white university.

That the tide has turned against black inclusion in the white university is exemplified most clearly in the California public college system. This most populous, liberal state with the most prestigious and extensive network of public institutions of higher education has a terribly low contingent of minority faculty. Congressman Gus Hawkins charged that minorities are an insignificant dot in the California system and that racism is rampant. To prove his point, he cited 1978 Equal Employment Opportunity Commission figures which showed that among the faculty, non-white minorities are at the lowest end of the spectrum in terms of numbers, salary, rank and tenure.[32]

In 1977, 1.9 percent of the university ladder rank faculty in California was black, compared to 1.8 percent in 1973. The number of assistant professors decreased by six during that period. Hispanics were 2.5 percent of the faculty. After disclosing these figures, the University of California's Affirmative Action Committee remarked, "With the dubious exception of the Asian faculty, the university's performance in attracting and retaining ethnic minorities on the ladder rank faculty is simply *dismal*."[33]

Moreover, it is significant that these dismal figures exist in a state where non-white minorities make up more than a third of the population. By 1990 minorities are projected to compose 45 percent of California's residents.[34] Most significantly, combined ethnic minority enrollments in California schools from kindergarten through high school in 1990 will total 25 percent more than Anglo enrollment.[35] In essence, the college system will mirror the secondary school system of that state, which has produced a situation in which as many as 90 percent of the students are non-white and 90 percent of the teachers are white. California represents a contrast to the Southern states where the population of black faculty is positively correlated with the proportion of black enrollment.[36]

Affirmative action rules were designed to facilitate the entry and retention of minority and female faculty. They were supposed to supplant the traditional practice of hiring beginning faculty through the old boy network. That affirmative action has not appreciably increased minority faculty can be traced to the lack of commitment among university administrators to a racially balanced faculty and weak enforcement by the federal government of affirmative action regulations. As the *New York Times* reported, "Five years after the federal government decreed that college and universities that discriminate against women or minority groups could lose their lucrative federal contracts, the nation's institutions of higher education remain largely unchanged."[37] While universities are required to complete affirmative action plans and file annual reports of progress on minority employment, this policy has not changed employment practices. No college has lost a contract because of failure to comply with affirmative action regulations, nor does the government follow up on how well schools implement their promises to remedy racial and gender imbalances in their work force.

Hence, the procedures of advertising all faculty and administrative positions, forming national search committees and interviewing minority candidates have become part of an arcane ritual in the academic world. In a situation where supply exceeds demand, universities have retreated to the old boy network for filling vacant positions. Many faculty positions are described to fit the predetermined candidate. Some universities hire and promote from within their ranks although soliciting applications from outside. Other universities, particularly private ones, favor their own alumni or favorite sons for vacant positions. Only white women have been moderately successful under affirmative action programs. Of course, their status as a minority to be equated with historically subjugated groups has served to obscure the fact that their economic progress mostly adds income to the already affluent white household. White women in academia represent somewhat of an exception to this rule. A fairly high percentage of female faculty are not married. The discrepancy between their percentage of the population and their representation on university faculties is often greater than that of racial minorities. Still, because white women are connotatively lumped into the minorities' category, white administrators point to their increase among faculty and students as an advance for minority rights.

After affirmative action regulations were put into place, academic departments learned how to manipulate them. A common ruse was to request additional faculty positions in order to increase minority contingents. In one such case, the University of California asked for 68 new faculty positions with language that suggested minorities and women would be recruited to fill them. At a later hearing, University officials reported that 49 of the 68 faculty positions had been filled by 42 whites, five Asians, one Chicano, and one East Indian.[38] This scenario has been repeated over and over again where the noble plan to recruit minorities has been used to enrich a department's own coffers. Some blacks and Chicanos who are already employed have ceased to accept interview invitations when they have found out their use as a statistic in affirmative action reports.

The percentage of black faculty members would not have declined if their attrition rate was not higher than average. Due to their recent entry into the white academic world, few blacks would have retired or changed professions. Many universities hired them only as lecturers, instructors or in soft money positions. Often, blacks had no real knowledge of the conditions of their employment. Those ranks have no security, few opportunities for advancement and a limited term of employment. For those blacks who are appointed to a ladder rank faculty status, fewer receive tenure than their white counterparts. One survey disclosed that among persons who received Ph.D.'s between 1960 and 1978, 61 percent of U.S.-born whites and 57 percent of U.S.-born minorities had been promoted to tenure by 1979. American Indians and Asian Americans were most likely to be tenured, and blacks least likely.[39]

The evaluation process for granting tenure is ostensibly an objective assessment of a faculty member's record in the area of teaching, research and service. A more accurate description is Burstein's observation that "university departments would be hard pressed to show that, rather than being subtle, professional judgments are not often capricious and have the effect, sometimes intended and sometimes not, of discriminating against women and members of minority groups."[40] While one might find it difficult, although not impossible, to defend tenure for some blacks who have not completed the terminal degree or published any articles or books at a publish-or-perish institution, the elements that go into denial of tenure for blacks are more complex than that.

Teaching evaluations may be used as the primary criteria at many liberal arts colleges. Although blacks are often regarded as skillful orators and humorous speakers, they may suffer from the negative evaluations of their teaching by white students. Several factors are attendant to these negative assessments. Many black faculty are engaged in teaching race related courses. In this conservative era, there are some white students who do not wish to hear of any white culpability for the condition of blacks, any defense of government social programs nor problems of the poor. A black professor who takes that approach may be seen as biased and having a vested interest in protecting his indolent black brother–thus pedagogically incompetent. Conversely, if a black professor is teaching a non-race related course (i.e., about whites), some white students presume the professor, *ipso facto*, to be incompetent in a subject mainly concerning whites. The black professor may also be the victim of the white students' perceptions of all blacks as being sub-par in intelligence. Just as white female professors are expected to project a nurturing personality to appeal to students, the black professor must demonstrate a non-threatening posture by resorting to racial jokes, frequent smiles and reasonably high grades.

Whereas teaching may be valued at a number of colleges, it has rarely been of any significance at elitist publish-or-perish institutions. However, publishing works that have an audience is not always sufficient for black faculty. The catch-22 has become the "quality," not the quantity, of a scholar's writing. Hence, there are increasing instances of prolific black writers being denied tenure because their written works did not meet "university standards."

Probably the most publicized case was that of Harry Edwards, a black sociologist at the University of California at Berkeley. One of the most popular teachers on that campus, Dr. Edwards had taught one-fourth of the students enrolled in sociology courses although he represented only one thirty-sixth of the sociology faculty. He was denied tenure because his three books and 50 articles were not of "scholarly caliber." Other comments made alluded to the fact that Dr. Edwards' specialty, the sociology of sports, was not a legitimate field of inquiry, and his articles were not in refereed, highly prestigious journals.[41]

Black scholars are victimized by a number of the standards used in evaluating a professor's written work. First and foremost is the suspicion that blacks are capable and interested only in studying their own racial group. Social scientists with broader theoretical and traditional interests in their disciplines are likely to be more successful at elitist institutions than those with interests in social problem areas affecting minorities. Since few established white journals will publish the works of black scholars, works that generally challenge the prevailing white view of the racial situation, most are forced to publish in black oriented periodicals. Such articles are presumptively dismissed as being unscholarly, containing political advocacy or polemical. Lately, tenure and promotion committees have begun to require that a candidate's books and articles be empirically based, preferably using quantitative methodology. Doing that kind of research often means obtaining a government or foundation grant, which also means being in a social network to secure access to those funds. While black scholars do obtain such grants, they are considerably less successful than whites, and many of them are forced to couch their proposals in terms acceptable to whites.

As is true of many aspects of American life, the rules of publishing scholarly articles are observed more in their breach than observance. Recently, there have been a plethora of newspaper articles on scientists falsifying data used to report significant research findings.[42] A more frequently used practice is known as "paper inflation." The term refers to the increasing tendency of professors to have co-authored papers and to publish the same data in a number of different papers. The length of published papers has been shrinking because authors have been publishing four short papers rather than one long one. By using multiple authorship for shorter papers, some researchers list as many as 600-700 papers in their vitae. With co-authorships, the contributions to an article, even a book, can vary widely. Sometimes a professor will secure a large research grant and hire a number of young Ph.D.'s under his or her supervision. Each paper the professor writes must contain the principal investigator's name as one of the authors. One man's sole contribution to an article that listed his name as a co-author was a few seconds of conversation in an elevator with the senior author.[43]

Few of these shortcuts are used by, or available to, black scholars. Most are not in a white social network to avail themselves of such techniques. They are most likely to write single authored, long and non-grant funded articles. Again, the rules of publication are often different from the practice. In one of the most systematic analyses of the scientific publication system in the social sciences, Lindsey discovered that, "The review process performs only a little better than random chance in assessing the 'true quality' of a manuscript. The review mechanism is apparently little able to differentiate the good from the bad paper." As for the objectivity of the refereed journal, he notes, "There is a confirmatory bias among reviewers; that is, they tend to support publication of papers that are in conformity with their own views and to reject papers that contradict their own methodological or theoretical views."[44]

Service, public or university, is rarely weighted very heavily by promotion and tenure committees. Where it might make a difference, black faculty can still be at a disadvantage. Being invited to present papers at a professional meeting is often a function of belonging to some academic network. The same is true of being elected or appointed to an office or committee of a professional organization. Sociology is a good example. It is considered the most liberal discipline in the academic world, a group of bleeding heart liberals who have compassion for the underdog. In the American Sociological Association's balloting for council and committee slots, pictures are published in its newsletter that identify each candidate's race and gender. The results of nominations and elections of 1970-75 for blacks revealed that 19 percent of the nominations to that body's council were black candidates. Only one black was elected. An update of black participation in Association activities showed there was one black on the 1982 council. The Association notes, without explanation, "Blacks had fairly substantial membership on elected committees during the early seventies, but this has now declined to *zero*." It also notes the relatively smaller proportion of black authors and presenters in the thematic sessions at its annual meeting.[45]

There are other miscellaneous problems confronted by black faculty on white campuses. They are often overburdened by counseling and service assignments since minority students and white faculty may rely on them for the only minority input. White students seemingly feel freer to challenge their grading system and to report them to white "superiors." An interesting development of late has been the well publicized charges of sexual harassment leveled at black professors and athletes by white coeds. While such charges may have been valid, it is ironic that similar charges have not been filed by black coeds, nor would they have been taken seriously if they were. So far, charges against black professors and athletes have resulted in one professor's suspension, a reprimand for another, and an out-of-court settlement of $100,000 won by a white coed from a black athlete. One may be firmly opposed to the sexual harassment of women and still recognize that the harsh penalties meted out to black males accused of such charges reflect the caste taboo on black men having intimate relations with white women. A black male executive committed suicide when told a white female employee had filed a complaint against him charging sexual harassment, a charge other black executives said was the most dangerous a black male executive can face.[46]

The issue of racism in the university is complicated by the fact that not all blacks are treated alike. In some cases, well-meaning whites are very sensitive to minority concerns and issues. That division in the white community partly accounts for the variations in institutional support for racial minorities, both faculty and students. In other cases, it is not an indiscriminate bias against all blacks, but certain ones are selected out for favorable treatment. In general, that black person will be one who denies race is a factor in his or her status, socializes occasionally with white faculty members, is willing to testify that blacks are incompetent, and is regarded as a team player or company "man" or "woman." These blacks are often promoted to high, albeit, powerless, administrative positions where they can be a token showpiece of the university's willingness to promote competent blacks. However, few qualify for that sort of reward. Of more than 4,000 top administrators in predominately white institutions, fewer than a dozen chief executives are black, and a slightly larger number serve as deans.[47]

THE MYTH OF DUE PROCESS

Figures on tenure and promotion tell us why the proportion of black faculty has declined at predominantly white universities. At most universities the rank of associate professor carries with it a tenure status, allegedly guaranteeing lifetime employment and, at most institutions of higher education, the right to determine university policy. A national survey reports that among sociologists, blacks have experienced an increase in the proportion they represent at each level *except* associate professor.

Moreover, the overall proportion of graduate faculty who are black has actually declined since 1974.[48] In the survey of black faculty at public universities in 14 Southern states, it was discovered that only 40 percent of black faculty are tenured, in contrast to 47 percent of white faculty. In relation to rank, 14 percent of all black faculty hold professorial rank in contradistinction to 22 percent of all white faculty. One caveat: Blacks were more likely to be tenured and to hold professorial rank in the black than in the white institutions. At the black colleges, 15 percent of black professors hold professorial rank while only nine percent of them attain that rank in predominantly white institutions.[49] As Congressman Hawkins has observed, "Since minorities don't have numbers, salary, rank and tenure in the system, they therefore have no real power base in the university. And, without a power base, minorities cannot effectively influence university policy dealing with educational issues which impact their presence as educators, students and advocates for their respective groups."[50]

One of the things senior faculty members influence is who else can join their ranks. Black scholars often suffer from the invidious standards applied to their application for tenure and promotion. In almost every case of tenure review, they will be judged by a cadre of senior white male faculty members. As Crosby has stated, "It is white people who determine what is important... to teach, how to teach, and whether that teaching is well done."[51] They make similar assessments in the area of scholarship, frequently forgetting or not caring about the peculiar history or circumstances of the black scholar. One of those special circumstances will be the clustering of black faculty in minority oriented programs. At the City College of New York in 1977, for instance, nearly 40 percent of its 93 black black teachers were in minority oriented special programs.[52] Furthermore, blacks have little control over the fate of their faculty in those programs designed to serve their needs. Few minority oriented departments will have senior level faculty qualified to serve on tenure review committees and, thus, will have their faculty judged by outside, mostly white male, professors. Not only will those black faculty members be evaluated by white standards but canons of another discipline as well.

The workings of a tenure review committee are subject to a number of biases—personal, racial, religious or political. Burstein claims that "if there is one thing universities typically do *not* have, it is clear criteria for tenure or promotion."[53] As is generally known, the teaching abilities of candidates for tenure or promotion are often not subject to any evaluation at the elite publish-or-perish institutions. The contributions to scholarship criteria are not precise, thus making their evaluations often arbitrary and capricious.

In addition, irrelevant criteria may be, and often are, applied in the case of black applicants for tenure or promotion. Such criteria may include the applicant's white spouse, non-attendance at faculty social gatherings, hostility toward whites, publications in black journals, and the onerous "not being a team player." According to Van den Berghe, there are two necessary and sufficient conditions under which one's colleagues will recommend him or her for tenure and promotion; enough publications to satisfy a tenure review committee and passing the test of "fitting into the department." The latter condition is basically a personality test and requires that you show a degree of humility, be noncommittal about important issues that divide the faculty, do not appear too aggressive or bright, and if black, stay in your place.[54]

While these irrelevant criteria may be, and are, applied in tenure and promotion decisions, the unsuccessful applicant is rarely aware of them. Under the cloak of confidentiality, college faculties highly protect the deliberations of these tenure review committees. This arcane method leaves the tenure applicant in the position of being found guilty without ever seeing the evidence or the jury. Universities zealously safeguard the identities of the committee members and the personnel files used in their deliberations. Only a court order can generally obtain them, and the courts have been inconsistent in allowing the injured party access to those data. The university's rationale is that the principle of academic freedom and autonomy outweigh the tenure reject's right to know. Yet, Scheppele makes the cogent observation that "there is a close affinity between the lie and the secret. After all, a lie is merely a secret with a story on top."[55]

Up to this point universities have succeeded in using arbitrary and imprecise criteria on objective grounds to deny tenure and promotion to people eminently qualified. The statistical evidence reveals that women and minorities bear an unequal burden under the current system. Despite the statistical pattern of gross discrimination against these traditionally underrepresented groups, any redress of grievance is hard to come by. Typically, university grievance committees are dominated by the same white males, who share a consciousness of kind with their counterparts on the tenure review committees.

Civil rights enforcement agencies are so understaffed and burdened with a backlog of complaints that they are unable to even review, much less investigate, charges concerning violations of civil rights and affirmative action regulations. Using the courts is a time consuming and costly process. Furthermore, there are indications that the federal courts will afford legal relief, in the professional and managerial occupations, only where abuses of civil rights are extremely obvious.[56]

SUMMARY AND CONCLUSIONS

Our analysis and the statistical evidence indicate that the university is a microcosm of the larger society in its attitude toward racial minorities and women. While this may not be surprising to anyone who is part of that setting, it departs from the conventional image of intellectuals as the moral antennae of society and clarifiers of fundamental moral issues. That image of intellectuals as supporters of the less privileged classes, if it ever was valid, lacks currency in contemporary America. Since the 1950's the university has been transformed into a huge bureaucracy designed to turn out trained and disciplined workers for the government and corporations. Professors are no longer a penurious class alienated from the society's values and leading the fight for social change.[57] They have become an elite class in society, not only gaining higher pay in the last couple of decades but supplementing that income by selling their services to the political and economic oligarchy. Some have contributed to the exploitation of the poor by selling their intellectual skills for C.I.A. activities against political radicals, devising counter-insurgency methods against peasants in Vietnam, and developing public policy inimical to the interests of the working masses.

As the market has grown for the products and services of the professional intellectual class, they have become committed not only to knowledge and skill but to their elite privileges. As Hoffer has stated, the intellectual is quite ready to join in and defend the interests of the ruling class when he or she gains acceptance.[58] After a period of liberal posturing, the intellectuals took a stand against affirmative action. Their stand curiously coincided with their move to the suburbs and its segregated schools, the entrance of minorities into the university, and intellectuals' perception that the white male's monopoly was at stake.

Hence, they joined the less knowledgeable white masses in the defense of white privilege and, moreover, made their resistance to racial parity respectable by developing standardized tests to prove racial minorities intellectually deficient. Some went so far as to write books on the evils of reverse racism and ethnic chauvinism, or they lauded black writers who claimed racism was moribund. Corresponding with these attacks on the small gains of racial minorities was the development of theories that claimed racism was the inherent antipathy of people toward groups with different physical characteristics and the re-emergence of a form of social Darwinism in the exposition of sociobiology, a perspective which asserts that genetics plays a significant role in human achievement.

Black students who entered the white university posed a class and cultural threat. They came not to passively accept prevailing Anglo-Saxon, capitalistic values from Euro-Americans but demanded the representation of their history and experiences in the classroom. They demanded the recruitment of black professors who also reflected their cultural and class interests. These demands defied the conventional role of students as acquiescent servants to the professorial hegemony. These demands, backed by organized student movements, were partially successful. Ultimately, they failed for a number of reasons peculiar to the university structure. Students are a transient group and found it hard to sustain their movement year after year. They never had access to the real mechanisms of control, which remained in the hands of white male faculty members. The university was never as vulnerable to strikes and demonstrations as a factory might be. Its closure only affected the students, and some faculty, since it was not a centralized system and produced no product of urgent need by the larger public. **While faculty members were adversely affected by student protests and strikes, the control of the university reverted to the administrators, Board of Trustees, Governors and state legislators in the case of student disruptions. When universities have become hotbeds of revolutionary activities in other countries, autocratic political leaders have been known to shut them down for years. The black faculty could not aid and abet their cause due to their own small numbers and the fact that many of those recruited had a greater commitment to Anglo-Saxon values and institutions.**

In the decade of the 1980's, the numbers of black students and faculty are in a stage of diminution, corresponding to trends in the larger society. Coterminous with the declining numbers and influence of blacks on the predominantly white college campus is the prevailing white view of black educational and economic opportunities as better than average. According to one study, 61 percent of whites believed black opportunities have improved greatly in recent years. Fifty-three percent agreed that blacks had an advantage over whites in opportunities due to reverse racism.[59] In the same year as that survey, the U.S. Civil Rights Commission issued a report that found "in good times or bad, at almost any age, when looking for a job in the United States, it's better to be a white man than a black or an

Hispanic or a woman." Among the Commission's findings were that black men are overeducated for their jobs and have greater difficulty translating education into suitable occupations, and that black women are often in marginal jobs and make up the group with the highest rate of workers in poverty.[60]

Unraveling this contradiction between white perception and black reality is not easy. There is no singular factor but a combination of forces that sustain these beliefs. Certainly, white racism plays a central role in this self-serving belief, since it frees whites from any responsibility for additional remedies to eliminate racial disparities in education and employment. Moreover, the general history of many whites in capitalistic societies has been the enjoyment of an exploitative position that yields an advantage in accruing money, power and prestige. Rather than give it up, white manipulate the rules in their favor and devise an ideology to justify their existence. Groups in the lower strata can rarely succeed by playing by the rules when the dominant group, whose power is threatened by their presence, not only created the rules but adjudicates them as well. Furthermore, it should be clear that the movement, if only a small number, of a different and highly visible group into the top echelons causes those at the top ranks to lose some power and centrality.

The ideology of equal opportunity requires people to accept anyone who succeeds if the competition is fair and others do not have an unfair advantage. Since affirmative action programs, racial quotas in employment and education and special admissions standards were all highly publicized by the mass media, it was convenient to assume that less qualified and competitive members of racial minorities were granted an inside track for the society's prestigious values. As Goode has asserted, "Men, like other dominants or superordinates, take for granted the system that gives them their status. They are not aware of how much the social structure, from attitude patterns to laws, pervasively yields small, cumulative and eventually large advantages in most competitions. As a consequence, they assume that their greater accomplishments are actually the result of inborn superiority."[61] This attitude, when applied to racial minorities such as blacks, is perpetuated by the societal stereotype of them as being intellectually inferior.

Finally, this ethnocentric attitude is enhanced by certain practices of the mass media. While blacks in general are under-represented in the media, what representation they do have is distorted toward the middle class. Rarely are the one-third of blacks still living in poverty depicted in the media. Most blacks on television, for example, are policemen, doctors and well-paid athletes. Success symbols are often highlighted whenever a black becomes president of a largely white organization or institution. These minor individual achievements are magnified into a normative event for the black majority. Meanwhile, the statistics which show black falling behind whites at every level and in every area of American life are ignored and minimized. Given these trends and tendencies, it is self-evident that the struggle of blacks for racial justice has just begun. The university is one more monument to racial inequality that must be dismantled before the ideology of equal opportunity is a reality for all Americans.

CHAPTER FIVE

Race and Crime in a White Settler Society

A number of factors are cited to explain the causes of crime in urban, industrialized societies. They range from the biological to the sociological. However, if one considers the societies with the highest rates of imprisonment, the one factor that is consistent among them is their status as a white settler country dominated by the ideology of white supremacy. Those two societies are the United States and South Africa.

Both countries were founded upon the displacement and subordination of non-white aboriginals. While differences in their historical evolution and demographic character make a direct comparison difficult, the two countries share the tendency to make racial differentiation the basis of social exclusion and a permanent underclass status. While other societies are not devoid of racial supremacist doctrines and some have eliminated problems of racial conflict through race genocide or biological assimilation, the United States and South Africa are unique in their systematic attempt to restrict class mobility to a sector of the population characterized by its light pigmentation.[1]

The case of South Africa is fairly simple: Its principle of white supremacy is embodied in its constitution. The United States, on the other hand, professes to be a color-blind democracy, after dismantling all the legal and official vestiges of racial inferiority among its citizenry. In reality, America only shifted from the practice of racial subordination based on physical characteristics to racial subordination based on class membership. The subordinate group remained the people of color, but it was their status as the underclass that determined their treatment, not their skin color.[2] In the United States, race and class have become synonymous.

By most indicators, America is the wealthiest country in the world. Yet, that wealth is more unequally distributed than in any other industrialized country except South Africa. Almost 13 percent of American citizens have incomes below the official poverty level. Among blacks, a third are in the poverty group. Hispanics number one-fourth of their people among the poor, and the majority of American Indians are poor. Only nine percent of Euro-Americans are counted among the groups with lower than poverty-level incomes.[3]

However, those statistics do not accurately reflect the racial differentials in standards of living, especially as they relate to the relationship between poverty, race and crime. By using a measure of personal wealth, a Joint Center for Political Studies survey revealed that the wealth of whites was almost three times that of blacks. The wealth of whites was concentrated in financial assets while that of blacks was largely confined to household assets. Attitudes of white superiority made black homes less valuable, and whites had more wealth to invest in other types of assets.[4] Moreover, poverty is a structural condition among the white group. Poverty is concentrated in rural areas, among female-headed households and the elderly, all groups with low rates of criminal activity.

It is clear that those who go to jail for criminal activity in the United States are the poor and uneducated. The demographic characteristics of jail inmates in 1978 showed that 61 percent had less than 12 years of schooling and an annual pre-arrest income of less than $3,000 a year. Four out of 10 were not employed prior to their arrest.[5]

While those are the salient characteristics of the groups most likely to be imprisoned for violating a law, they are actually only a fraction of the law violators in the United States. According to one study, one-third of retail, manufacturing and hospital workers admitted stealing from their employers. Most of those workers were motivated more by the feeling that their employers were exploiting them than economic compulsion.[6] The magnitude of employee theft is so great that it is estimated to cost American businesses more than 44 billion dollars a year.

Much of employee theft is of a petty nature although the aggregate sum is quite high. White collar crime may cost the

American economy as much as 100 billion dollars annually. The definition of white collar crime may range from the account-ant's manipulation of his/her books to steal a few thousand dol-lars, to giant corporations who gain billions of dollars through monopolistic practices and violation of anti-trust regulations. The advent of high technology has created new opportunities for white collar crime. Computers are now used to illegally take and transfer funds by employees who have access to them. In one case, as much as 21 million dollars was stolen through use of a computer.[7]

When white collar crimes occur, it is a common practice to avoid bringing criminal charges against the employee. In order to maintain a respectable corporate image and avoid embar-rassment, many companies actually promote or terminate indi-viduals and send them on to another company with excellent recommendations. It is safe to assume that few of the jail in-mates were imprisoned for a white collar crime. As many as 98 percent of the white collar criminals are white and largely go unpunished. Given that racial distribution, it was a cruel irony when a black professor was sentenced to five years in prison for exacting kickbacks from graduate students in exchange for jobs or course credit. The judge's rationale for the unusually harsh sentence was, "It (the sentence) would seem to signal the com-munity that white collar crimes simply cannot be tolerated. When you steal with a pen, you're going to get the same punish-ment as when you steal with a gun."[8] As the black man was car-ried off to a prison that was already 90 percent black, the more likely signal to the community was that not even a black person with a Ph.D. can expect the same justice as his or her white counterpart.

CRIME IN AMERICA

Other societies may have greater disparities between the poor and the wealthy. However, the United States has long had an ideology of equal opportunity for all its citizens, regardless of race, creed or color. That creed is observed more in its breach than its practice. Peoples of color have watched European im-migrants come to the United States in the 1940's and receive political and economic opportunities denied some Americans for centuries. Consequently, alienation is added to poverty as a root cause of crime. The poor people of color do not consider their country to be a fair and just society, hence feel no obligation to obey its laws. As the political scandals, such as Watergate, have gained publicity and it becomes common knowledge that many of the wealthy have engaged in fraudulent schemes to avoid paying income taxes, the criminal class is made aware of the double standard of justice applied to the poor.

While the United States may not have the highest crime rate in the world, no other Western nation has as high a percentage of its people in prison. The fact that a disproportionate number of those imprisoned are people of color, along with South Africa's rank as the second largest jailer in the industrialized world, gives eloquent testimony to the role of race in the criminal justice system.[9] Although the poor people of color bear the brunt of white supremacist attitudes, the American Constitution and respect for civil liberties has forced all U.S. citizens to bear the consequences of America's racial ideology. Crime, and the fear of it, have become so rampant in the United States that one citizen was moved to note, "I've got bars on all my windows. The only difference between me and the boys in prison is that I've got the keys to 'MY' cellblock."[10]

A couple of factors distinguish the United States from both South Africa and other Western nations. Unlike South Africa, U.S. courts do not blithely ignore civil liberties and put people in prison without due process. In 1982, South Africa arrested 200,000 blacks for violating residence and travel restrictions.[11] Whereas blacks suffer numerous inequities in the American criminal justice system, constitutional safeguards prevent massive abuse of an individual's civil rights. In 1983, the Supreme Court upheld the right of a black man to walk the streets of white neighborhoods without being accosted by the police.

On the other hand, the social welfare system in the United States is less developed than those of European nations. The American government spends proportionally less of its gross national product for social insurance schemes than other Western nations.[12] Hence, those without jobs often have no alternative other than to engage in criminal activity as a means of survival. It should be noted that the lesser health, welfare and education benefits are also intricately linked to the notion of white supremacy. Because so many of the poor in America are people of color, white voters resist the idea of welfare increases that they believe will largely benefit the "indolent coloreds."[13]

Consequently, Americans are placed in the dilemma of suspending civil liberties for everyone or tolerating a crime-ridden environment for themselves and their families. Attacking the root causes of crime-racism, unemployment and poverty seems to have been ruled out by the majority of white citizens. So, they vote to strengthen existing laws, build more prisons and reinstitute the death penalty, none of which serves to deter the criminal class. To the underclass, there is nothing to lose. To someone who cannot find work, a place to live and has nothing to eat, freedom is worth nothing.

Meanwhile, in New York City an estimated 100,000 drug addicts and hard-core criminals stalk the streets in search of unsuspecting victims. They walk into and out of other people's homes as though they have keys. Chains dominate the doors of the high rent districts, and private guards patrol almost every place of business, sometimes even called to escort men and women to their apartments. One weekend New York City experienced 17 violent deaths and simply listed them like the war dead on one page.[14]

America spends 10 billion dollars a year on a wide variety of security equipment and services, ranging from $5-an-hour private guards to $1,100 for a hand scanning lock. The United States is expected to spend 23 billion dollars by 1990 to fight crime. Security is one of this country's few growth industries.[15] The other responses of Americans are to take self-defense classes, arm themselves and teach their children how to scream for help. It is a silent class and racial war reminiscent of France in 1789 and 1917 in Russia.

Obviously, America has become a society of adversaries because it lacks the moral anchor of a common heritage, traditions and racial backgrounds. There are 622,000 lawyers, more than one for every 375 Americans.[16] This ratio is far more than any comparable nation and is projected to number one million by the mid-1990's.

The indication of crime's far reaching impact is illustrated by the most comprehensive crime data available. Figures compiled from the Bureau of Justice surveys in 1981 revealed that nearly 25 million households, or 29 percent, suffered violent crime or theft in that year. The most common crime was larceny, and the most vulnerable households were those with high incomes, those in central cities and those headed by blacks.[17] These figures are considered most reliable since they are not based on crimes reported to the police but are compiled from a random survey of 50,000 Americans. However, even these figures understate the magnitude of "serious" crime in the United States. Few white collar crimes are reported through this method, and other crimes such as rape are vastly underreported.

According to the F.B.I.'s annual Uniform Crime Report of 1981, 13 million serious crimes were reported in 1980. This figure was a 55 percent increase from the past decade. Only one out of five criminals was apprehended, and there was an arrest rate of 10 percent for all serious crimes. The report revealed that the crime rate increased four times faster than the increase in the population. "Serious crimes" rose fastest in the suburbs where they increased by nine percent, compared to seven percent in metropolitan areas and six percent in rural areas. Murders occurred every 23 minutes on the average in the United States, and murderers killed 23,044 people—one out of every 10,000 residents of the country.[18] These figures, bad as they seem, vastly understate the magnitude of serious crime since they are based on reports to the police. Due to the large number of crimes unreported, the inconsistency among police jurisdictions in classifying crimes, and the politicians' need to manipulate crime statistics, these figures only reflect the minimal level of criminal activity.

RACE AND CRIME IN AMERICA

While most white settler societies have effectively annihilated, amalgamated or subjugated their non-white subjects, the United States continued to increase its non-white population through slavery and immigration. The black population's increase in recent years has been through a birth rate higher than the Euro-Americans'. In the last decade, the white population has declined proportionally due to the changing character of immigration trends. More than 75 percent of America's legal immigrants—and almost all of its illegal ones—are people of color. The largest number come from Asia and Latin America. Africa accounts for only two percent of immigrants to America.[19] These new immigrants will begin at the lowest paying jobs, and most will eventually end up in the nation's largest cities.

As a result of this immigration trend and the higher fertility rate of third world people, the white population officially declined, between 1970-80, from 83 to 80 percent of the total population. Given the undercount of non-whites in the U.S. census and the problems of racial classification, a more accurate representation for the white population should be about 70 percent. Moreover, it should be noted that the non-white population is considerably younger than its white counterpart, a partial factor in the former's higher crime rate since young males commit a disproportionate share of the nation's serious crimes.

The crime statistics graphically describe the relationship between race and crime. Between 1980-84, urban blacks, who officially constitute 12 percent of the nation's population, made up 48.5 percent of all arrests for murder and non-negligent manslaughter.[20] Although whites are still a majority of those arrested for criminal activity, it is ingrained in the American consciousness that the criminal and black male are one and the same. The fact that black males are a disproportionate percentage of the street criminals led one student of the subject to state, "There is no escaping the question of race and crime." He then summed up the issue by quoting from one of James Baldwin's earlier works: "To be a Negro in this country and to be relatively conscious is to be in a rage almost all the time."[21]

The caveat is issued, however, that violence cannot be excused because black offenders are victims of poverty and discrimination. While the concern over "black crime" is mostly related to its impact on the white population, it is other blacks who are most likely to be victims of crimes committed by blacks. Surveys reveal that blacks are more likely than whites to have been victims of personal crimes. One survey reported that black males had a victimization rate of 85 per 1,000 of the population as compared with 75 per 1,000 for white males.[22] In fact, the poorer a person is, the more likely he or she will become a crime victim.

It is interesting to note that the proportion of blacks arrested closely parallels their numbers among those officially listed as having incomes below the poverty level. Certainly, few blacks with a college education or gainful employment fill the ranks of the nation's jails. In 1983 the official unemployment rate for adult black males was 22 percent. Black youth had an unemployment rate of 50 percent.[23] As federal Judge A. Leon Higginbatham sagely noted:

> History tells us that a nation can survive for years by shifting the burdens of life to the people confined by force and violence to the bottom. But history also tells us that this process, with inexorable logic, rebounds against the oppressor. For at a certain point, the people on the bottom begin to straighten their backs and the burdens rise to the top of society, affecting everything and sparing nothing. That's where we are today.[24]

A report issued by the National Minority Advisory Council on Criminal Justice condemned the United States for its heavy handed use of state and private powers to control minorities and suppress their continuing opposition to the influence of white supremacist ideology. The report noted the hypocrisy inherent in the public declaration of freedom by a nation that has blocked economic opportunities for peoples of color and prevented their upward mobility in ways not experienced by Americans of European descent. As a result, with few exceptions, minorities remain segregated, powerless and at a marginal level of existence as a result of America's socio-economic system and political practices.[25] It is that fact, and that fact alone, that explains why the rate of imprisonment for blacks exceeds that for whites by 9-1. In 75 percent of American states, the black rate of imprisonment is higher than the national incarceration rate of South Africa. In 10 states, the black rate of incarceration is more than 15 times the rate for whites.[26]

What determines a state's likelihood to imprison its residents is not its crime rate but the size of its non-white population. The higher the non-white population, the higher the incarceration rate. Colorado, for instance, has a very small black population, a very high crime rate, and a very low incarceration rate. Conversely, Mississippi has a very low crime rate, the highest proportion of blacks of any state, and a very high imprisonment rate.[27] The demographic ratio of blacks to whites appears to pose a threat to the hegemony of whites. Hence, imprisonment is used as a form of social control, just as political and economic disenfranchisement is. As one former prison warden concluded, "Racial composition is the only important cause of incarceration rates in our analysis."[28]

Although the harshest treatment is reserved for blacks, due to them being defined as "the race problem" and because they are the only racial minority spread throughout the United States, other peoples of color are also the objects of greater crime and imprisonment rates. In the states where they dominate the population, Chicanos, Puerto Ricans and Indians have an incarceration rate higher than whites. American Indians, for example, are regularly picked up off the streets by policemen in many towns in Oklahoma. The Indians are jailed for a short period of time and then released to perform forced labor such as cleaning the streets and collecting garbage.[29]

Only Asians have a low incarceration rate among the peoples of color. That fact seems to be a function of the underreporting of crime by the Asian community. Juvenile delinquency has increased among Chinese youth, and Southeast Asians have experienced a rash of crimes by some of their members. Asians remain a close knit culture, and many crimes among that group are internal and hence not a source of concern to the larger white community.

Since crime is often interpreted as a function of moral flaws among the "barbaric" coloreds, the white public is largely indifferent to the underlying causes of the political and economic conditions that propel individuals into criminal activity. Instead, whites rely on the politically motivated cry for more law and order and even harsher punitive measures. Contributing to the feelings of alienation among the underclass is the double standard of justice applied when the perpetrator is white and the victim is non-white. One such case was that of Vincent Chin, a Chinese man brutally beaten to death in Detroit by two white auto workers who blamed all Asians for taking their jobs away from them. For no greater sin than being of Asian descent, Chin was killed, and the only punishment his white attackers received was a fine of $3,700 and three years' probation.[30]

THE ECONOMIC ROOTS OF CRIME

Students of criminal activity in the United States have shown a strong correlation between rises in crimes and unemployment. The *Washington Post* compared the incidence of crime in seven categories with nationwide unemployment rates from 1960 through 1980. In the recession year of 1975, when unemployment reached 8.5 percent, the total crime index reached a peak with historic highs in violent crime, robbery, burglary and auto theft.

Based on statistical analysis, one sociologist, M. Harvey Brenner, has published findings indicating a strong link between unemployment and many crimes, particularly murder. His analysis revealed that a one percent increase in the unemployment rate is associated with a 5.7 percent increase in homicides and a four percent increase in the number of people in state prisons. According to Brenner, a principal reason for this relationship is stress. When people are unemployed, they feel tension. They may also feel victimized, and there may be economic reasons for committing thefts or burglaries.[31]

Certainly, the factors of stress and alienation can be found among the black American population. Psychiatrist Thomas Parham claims that while all Americans have some degree of stress in their lives, environmental stress is a lot higher for black people. The reason for the stress differential, he says, is that blacks still have to function in a white dominated and oriented society. How successful they can be in life is contingent on how well blacks can assimilate into what the white culture suggests is the norm.[32] The fact that there is often a discrepancy between the societal norm of equal opportunity and its treatment of blacks serves to fuel their feelings of alienation. One study concluded that blacks believed the economic gains of the 1960's have diminished to the point where they again are at the bottom of the heap. The survey found that 72 percent of the black respondents felt they had little or no power in today's society, and 64 percent blamed the system for their difficulty in finding jobs.[33]

Added to the high unemployment rate the feelings of stress and alienation, the outcome is a highly disproportionate number of blacks among the criminal population. Blacks constitute about 12 percent of the United States population, but 36 percent of them are officially classified as poor. Blacks also make up about 30 percent of those arrested for the three property crimes in the F.B.I.'s Crime Index (burglary, larceny theft and auto theft). For violent crimes, black percentages are even higher. According to 1981 F.B.I. reports, blacks represented 57 percent of those arrested for robbery, 48 percent of those arrested for murder or rape, and 37 percent of those arrested for aggravated assault.[34]

The relationship between crime and race is a spurious one. As our analysis has shown, the more salient relationship is between race and class. Using the dual labor market model, one can understand the relationship between race and crime. The unemployment problem of non-white males is a direct result of their systematic exclusion from jobs in the primary sector and their concentration in unstable secondary sector jobs. A central assumption is that two largely separate labor markets exist: Primary sector jobs have a future, while secondary jobs are dead ends. The primary sector offers high wages, good working conditions, advancement, equity and employment stability. Jobs in the secondary sector are low paying, or involve poor working conditions, offer limited advancement, instability and a high turnover rate.[35]

Researchers have documented that several aspects of this dual labor market are stressful for non-white males, who are overrepresented in the secondary sector and encounter hiring discrimination, isolated job contacts and other barriers that restrict entry into primary sector jobs. Additionally, the rising joblessness rate among non-white males is a function of the instability of secondary sector jobs and their vulnerability to technological change and economic risk. Consequently, many drop out of the labor force and experience persistent economic hardship.[36]

Nowhere is the effect of the dual labor market more evident than among black Americans. According to 1980 census statistics, blacks in the experienced civilian labor force were concentrated in three summary occupational groups: operators, fabricators and laborers (27 percent); technical, sales and administrative support (24 percent); and service occupations (23 percent). Between 1971 and 1981 the real median income of all black families dropped 8.3 percent, from $14,460 to $13,270 in constant dollars. The ratio of black to white median family income was .56 in 1981. Unemployment among blacks increased 140 percent between 1972 and 1982—from 900,000 (10.3 percent) to 2.1 million (18.9 percent). In 1982, one-third of all blacks in the labor force were jobless at some point in the year.[37] Thus, we see the indirect effects of the dual labor market in the destructive stress for blacks, who may cope through criminal activity. Economic hardship, environmental stress and employment inequalities are all translated into higher rates of crime.

Not only is crime in the United States a function of race and class, but it reflects age and gender factors as well. Most of the convicted criminals are men. Women represent less than four percent of the incarcerated population, but the racial and class bias is still maintained. In 1977, 50 percent of the imprisoned women were black. Indian women were also overrepresented. Over half of them had a high school education or less. Fifty-six percent had received welfare during their adult lives. Black women made up a larger percentage of the female inmate population than their male counterparts.[38] Studies suggest that judges and juries treat women defendants more leniently than men who come before the court. Apparently, this leniency is not extended as often to non-white women. In some highly urbanized states, the female inmate population is so heavily dominated by non-whites that judges are reluctant to send a white female into such a setting.[39]

Crime has sharply divided along age lines in the last three decades. Between the 1950's and the 1970's, crimes committed by juveniles in the United States tripled. Chronic offenders—those with five or more offenses—now are mostly under the age of 25. Police statistics suggest that young men under 18 commit nearly half of all serious crimes—murder, rape, armed robbery and arson. Eight and one-tenth percent of all property crimes and 60 percent of all crimes of violence are committed by persons under the age of 25. These same data show that the typical young offender is a non-white male residing in the slum area of a large city.[40] That is the same person whose age cohort experiences a joblessness rate of about 70 percent, compared with 20 percent for white youths. In fact, white high school dropouts have a lower rate of unemployment than black college graduates.

In the last decade, some have asserted, the crime rate fluctuations were a function of the proportions of teenagers and young adults in the general population. As the birth rate declines, so will the proportion of young people in the country and consequently, so will the crime rate. The problem with this predicted scenario is its failure to account for: (1) the higher fertility rate among non-white women; (2) immigration, accounting for a substantial proportion of the increase in the non-white population, most of them young families with children; and (3) the jobless youth of today, who may never obtain gainful employment and will simply become more sophisticated criminals as they grow older.

Whatever may happen in the future, the young, non-white male is a source of tension on the urban scene. His lack of educational credentials and marketable skills has rendered him redundant in a society increasingly geared toward the use of high technology. Some see the young, non-white male as the vanguard of a worker's revolt in the United States because he has nothing to lose. As psychologist Kenneth Clark testified before a Congressional committee in 1981:

> You gentlemen in the middle class have a particular respect for punishment, for penalty. That is a measure of your faith in society. You have something to lose. What is difficult for you to understand is that this society has made it possible for too large a group of people not to have this respect.[41]

Certainly one could interpret urban crime as a kind of guerrilla warfare with political excuses but not clear cut political objectives. The adversary tension between the underclass and society represents sort of a class war. In an affluent society such as the United States, the promise of material abundance is held out to everyone as a desirable goal. But the means for obtaining that goal are unequally distributed. The young men of color will not have the access to conventional means of obtaining even a middle class standard of living. Hence, they resort to illegitimate means.

When the Carnegie Council of Policy Studies examined youth employment and educational problems, it concluded that "the role of illicit earnings might be possibly more significant than welfare payments in America's inner cities." Another study found that 20 percent of the adults in Harlem lived entirely on illegal incomes.[42] They exist entirely outside the boundaries of the wage system because it is clear that illegal activities, in many respects, provide a more lucrative alternative to low wage employment.

RACE AND THE CRIMINAL JUSTICE SYSTEM

Historically, the police departments and other adjuncts of the criminal justice system have been viewed by peoples of color as enforcers rather than protectors in the non-white community. Because it is the police force that comes into direct contact with the non-white populace, most of the police opprobrium is reserved for that group. Frantz Fanon, the black psychiatrist, once said of police: "In the colonies it is the policeman and the soldier who are the official instituted go-betweens, the spokesman of the settler and his rule of oppression."[43] Certainly it is arguable that the police in racial minority areas are only there to serve the public interest. Until recently, most of the police assigned to non-white communities were white, and studies reveal those white police officers expressed highly prejudiced attitudes toward racial minorities.[44]

Probably the best barometer of the white police officer's role in minority communities is the complaints of police brutality. Wallace Warfield, Associate Director for the Justice Department's Community Relations Service, said that both the incidence of police brutality and the reporting of such episodes were increasing throughout the country, with minorities most frequently the victims. In 1980, the complaints of excessive force by police officers increased by 93 percent over the previous year.[45] A survey of selected American cities showed a positive correlation between the percentage of the black population and the average annual complaints of police brutality.[46] It was generally an act of police brutality that triggered the race riots in American cities during the 1960's and 1970's. As Earl Shinhoster, an official of the N.A.A.C.P., has noted, "Police violence and minority violence go hand in hand. Miami gets the headlines, but the potential for a racial explosion triggered by police violence exists in many communities."[47]

Despite the ostensible political and economic gains of America's racial minorities, the basic issue of police brutality toward them is as much a fact of life as it has ever been. Any minority group can offer up a litany of horror stories. And, brutality knows no class distinctions when it comes to people of color. Famous and wealthy black celebrities such as Lynn Swann, the football player, and Smokey Robinson, the singer, have filed lawsuits against police departments for brutality. Such indiscriminate use of police force against the black population once led author Louis Lomax to comment, "I don't know a single black who doesn't get a flutter in his stomach when approached by a white policeman."[48]

Distrust of the police is widespread in the minority communities, and for good cause. During 1973-74, a Police Foundation study found that 75 percent of the civilians killed by police in seven cities were black males. The study concluded that many police shootings did not appear to have served any compelling purpose. In nine out of 10 cases, police who shot civilians were not punished.[49] While it is often argued that blacks are over-represented among the violent criminals (the percentage of black civilians killed by police is a function of that fact), that hardly explains three cases in southern California where an old lady, a seven-year-old boy and a football player, none of them armed or violating the law, were summarily killed by the police.

The racial issue is put into clearer focus when it is revealed that a study of black police officers found that the majority of them did not trust their fellow white officers. As one black police officer was quoted, "Black policemen recognize separation and insensitivity of policing as it relates to blacks and other minorities from the inside (of the department) more than the community does."[50] In New York City, about 3,000 black police officers resigned from the predominantly white policeman's association in protest over the union's support of a white officer accused of killing a black youth.[51] In the words of author John Williams,

> Cops in the U.S. have a lot to answer for. The jails, as noted by nearly everyone, would otherwise not be quite so filled with "dark spots" were it not for the tacit agreement, it appears, between the police and other elements of the criminal justice system, which carry out the mandates of a society verging on collapse.

Most of the studies of the American criminal justice system have concluded that racial minorities are over-arrested, selectively prosecuted and receive longer sentences than whites. Blacks, for instance, comprise only 12 percent of the nation's population, but nearly half of those in prison. A recent study by the Rand Corporation found that blacks and Hispanics receive stiffer prison sentences and serve more time in jail than whites convicted of similar felonies.[53] Another study of all-white juries disclosed that they tended to hand down more guilty verdicts for black males, although the basic information was the same for all racial groups.[54] In a survey of the racial composition of the law enforcement personnel in the United States, it was revealed that minorities comprise 50 percent of the country's jail inmates but only four percent of its law enforcement personnel.[55]

It is in the area of capital punishment that racial disparities are most evident. Only the Soviet Union, South Africa, Japan and the United States, of the industrialized nations, retain the death penalty. Japan, however, only executes about one person a year while the United States has a total of 1,202 prisoners on death row. About 42 percent (508) of those awaiting execution are black, 59 are Hispanic, seven are American Indian, and five are Asian.[56] A large proportion of the black males sentenced to death were convicted of raping a white woman or killing a white man. The ideology of white supremacy places little premium on the lives of people of color in the United States. There is also evidence that the death penalty in the southern United

States is reserved exclusively for blacks who rape or kill whites.[57]

Those who escape the death penalty must suffer the degradation of being housed in America's prisons. Prison confinement is a brutal, dehumanizing experience where inmates are subjected to overcrowded and unsanitary conditions, random attacks and homosexual rapes. In fact, in 1982 more death row inmates were murdered than executed.[58] Due to the economic recession from 1980-83, the number of prison inmates rose by a record 42,915 in 1982, to reach an all-time high of 412,303, the highest of all the industrialized nations. Federal prisons are nearly 24 percent over capacity. At the state level, inmates have been housed two and three to a cell or in tents, sheds and military stockades. At least 31 states are under court orders to reduce overcrowding because their prisons have such bestial conditions that they violate the Constitutional safeguard against cruel and unusual punishment.[59]

The drain on government treasuries to maintain the race and class inequality of American life is enormous. It costs at least $10,000 a year, sometimes three times as much, to house, feed and guard a single inmate. We have already noted that racial minorities comprise the majority of the nation's inmates. In the federal system, for example, the white population has risen 22 percent, while the black population has risen five times faster, or 111 percent during the last decade.[60] The heavy concentration of non-whites in New York's prisons led one criminal court judge to free a white defendant because the Department of Corrections could not guarantee a white man's safety, indicating that whites should get special treatment.[61]

POLICY IMPLICATIONS

Our analysis of the relationship between race and crime indicates that the United States' excessive rate of criminal activity is a function of racial and class inequalities that exist in its political, economic and criminal justice systems. Given that the class inequalities alone were extant, the crime rate would be reduced because the burden of economic hardship would be equally distributed among the various racial groups. Since the problem of poverty is so disproportionately laid upon the non-white population, members of that group feel little need to obey the society's laws. The fact that large numbers of non-white people are mired in poverty for no reason other than their race contributes to their feelings of alienation and stress. Thus, it is incumbent upon policy makers, political activists, and community groups to develop intervention strategies to promote meaningful access to primary sector jobs and constructive coping experiences.

For those unable to secure jobs in the primary sector, social insurance schemes should be developed to cushion the blow of unemployment and underemployment. Most current welfare measures are woefully inadequate in providing a decent income for young minority males. A floor underneath individual incomes should be provided for all citizens regardless of age, gender or marital status. Scholarships for a college education or remedial or vocational training should be made available to all who desire it. To undermine the arbitrary arrest by police officers, an ombudsman's office should be established to review all arrests of those who claim innocence and the arrest procedures. Civilian review boards should be created where they do not presently exist, in order to render judgment on complaints of police brutality or other inappropriate police practices. The police force, judiciary and juries should reflect the racial and class composition of those arrested and brought to trial. Should these policy recommendations not be enacted, the United States will remain a country whose inhabitant have the key to their cells, and the country's image as the bastion of democracy will forever be tarnished.

CHAPTER SIX

Culture, Ideology and Black Media Images

Human society has been characterized throughout history by unequal access to its values. This inequity is often accepted by the denizens as the natural order of life. Since the inequality enhances a small minority at the expense of the masses, it is necessary to erect some kind of cultural apparatus which services the function of convincing the exploited groups that their condition is necessary and natural. Marx called this cultural apparatus the superstructure, wherein the ideas of a society, of necessity, reflect the values of the ruling class.[1]

These ideas, historically, were expressed through the political, religious and legal institutions as well as the images and ideologies through which social reality was constructed. In the 20th century, other mediums emerged to serve the function of purveying the bourgeois and racist ideology to mass publics throughout the world. Those mediums, generically labeled as the entertainment and arts complex, have typically operated negatively for groups at the bottom rung of the social strata. As the most oppressed of the exploited classes, black Americans have been portrayed in the media in ways which reinforce the image of white superiority and black inferiority, the purpose of which has been the stabilization of status quo relations between the races.

In one of the most important mediums, movies, blacks have been blatantly subjected to exploitation and dehumanization. More than any other medium, the film industry has shaped and reflected racist attitudes toward blacks. Sterling Brown has listed seven stereotypes of blacks found in literature and films: the contented slave, wretched freedman, comic Negro, brute Negro, tragic mulatto, local color Negro and the exotic primitive. In these types, one finds the characteristics of laziness, filth, sensuality and crime.[2] Until 1954, these images of blacks were projected in American films, and they served to create and maintain the myth of white purity and superiority.

During the latter part of the fifties and early sixties, blacks were portrayed as social problems and super-heroes. Seldom did one ever see an average black family that worked hard, engaged in normal love and marital behavior, or enjoyed life.[3]

It was in the late 1960's that a new form of exploitation emerged in the shape of black films directed toward increasing black audiences who were hungry to see their images on the cinema screen. Most of these movies ("Superfly," "Shaft," etc.) contained heavy doses of sex, crime, violence and drugs in a way that suggested approval of them.[4] In most cases these films were nothing more than a continuation of past stereotypes of blacks as criminal and sexy savages, related this time to the nitty-gritty black cultural lifestyle.

Most of the producers of these films were whites who claimed that black audiences desired these types of films. Few black leaders outside the movie industry agreed. One reviewer asserted that the films were not only an insult to black intelligence, but subtly harmful to the interests and well-being of blacks and whites alike.[5] He nevertheless defended the films because of his belief that it was unfair to expect the downtrodden to be more upright than the oppressor.

The blacks who participated in the production of "Blaxploitation" films were, in reality, that sector of the bourgeoisie which had internalized the values of the white oligarchy. Hence, they seized the chance to make a profit out of movies that encouraged drug use, violence and the sexual exploitation of black women.

Black audiences eventually tired of the constant diet of sexual violence as the only content of most black films. Although black audiences did not disappear, the "Blaxploitation" films faded away, and few blacks appeared on the silver screen after 1975. Hollywood took the position that movies with black heroes were not working (i.e., not appealing to white audiences), and that black audiences would continue to patronize movies with all white characters. Thus, there was no need to cater to the aspirations of blacks to see their images on the screen. While blacks constituted 12 percent of the U.S. population, they accounted for more than 20 percent of the movie-going audience.

Still, there was scant evidence that black movies of a high quality could not attract a cross section of the movie-going public. Richard Pryor and Eddie Murphy became two of the biggest box office attractions of the 1980's. Yet, an industry, known for imitating trends that were financially successful, did not rush out to sign future black stars and develop projects to suit their talents. According to a survey of 299 Hollywood films made between 1979 and 1981, less than three percent of speaking roles went to blacks.[6]

The films of the late 1970's and early 1980's depicted even box office attractions such as Pryor and Murphy in limited roles. They, and other black male actors, were subject to the "eunichization" process, wherein the black actor is reduced to playing the sidekick to a white male actor. The black actor is sexually neutered and stripped of any romantic or sexual involvement.[7] This kind of portrayal is a reinforcement of racist stereotypes that derive from the myth of black sexual prowess and reflects Hollywood's desire to subjugate black actors in side-kick roles. As one of the stars of the movie "Ghostbusters," Ernie Hudson, notes:

> Hollywood is afraid, I mean petrified of black sexuality. They think we're different, sexually, from other people. They can't let us be tender and kiss women on the screen. They want me to be angry and break things.[8]

Black women fare even worse. Even more absent from films than the black male, they are reduced to playing the roles of harlots and maids whenever they can get roles. In 1981, when 240 films were released, only one black actress, Cicely Tyson, held a major role.[9]

Another ominous trend is the legitimization of the shooting and killing of blacks by macho white males. In the movie "Taxi Driver," the white hero critically wounds a young black man who attempts to rob a delicatessen and is commended for his heroics by the proprietor. Later, the proprietor bludgeons the unconscious black man with a tire iron. A similar scene exists in the movie "Sudden Impact," in which Clint Eastwood confronts an unarmed black criminal with his pistol and taunts,

"Go ahead, punk, make my day," a phrase later repeated by President Reagan. Blackness is becoming synonymous with bestiality, and it becomes legitimate activity for any armed white male to shoot black men. The case of Bernard Goetz, who shot four unarmed black youth in a subway, is an example of life imitating art.[10]

It is possible in a racist culture for whites to be socialized to expect their race to appear in dominant media roles and blacks in stereotypical, subordinate roles. A more likely explanation is that the whites who control the film industry see themselves as the gatekeepers of the image of white superiority. Hollywood has a long history of exploiting racial slurs and stereotypes, beginning with the D.W. Griffith film, "Birth of a Nation," in 1915 that depicted blacks as fun-loving, lazy, shiftless and foolish. In fact, the film industry's production code, set up in the 1930's to guard the manners and morals of moviegoers, forbade miscegenation between the races in films.[11]

The racist gatekeepers maintain their vested interests by limiting blacks to roles as actors and keeping them out of areas where they might exercise artistic control. Of some 5,700 writers in the Writers Guild of America-West, only 70 are black. Only 252 of the 6,672 members of the Directors Guild of America are members of minority groups.[12] As a white female member of the Writers Guild of America comments: "Most people who control the work here are men, and they hire their friends and their friends are men" (and white).[13] With white males in control, the images of women and blacks continue to be shaped out of stereotypical portraits that form the superstructure of a bourgeois society.

MUSICAL APARTHEID

No other entertainment medium has the shameless history of racial exploitation as popular music. The most popular musical form, rock and roll, has its roots in the musical tradition of black Americans. It took a white male, Elvis Presley, to popularize black music in the 1950's, since black singers had no access to most of the nation's airwaves. At least Presley retained the primal force of black music and recorded songs long after the original versions had been released.

Other white singers, such as Pat Boone and Georgia Gibbs, engaged in the practice of "covering" a black singer's song immediately after its release and having the white version played on 95 percent of the radio stations. The white version was usually a sanitized, bland imitation of the original black edition. Highly risque lyrics were replaced, and titles changed that were considered too ungrammatical to suit the white audience. As one white rock critic observed: "America loves the bogus, celebrates the imitation and adores British musicians who can take the danger and threat out of exotic black music, be it the Rolling Stones playing Bo Diddley or Eric Clapton doing B.B. King."[14] While Pat Boone had a nice clean-cut image that white parents found acceptable, Little Richard seemed like a man you wouldn't want to see in a dark alley.

Nonetheless, blacks did gain a niche in the music world of the 1950's and 1960's, although no black singer or group ever attained the popularity of Elvis Presley or the Beatles. Just as occurred in the movies, in the 1970's there was an erosion of the tenuous toehold blacks had reached in the arena of popular music. As one observer of the music scene noted: "The listening habits of most of pop's audiences are more strictly segregated today than they were 10 or 20 years ago, when black music was a common place on Top-10 sales charts and Top-40 radio playlists."[15] Record producers and radio programmers claimed that white audiences automatically rejected music by black performers. Music awards shows and magazines ranking sales of records actually separated music into black and non-black categories. This strategy had the effect of restricting black musicians to the 400, out of 9,000, radio stations in the United States, reducing their potential audience to less than 30 million people in a country of 230 million.[16]

The problems of black artists were compounded with the advent of music video. Since white funk and black funk can sound similar, a black band had a better opportunity of getting exposure when it was only heard, not seen. The most popular music video channel, MTV, seemed to have a "white artists only" policy for which it was widely criticized by music critics and black musicians. In March 1984, in MTV's heavy rotation,

meaning the videos most played and played most often at op-
timum times, there were 21 names listed, not one of them
black.[17] When questioned about the absence of black artists, an
official of MTV replied: "MTV is not racist. It is merely the format of the show. The viewers don't want to see black acts on
MTV, and in America the people rule."[18]

Since a small number of white males made that decision,
white audiences voted with their record purchases. They became
aware of black music through its increasing use in popular
movies, and from 1982 to 1983 the percentage of dollars spent
on black music increased from seven percent to 11 percent–half
of the records purchased by whites.[19] As MTV relented on its
"whites only" policy, blacks made music videos deemed more
palatable to white audiences. Herbie Hancock, the black jazz
musician, used robots in his video instead of blacks to improve
its chances of being played on MTV.[20] Other black artists used
mostly whites, other than themselves, in their music videos.

Again, as true of the movies, the overwhelming success of
black music had little ripple effect for black performers. Between 1982-85, the most popular records in the U.S.A. were by
black artists. Yet, as Roberta Flack has stated:

> Black artists are not afforded the same opportunities as white artists.
> People who are not black take our ideas and put them on the vinyl, and
> it becomes very, very successful and we're not allowed it.[21]

The eunuchization process is also operative in the music
world. In 1981, whites purchased 93 percent of all records sold,
and women bought 51 percent of them.[22] Since people are often
not buying just a music form but a romantic fantasy attached to
the singer of the songs, the sexual neutering of black male singers
must occur. It may be no accident that the black male singers
with the largest cross-over appeal (i.e., white audiences accept
them), in the last 20 years were blind, admitted or alleged
homosexuals or married. The most successful black male singer
in recent years knew the formula for cross-over success. Michael
Jackson Anglocized his facial features, straightened his hair
and took a white woman to public events, the latter an act that
caused no public outcry since rumors of his homosexuality were

so rampant that he had to publicly deny them.

Illustrative of the limitations placed on black male singers is the complaint by Peabo Bryson:

> I don't know if white America is ready to fully accept a black matinee-idol type, the soul singer who sweeps women off their feet with love songs. On a deep level, many white Americans are threatened by blacks. When you have a black ballad singer, somebody with great physical appeal, that makes some whites uncomfortable.[23]

The fantastic financial successes of black artists rarely have economic side effects for other blacks. As Ewart Abner points out, "Black music accounts for 10 to 20 percent of the profits of many record companies. Yet, blacks don't represent one percent of anything in the industry, not on the wholesale level or the retail level or the manufacturing level."[24] While the black musician may receive only 10 percent (or less) from the gross sales of his or her product, even the 10 percent will be divided among managers, accountants, lawyers, promoters and others. With the exception of racially conscious artists such as Stevie Wonder, the supporting staff of black superstars are largely white. The reverse is rarely true as even liberal white entertainers employ only a token black in their bands. Some black entertainers believe that being surrounded by white managers and lawyers guarantees them greater access to the white media, a belief hardly validated by black people's sparse representation in the music world.

However, certain accommodations have been made to attract white listening audiences. The music of black cross-over artists in the 1980's is a blander version of music presented to black audiences. One white disk jockey claimed that, "An obvious black sound is the kiss of death for Top-40 radio." Even the reigning king of contemporary pop music, Michael Jackson, had to enlist the assistance of white artists such as Eddie Van Halen and Paul McCartney to have his records played on white radio stations. Certain observers thought it was an act of courage for white singer Paul McCartney to risk his standing with white audiences by recording songs with black artists such as Stevie Wonder and Michael Jackson.[25] In contrast to their white American counterparts, British artists have been candid about borrowing, even stealing, elements of black music to refashion for white audiences.

By banishing black music to black stations, white stations have been left free to play music by whites without effective competition from blacks. Since whites purchased 95 percent of all records in the United States, the white artists enjoyed a strong economic advantage. Black dance music and jazz accounted for only six percent of the records sold in 1983.[26] Most of the whites purchasing black records were women, indicating continued hostility to black music by white males.

At least black musicians had 400 black radio stations as an outlet for their products. Unlike blacks in television and movies, exclusively controlled by whites, black musicians were not consigned to the unemployment lines when blacks became "unfashionable" in those mediums. Most of the 400 black radio stations are owned by whites, some of whom have become millionaires through their control of the black communications media. Some of the black "soul" stations have achieved the number one spot in their market. A black owner seems to be no guarantee the black community's needs will be met or even the job stability of black personnel at these stations. The son of Adam Clayton Powell purchased a black soul station in Oakland, California, converted it to an all-news format and replaced most of the black employees with whites.

Other soul stations have been criticized for playing rhythm and blues to the almost total exclusion of other black musical expression, reading news from the wire services that relates little to black problems, and playing music that glorifies drugs and promiscuous sexuality. Soul music is politically neutral and hymatic. As true of alcohol and drugs, soul music is a psychological depressant and hallucinatory, which releases the inhibitions and retards the thinking process.

Whereas music has been used as a liberating force in the past with the songs of Woody Guthrie, Pete Seeger, Bob Dylan, Marvin Gaye and Stevie Wonder, in the 1980's it has become another opiate of the masses. New racial and sexual stereotypes are embodied in pop singers such as Boy George, Prince, and Michael Jackson, which reflect the alienation of American youth. In a bourgeois society in a declining state, the media oligarchy prefers music and performers that bear little resemblance to social reality. In that endeavor, blacks play a crucial role.

THE LOOKING GLASS SELF

With the coming of television and the electronic revolution it spawned, the concern over the level and quality of black participation in the film and video industry has significantly escalated. From an early concern about getting blacks on television, that concern has expanded to include the quality of that participation. While the number of blacks has increased since they first began to appear on television in the late 1940's and early 1950's, the quality of their portrayals has been uneven.

The decade of the 1980's found elusive anything approaching a decent portrayal of black life and culture on television. The people who control what is shown on TV seem to believe that whites feel most comfortable with blacks playing the roles of fools, maids, funny men, and small time hustlers, and are most uncomfortable with blacks in romantic roles. For example, a recent survey of ABC television programming revealed that blacks are generally stereotyped, with 49 percent of all blacks playing roles of criminals, servants, entertainers or athletes. Rarely are blacks portrayed as loving, sexual, sensitive or cerebral people.[27]

According to a recent A.C. Nielson survey, blacks watch television an average of 10 percent more than whites. Other Nielson Index figures indicate that by the time the average child has graduated from high school, he or she will have viewed 15,000 hours of television.[28] Since a good percentage of this 15,000 hours shows black people in a negative, distorted light, it may not be unreasonable to argue that with all its promise, television serves no greater purpose than to create a false sense of superiority on the part of white people and a false sense of inferiority on the part of blacks.

In the pages that follow, we will provide an historical overview of blacks in television, discuss the significance of black roles in television, examine white cultural ideology as it relates to black roles, and explore the impact television has on black culture.

Television came on the American scene in the 1950's with great promise for what it could do to promote world harmony, peace, understanding and goodwill. In his award winning book, *Black and White TV, Afro-Americans in Television Since 1948*, J. Fred McDonald captures the optimism of both blacks and whites for the potential of television as a great unifier. He writes:

> Television had the potential to reverse centuries of unjust ridicule and misinformation. In terms of utilization of black professional talent, and in the portrayal of Afro-American characters, TV as a new medium had the capability of ensuring a fair and equitable future.[29]

Since television was controlled by the same groups that controlled radio, i.e., ABC, CBS and NBC, this optimism may have been somewhat naive, given the networks' track records in the portrayal of blacks. Radio had a long history of confining black talent to demeaning roles. To obtain steady employment on radio or in film, blacks were relegated to roles of Uncle Toms, Aunt Jemimas, or dancing dandies, and these roles worked to foster the image of blacks as loyal, childlike and semi-human. Television, the medium, may have been new, but those who controlled it were products of a racist society and, as such, found themselves trapped by the cultural, political, economic and social ideology of that same society. It would be unreasonable to expect that the products of television would somehow escape the human limitations of its managers, producers and advertisers.

Blacks were there in the beginning of television, and while there was great hope for progress in race relations through television, actual practice fell far short of this dream. In the early days of television, blacks were more likely to appear on television in some musical context and usually as a guest, not a regular.[30] In addition to the dancing and singing black guests who appeared on television, the next most popular format for the black entertainer was that of subservient clown. In short, blacks were allowed to appear on television as long as their roles fostered the traditional stereotypes of blacks as happy, carefree, musical and lazy. Fitting this mode almost perfectly were such television characters as Rochester on the "Jack Benny Show," Louise the maid on "The Danny Thomas Show," and Willie on the "Trouble

With Father Show" of the early 1950's. These roles had previously been made famous on radio by such people as Eddie "Rochester" Anderson, Butterfly McQueen, Ruby Dandridge and Lillian Randolph.[31]

When the promise of television settled into its reality, the demeaning stereotypes of black characterizations became common place. Despite the efforts of such personalities as Ed Sullivan, Steve Allen, Arthur Godfrey and Milton Berle[32] to showcase blacks in a positive and non-stereotypical light, the dye had been cast, and the black stereotype had won out over multi-dimensional black humanity. Two of the most notable examples of the stereotyping of blacks are found in the "Amos and Andy Show" and "The Little Rascals," the latter a successful television attempt to revive the film shorts of the "Our Gang" series of the 1920's and 1930's.

While there are many examples of television's insensitivity to the need for honest and realistic portrayals of black characters, one very good example of this phenomenon is that of the "The Little Rascals" series. The intent of "Our Gang," as the original 221 film episodes were known, was to capture the innocence of "just plain kids" in a film series.[33] While the series may have partially accomplished that goal, it also perpetuated racial stereotypes through the characters of Sunshine Sammy, Stymie and Buckwheat. The series was laced with examples of these black characters acting out negative stereotypes. Examples include rolling their eyes, being frightened to the point that their hair would stand on end, and uttering lines almost always meant to demean. In short, the black characters on "The Little Rascals" almost invariably were cast in a way as to make of, ridicule, or demean black people. While many whites may have found some joy in these portrayals, most blacks found them to be highly offensive.

However, it wasn't until the 1970's that civil rights groups were able to have an impact on the "Little Rascals" series. King Productions, who produced the series for television, realizing that the growing minority opposition to the "Little Rascals" might drive it off television, invested a great deal of time and money to re-edit the series.[34] According to Maltin and Bann, King World Productions removed the racial and other gags that could be interpreted as being in bad taste. Maltin and Bann also note that:

> Some twenty-minute episodes were cut by as much as ten minutes, while others ("Little Daddy," "The Kid From Borneo," "A Tough Winter," "Lazy Days," "Little Sinner," "A Lad as a Lamp," "Moon and Groan, Inc.," "Big Ears") were eliminated from the TV package altogether.[35]

The "Little Rascals," shown at prime time for children (weekdays between 3:00 to 5:00 and Saturdays), has been a living monument to the film industry's inability or unwillingness to portray black characters as whole human beings.

In 1951, television unveiled the "Amos 'n' Andy" show to the American public. What many thought to be black characters were actually white. In fact, for radio and stage productions, using white actors to "imitate" blacks was a common occurrence. In the case of the "Amos 'n' Andy" show, its stars were Freeman Gordon and Charles Correll, two white radio men who perpetuated white stereotypes of blacks through "talking black." According to historians W. Augustus Law and Virgil Clift, the "Amos 'n' Andy" show, in spite of its stereotyped imagery, became a favorite of both black and white audiences during the 1920's and 1930's.[36]

When the "Amos 'n' Andy" show was being prepared for national television, Gordon and Correll decided to use black actors to continue the stereotyped characters. In spite of NAACP protests, the show premiered in June 1951 on CBS television. MacDonald vividly reminds us that:

> The roles they sought to case were classical minstrel figures. Amos Jones (played by Alvin Childress) was a low key, compliant Uncle Tom. He and his wife, Ruby, were an unhumorous twosome who tried to bring reason and level-headedness to bear upon rascalish Harlem friends. Andy, whose full name was Andrew Hogg Brown, was an easy going dimwit...In George "Kingfish" Stevens, the show presented the stereotyped scheming "coon" character, whose chicanery left his pals distrustful and the audience laughing. Added to the three mainstays were Kingfish's shrewd wife, Saphire Stevens, and domineering mother-in-law, Mama, a feeble-minded janitor, Lightenin, and a thoroughly disreputable lawyer, Algonquin J. Calhoun.[37]

In effect, the "Amos 'n' Andy" television show brought the

image of the old minstrel stereotype of blacks as slow, foot-shuffling, fun loving, and slightly dishonest people from the radio to television for all the world to see. Protests against the show (produced from 1951-1953) began even before the first television broadcast and continued until CBS agreed to withdraw it from circulation in 1966.[38] While there were many defenders of the "Amos 'n' Andy" show, the critics, both black and white, objected to the program because of the way it negatively stereotyped black Americans and black American life.

"The Little Rascals" and the "Amos 'n' Andy" show were not the only programs with black characters during the early days of television, but, some argue, the stereotypes they presented represented the worst of the lot. In continuing with the pattern of stereotyping blacks, ABC was the first network to star a black actress in her own regular television show. "Beulah," starring Ethel Waters and later Louise Beavers, was first broadcast in 1950. While favorably received by the general public, the show was not devoid of stereotypes.[39] Beulah was a maid for a white family and, as such, carried out the stereotype of the black woman as "mammie." She was warm, loving, caring, funny, and very dedicated to her white employers and their children.

In 1956, the "Nat King Cole" show premiered on NBC. For the first time on national television, a black man had his own show and was not portrayed as a clown. From the beginning, the show met with problems and never really did well in the ratings. By 1957 the show died for lack of a sponsor.[40] The speculation was that the American public was not yet ready for a black performer in other than a stereotyped role, and that corporate sponsors were reluctant to back such a show out of fear of offending white audiences.

It took until 1965, but Bill Cosby, in the adventure series "I Spy," demonstrated that the American public would accept a black actor in a non-stereotyped role. "I Spy," starring Cosby and Robert Culp, was televised on NBC from 1965 to 1968 and showed the black male in a rather positive manner. Cosby was the first black to star in a network series, the first black to win two Emmy Awards for best actor in a running series, and the first black to star in a series where race was not the controlling force.[41] Though very successful, "I Spy" was not without its stereotypes. For example, Cosby was cast as the trainer for a world class tennis player and rarely got romantically involved. Occasionally, there was the illusion of romance when black women stars such as Pam Grier and Denise Nichols would appear on the show.

By the late 1960's, with the civil rights movement in full swing, blacks were becoming commonplace on American television. Though black percentages on television never matched their percentages in the American population, there was the establishment of a definite black presence on American television. In addition to the above mentioned shows, Diahann Carroll, Teresa Graves, Leslie Uggams and Flip Wilson were given their own series. Couple this with such shows as "Room 222," "Mission Impossible," and "Baretta," all of which had regular black supporting actors, and it began to appear that blacks were making progress in the television industry.

By the early 1970's America fell in love with situation comedies such as "Maude," "All In The Family," and the "Mary Tyler Moore Show." Following close in popularity behind these shows were such programs as "That's My Mama," "Good Times," "Different Strokes," and "What's Happening." These shows either had all black casts or blacks in central roles, and they relied very heavily on a "black humor" that came dangerously close to being as demeaning and stereotypical as the old "Amos 'n' Andy" show. In fact, some argued that the shows of the '70's that featured blacks were every bit as demeaning as "Amos 'n' Andy."

By the 1980's, continuing in this trend of stereotyping blacks on television, the networks bought "Gimme a Break" with Nell, the black, live-in housekeeper, and the "A Team" with the very muscular Mr. T. The role of Nell is little more than that of a sophisticated mammy of earlier TV days, and the "A Team's" Mr. T. casts a black male in the role of a super masculine menial, a brainless eunuch who is no real threat to the white male.

What appears to have happened, as we move into the latter part of the 20th century, is that we have gone full circle in terms of the roles blacks play on TV. From blacks in stereotyped, demeaning minstrel-like roles, to some attempt to portray blacks with some dignity and depth in the late 1950's and 1960's, we are now back to the stereotypes and minstrel-like portrayals of the 1950's.

In this cyclical trajectory of black television history, there has been one significant exception. "The Bill Cosby Show," the number one television show in America in 1984-85, was seen by some 30 million people a week. The show is about a middle class black family and that family's experiences. The show is a move away from stereotyping blacks. There is no ghetto, the family lives in a fashionable New York neighborhood, the father is in the home, and there are no drug deals or killings. "The Bill Cosby Show" has been an exceptional program and demonstrates that the American public will watch a television show about unstereotyped black Americans. On this point, Cosby notes:

> This is a major, major step, not just for American people but for those who control what goes on the air. The truth is in the numbers, and this helps straighten out non-believers concerning what an American audience will watch.[42]

It is difficult to assess why the show is so popular, beyond the fact that Bill Cosby is an extraordinary talent. Some argue that the show is popular because of the universal appeal of the situations in which the family finds itself. It is a show featuring black people, but it is not a black show. Everyone can relate to the predicaments Dr. and Mrs. Huxtable encounter with their five children. While critics argue that it is not black enough, does not deal with racism and poverty, or make a social statement, few can argue that it is not a move away from the demeaning stereotyping of black Americans.

In spite of "The Bill Cosby Show," television has not been kind to black America. Its continual portrayal of black people in demeaning roles has had a negative impact on both black and white America. In order to understand white America's need to denigrate black America, it is necessary to examine white cultural ideology and its relationship to the television industry.

It is very important to recognize that we live in a highly ethnocentric and racist society—two Americas, if you will, one black and the other white. The social distance between the races results in distinct cultural differences between blacks and whites in America. Culture plays a significant role in our perception of others and the world around us. Since we are influenced in our perceptions of others by our culture, it would appear that the greater the distance between cultures, the greater the room for misinterpretation, distortions or negative perceptions to develop.[43]

In short, one's culture is pretty much like a road sign, guide or anchor. It helps to keep one on course. We rely heavily on these signs, guides or anchors and in our daily lives use them to make our way. Usually, in a subconscious way, we judge other situations, other groups and individuals by these guides. The more distant these people are from us, the more likely it is that our signs or guides may not serve us well. Our culture may cause us to develop inadequate or inappropriate perceptions of others.

If there were were equal power amongst the races, these misperceptions would be unfortunate, sometimes painful, but in general they would probably balance out in some rough way. Unfortunately, there is not equal power between the races, and these misperceptions often lead to great pain and turmoil for the least powerful in American society, blacks. The powerful, mostly whites, in the United States are so engrossed in their power and perpetuating it, that their perceptions of others, especially minorities, are severely distorted. Karl Mannheim once noted:

> The ruling groups in their thinking become so intensely interest bound to a situation that they are simply no longer able to see certain facts which would undermine their sense of domination.[44]

The mass media, especially television, has helped to perpetuate this ignorance and distortion. Harold Cruse, in *The Crisis of the Negro Intellectual*, observes that:

> The mass media would seriously distort the Negro Cultural Image; make the Negro style banal and trivial, thus ripe for low level entertainment values; low originality; and intensify the cultural exploitation already at work.[45]

Some of these distortions are out of ignorance, based on cultural distance and difference. Others, no doubt, are based on ethnocentrism and racism and the need to maintain control and keep a social distance between the races.

Ralph Ellison makes this point another way when he states that white social scientists have generally accepted the stereotype of the black community, or Harlem, as "piss in the halls and blood on the stairs." While such stereotypes may hold some element of truth, they significantly oversimplify the richness and diversity of black life.[46]

Television, controlled by American advertisers, regulated by the Federal Communications Commission, and influenced by the American public, has chosen to adapt a white American cultural ideology based on the glorification of white norms, mores and values. This ideology glorifies whiteness and demeans blackness by establishing, maintaining and refining a society based on race and racial privilege. In television programming this is evident in the historical portrayal of blacks and other minorities in a patronizing, demeaning, childlike and stereotyped way. Television, then, like radio and even newspapers, supports this white cultural ideology that works to maintain a status quo for black Americans as second class citizens.

Whites are always in control and portray the central characters in most television productions. Blacks, when they do appear, appear in supporting roles, quite frequently in demeaning roles, and often as stereotypes of white ideas of what blacks are like. Mostly, blacks portray updated versions of the happy, shuffling, darkies, mammies, pickaninnies, and loyal assistants.

The situation is no better for other minority groups. No lead character of any of the top entertainment shows is Hispanic. Only three of the 264 speaking roles in 1984 were played by Hispanics, and two-thirds of the Hispanic characters were cast as criminals. It was even worse for Asians in that none of the 173 major roles cast last year were portrayed by an Asian actor or actress.[47]

At work here is a not so subtle attempt to reinforce white domination through the medium of television. Prime time television watchers get a distorted view of the real world. More specifically, television is damaging to black children in that most of the people they see doing interesting and important things are white, and when black people are seen, it is likely to be in a stereotyped supportive role. The areas of sex and romance, in particular, have been forbidden territory for the black actor. Until the addition of Billie Dee Williams and Diahann Carroll to "Dynasty," blacks have been virtually cast as sexual eunuchs on television. This absence of a love life for the black actor is another of the missing pieces of a fully developed role for blacks in television.

While the "Amos 'n' Andy" show has been viewed as one of the most obvious examples of the results of white cultural ideology, almost nightly, American television exhibits examples of the demeaning results of such an ideology. One of the most recent examples of the results of white American cultural ideology is the "A Team," with Mr. T. as one of its major characters. The "A Team" comes to us weekly in living color. To some extent it could be argued that the "A Team" is just one more symbol of the violence that the American public receives in its television programs. Why does Mr. T. stand out so significantly, and why has he become the darling bad boy of American television audiences?

Mr. T. is projected as super-masculine, loyal, short tempered, tough, kind, smart, simple, loveable, aggressive, intimidating, flamboyant, savage, and streetwise. His image, from the gold jewelry to the haircut to his costumes, is deliberately projected as bizarre. He is the latest, but probably not the last, of a long list of "acceptable" black television personalities. These personalities, whether they be pimp, prostitute, soldier of fortune, or helicopter pilot, are always portrayed as the friendly, loyal, and trustworthy outsider.

It is imaginative to see Mr. T. and these other black television personalities, who proceeded him, as loveable pets. This is the heart of the white cultural ideology at work. Blacks are cast as inferior and obedient, and even though on the "right side," they are not quite capable of making a go of it by themselves. They, like a loyal pet, need the help of the master. As pets they are nice and have human-like characteristics, but they are not quite human. They are stereotypes. Mr. T. and the "A Team" are a prime example of this phenomena. The image of Mr. T. is the result of white cultural ideology as filtered through the eyes of white writers. In short, Mr. T. and most black characters on television evolve out of the white mind and white culture, not the black mind or black culture.

In analyzing the role of Mr. T. and black roles in television, one might well conclude that these stereotypical roles blacks play actually tell us more about the white people who create them than they do about black people. On the one hand, the creation of Mr. T. as a super masculine menial is something the white mind can handle; one only need rationalize that while Mr. T. has the muscle, the white intellect will win out in the long run. In contrast, think of the anxiety that could be generated in white minds if Mr. T. were beamed into our living rooms as a Don Juan with an affinity for white women.

It is incumbent upon us to remember that television is more than just fun and entertainment. It is big business. The network which brought us the Superbowl in January, 1985, sold advertising time at close to a million dollars a minute, and in 1985 ABC was purchased by Capital Cities Communications, Inc. for $3.5 billion dollars.[48]

Where there are large sums of money at stake, people tend to want an atmosphere of predictability and stability. Since television has become a vehicle for the generation of these large sums through advertising, it attempts to be a rather timid, conservative and inoffensive medium. Advertisers, either directly or indirectly, attempt to influence the information presented in the media that their dollars underwrite. The advertisers, in trying to match their products to programs the public will find satisfying, are quite conscious of public opinion, or at least they attempt to be. They do not want to link their products with anything that will be too offensive, too radical or in bad taste. Television writers, producers and advertisers have traditionally been quite conservative in their approach to themes that have a controversial air to them and how blacks and other minorities are cast. The general rule of thumb has been, and continues to be, don't do anything that will be too offensive to the general television watching public, mainly the white watching public. Offensive programs could start a backlash against the sponsors of these programs.

In the early days of television, Ed Sullivan, Steve Allen and Milton Berle were subjected to this type of pressure. Mac-

Donald has noted that television producers were especially wary of their Southern audiences. Television executives, not wanting to alienate their Southern white audiences, tried to avoid programs that cast black people in too favorable a light.[49] While present day television executives have, no doubt, become more sophisticated over the years, they are still concerned about what television viewing audiences will find acceptable. Most networks use some manner of marketing or survey research to determine just what the American public will find acceptable. Using a slightly different twist, networks also want to make sure they present what they think the audience wants. The CBS network, at one time, used a British-based company, TAPE Ltd., to evaluate television movies, with the thought that they knew just what the American public would find acceptable. One example of their conclusions was revealed in a *National Leader* article in October 1982:

> It was revealed that TAPE uses a formula that deducts points for ideas whose central characters are Negroes, Jews, Italians, Mexican, etc...Thomas McManus, North American sales representative of TAPE, stated that if networks wanted to reach a mass audience, then they would need to take into consideration the fact that the mass audience is a white audience.[50]

The conventional wisdom, supported by such information provided by companies like TAPE, has it that television and its advertisers, in attempting to sell to national markets, should attempt to avoid themes that focus on minorities and certain controversial subjects. Many years ago, sociologist W.I. Thomas talked about the "self-fulfilling prophecy" or the Thomas theorem, which, in short, states that "if men define situations as real, they are real in their consequences."[51] It follows that if television executives are convinced that whites will not accept blacks on television, or will accept them only in certain stereotyped situations, blacks will routinely be denied opportunities for other kinds of roles, no matter what their qualifications.

In essence, the definition that whites impose on blacks has powerful social consequences because whites are in a position to translate the definition into reality. "The Bill Cosby Show," with its all-black cast, has challenged the traditional wisdom that a white audience will not buy a black show in which the characters are not placed in stereotyped roles. Is this the beginning of a breakthrough in television, or is it only an aberration? Only time will tell.

THE IMPACT OF TELEVISION ON BLACKS

It is difficult to make an overall assessment of the impact of television on blacks. The constant bombardment of white cultural ideology through television is bound to have had some impact. As has been noted, blacks watch more television than whites. The meaning of their greater television viewing habits has yet to be determined. Television is such a new force in our socialization process that we are still trying to measure its effect.

What is clear, however, is that 98 percent of all homes have television sets, and the average home viewer watches six hours of television a day. Furthermore, by the time the average American child reaches 18 years of age, he or she has watched 22,000 hours of TV, as compared to 11,000 hours of school, and seen 350,000 commercials.

The significance of such television viewing habits is summarized by Tony Brown: (1) Blacks are more likely than whites to use TV as a source of information when buying a product. (2) Blacks most often turn to TV rather than newspapers or other people for news of the black community. (3) Black adults prefer programs which feature blacks. (4) Blacks perceive TV as a representative of real life more than whites. (5) Black children learn aggressive behavior from TV role models, and they are more likely to imitate a white role model than a black one. (6) Black adolescents are more likely than whites to use TV to learn how to behave with the opposite sex, to develop codes of social conduct.[52]

Richard L. Allen, a researcher on minorities' use of television, takes exception to some of these findings. He believes that blacks do not watch television passively, that they tend to be critical of the programs they watch.[53] From their perspective, blacks do not helplessly soak up all that is put before them and become puppets of white cultural ideology. They filter what they view, accepting some, intellectually filtering out others, and possibly accepting still some others as just fun with no socially redeeming value.

We are clear that television has certain negative impacts on the present condition of 1980's black America. The greater frequency of television viewership, in part, is due to the high rate of unemployment among black males. According to Joe and Yu, about 46 percent of black males between the ages of 16-64 are not in the labor force.[54] It is black males who form most of the black television audience since black women are least likely, of all groups, to watch television. The frequent television viewership of black males may have as one of its consequences the high illiteracy rate of that same group. People who watch television constantly are not developing or cultivating reading skills. Among black males the national illiteracy rate is 44 percent.[55] That fact renders them largely ineffectual in the expanding sectors of the economy, service and information processing.

Television fare has no socially redeeming values, while inculcating negative social values in impressionable black youth. Because half of black families are headed by a single parent, many of them suffering from role overload, television often serves the role of custodian and socializer of black children. What they learn from television is that many people, primarily whites, live much better than they do. Television shows such as "Dallas" and "Dynasty" illuminate the opulence of America's bourgeoisie. Thus, black children may acquire the desire for material goods without the means (legitimate means, that is) of achieving them. However, the abundance of crime and violence on television shows teaches black children that there are illegitimate means for achieving the same goals. Since these same shows do not convey the consequences of criminal behavior or transmit any sense of morality, black youths reach the conclusion that it normally acceptable, and effective, to rob and murder people. Certainly, the responsibility for some of the petty thefts, rapes and murders perpetrated against the black community must be shared by the television perpetrators of such crimes.

Other lessons are mediated to blacks by standard television

fare. Most television shows depict blacks as being in single parent homes or unmarried, thus providing no model of a stable nuclear family for the viewing audience. When a black married couple is shown, it is the most persistent and damaging of all black stereotypes—the weak man-strong woman concept. Furthermore, these black couples are rarely shown in a loving relationship but tend to exchange insults with each other. It was his reaction to those depictions of black families that caused Bill Cosby to develop his show. He said:

> I would rather hug and kiss and romance my wife as opposed to showing that we argue. I would rather show life in the positive sense...I want to show that we have the same kinds of wants and needs as other American families. I'm going to take this show and make it last as long as I can to show black people that they have something to be proud of.[56]

Unfortunately, "The Bill Cosby Show" may remain an oasis in the vast wasteland of black comedies. Cosby has the advantage of being an established entertainer with a huge following, who sold his show to a network that was dead last in the ratings. Cosby's stature and the network's desperation allowed him to conceive the show, select the other members of the cast, and even hire a black psychiatrist to insure the show did not bow to negative racial stereotypes. In other words, Cosby maintained artistic control over the content of the show, something other black actors could not yet or did not want to exercise. The outcome has been the show's ranking as the number one television program in the country and the NBC network's rise out of the bottom of the ratings race. This show has managed to be genuinely funny without being demeaning, and exemplifies the aspirations of all racial groups for a happy family life. It also belies the television programmers' claims that mindless sitcoms, sex, wealth and violence are what the public wants.

While "The Bill Cosby Show" promises a progressive trend toward positive portrayals of blacks on television, most TV shows still present blacks in demeaning and subordinate roles. Since most blacks on television are shown as funny, stupid, singing or dancing, these images teach blacks not to take themselves or their plight seriously. Life is nothing but laughs, music and dancing in urban ghettos plagued by high unemployment, drugs, crime and violence. The other role reserved for blacks is that of the loyal sidekick, which teaches blacks to accept their minority status as naturally inevitable and even deserved. The purpose is to show blacks that heroes are always white. By being deprived of black heroes, blacks' reflections of themselves will be developed and their capacity to resist their oppression eroded. As playwright Charles Fuller has observed: "Americans trust black people when we sing, dance or tell jokes. It's when we stop laughing that people get itchy."[57]

CONCLUSION

The role of blacks in the media is a complex one. While constantly being told that blacks are not saleable to the white audience in music, films and television, the facts tell a different story. While "The Bill Cosby Show" was ranked number one among all shows in 1985, at least three other black shows held that ranking in the 1970's. The black shows have generally had higher ratings as a genre than comparable white television shows because the former have attracted a vast white audience and keep a loyal black viewership. In fact, the most watched television program of all times, "Roots," had a black theme and starred black actors.

The same is true of movies. Sidney Poitier was a number one box office star in the 1960's, and Richard Pryor and Eddie Murphy attained the same ranking in the 1980's. In 1982, black actors starred in three of the six biggest hits of the year.[58] While blacks were assumed to be successful only in sidekick roles, Eddie Murphy's break with tradition in the film "Beverly Hills Cop" made it the most financially successful non-summer movie in film history. It should be noted that almost every film critic credited Murphy's comedic ingenuity for the movie's success.

Popular music is certainly no exception to the rule of black acceptability to white audiences. The largest selling record album of all time was made by a black performer, Michael Jackson's *Thriller*. Ranked first and second among best selling record albums in 1984 were works by Lionel Ritchie and Prince, both black.

Being an entertainer has been one of the few accessible

means of attaining success for American blacks. With the exception of sports, blacks have more significant participation in this area of the white world than any other. It is practically the only path to financial success for young blacks. In an article on young black millionaires in *Ebony,* almost all of them were athletes or entertainers. While blacks bring a certain creativity to the arts based on the expressive orientation of their culture, entertainment is also the only arena they were allowed access to, restricted as it is, in American society. The white world would accept blacks as entertainers when they could not be businessmen, political leaders, scholars or even athletes.

Only through the gatekeeping role of white media leaders has the dominance of blacks in the entertainment complex been prevented. The entertainment industry is a multibillion dollar field, and black participation has been limited. Black successes in each medium have rarely been followed by other black successes because the media gatekeepers have practiced tokenism in the entertainment world, as they have in other sectors of the society. Black entertainers often rise to the top of the field because so few are permitted access or exposure to white audiences that the blacks command more attention when they do so. Only a few are selected for such exposure, and most mediums remain dominated by white artists. Radio does it by playing only the songs of a few black artists. The movies accomplish it by consigning black actors to sidekick roles, while the white male actor is the main hero who romances the white female lead. Television allows more access but restricts most blacks to demeaning comedies that eventually become the same, and tiring to the viewing audience.

While this pattern reinforces the cultural ideology of white supremacy by retaining most positive values for members of the white group, we should not be deluded into thinking the media operates that positively for whites. The entertainment complex is selling a fantasy for the mass public that obscures class inequalities in the economic substructure of American society. Most of the media reflect bourgeois values. Rarely are the lives of most working class Americans, white or black, reflected accurately in films or television. Instead, we are shown the lives, loves and problems of the bourgeoisie and taught to identify with their lifestyles. As as result of the fame that comes to actors and actresses portraying these roles, a whole industry develops around providing vicarious thrills by showing glimpses into their intimate lives and affluence. Radio serves the same function of perpetuating false class consciousness by providing its listeners with a steady diet of songs about romantic fantasies and bitter and unrequited love, while most couples lead lives of quiet desperation. The ultimate fantasy is fed to an unsuspecting white public, which is led to believe that the world they live in is inhabited by other whites who remain in firm control of the destiny of other races. It is a fantasy that even white cultural ideology cannot prevent from its inevitable collision with social reality.

Part III:
Black Institutions
and the Colonial Order

CHAPTER SEVEN

Colonialism and the Crisis
of the Black Family

The decade of the eighties finds the black family a fluid and complex institution. Our understanding of this group has been impeded by the obtrusion of alien values and political motivations in research on the subject. Hence, we have to sift through an array of literature which is in conflict in its findings and interpretations on the nature and significance of Afro-American family life.

While some of the discrepancy between the black family reality and its depiction in the social science literature may be altruistically attributed to adherence to the conventional wisdom of the times, much of the discrepancy is a function of what Nobles labels "conceptual incarceration."[1] As a result, the black family's well-being is measured in terms of its statistical approximation to the white middle-class.

It helps us little to recapitulate the history of that research. Perhaps we have already labored too long in refuting the research which generally indicts the black family as pathological or sees it only as the darker skinned counterparts of the white family and the black family's concentration in the underclass of the American social structure. The alternative framework suggested by young black scholars may be characterized as the Pan-African conceptual model.[2] This model views the black family in the context of Afro-American or African values and largely confines itself to presenting the strengths of the black family that are responsible for its survival. While the elaboration of black family strengths is a necessary task, it still limits our understanding of black family life in a dynamic society. In fact, it threatens to reimpose a conceptual incarceration upon black scholars because, as applied, the model is often static.

The Pan-African approach is most germane when we look at lower income Afro-American families in the rural South. With a singular focus on the strengths of black families, can we develop a holistic theory of black family life? Or, as Lieberman (1973) poses the question: Can the model of the ethnic group rest solely, or even largely, on strengths when all human social systems have numerous weaknesses?[3] What is required is an historical, dynamic and process-oriented model which sees blacks as being victims of larger, external forces but also makers of their own history. In this author's opinion the internal colonialism framework holds the promise of such a goal. It allows us to depict the alternation between black values which shape their family lifestyles and the forces in colonial society which produce weaknesses in the family structure.

Although not a full blown theoretical system at this juncture, internal colonialism is a perspective that recognizes the existence of an Afro-American culture that has value. However, it also acknowledges that in a colonial setting those cultural values of the native are constantly under attack. The colonial structure inhibits expression of the native's values by an elaborate system of rewards and penalties. More importantly, this structure socializes a segment of the colonized group into its own values. The interaction between the acculturation process and colonial status might be viewed as the locus of conflict between Afro-Americans and their own cultural imperatives. And it might be most boldly viewed in objective indexes of family disorganization such as male-female antagonisms, divorce, child abuse and other problems. These are very real problems in the black community and cannot be subordinated to our attempt to delineate strengths of the black family.

In our discussion of colonialism and black family life, we shall be concerned with how the family promotes emotional well-being in individuals. Our basic thesis is that the black family has been a sanctuary which has buttressed individuals from the pervasiveness of white racism, provided needed support systems that were unavailable in other majority group institutions, and socialized and nurtured the young. This creation of a sanctuary was possible as a result of black values that related to the family. However, as the black population has dispersed from its original location in the rural South to urban ghettos and differentiated into different class strata, new values—alien values—replaced traditional ones regarding the family and black people's role in it. Hence, culture is a dichotomous phenomena: it enables a people to adapt to oppressive conditions, but the imposition of new institutions and value modalities can perpetuate their oppression in the colonial context.

Whereas Afro-Americans were a peasant class in the rural South, their evolution into an urban people divided by subjective affiliations into socio-economic classes was to alter their collective orientations to an individual one among some of their members. At the same time, they all remained members of a colonized group with its attendant liabilities. Although taking on the values and trappings of the colonizer, black Americans do not have the structural underpinnings of the ruling group which will compensate for the loss of their traditional values. Once blacks detach themselves from the emotional and spiritual support of the collective black community, the gains allowed them under internal colonialism are not sufficient to serve as adequate substitutes. The result is a decline in the positive strengths of black families. It is in light of such a theoretical perspective that we examine the contemporary black family and its relationship to internal colonialism.

HISTORICAL REFLECTIONS

There is little doubt that North American slavery was one of the harshest forms of involuntary servitude, and its impact was most vividly reflected in Afro-American culture and family life. Enough historical evidence exists to show that slave families were separated for pecuniary motives; slave women were used as breeding instruments to produce future slaves; males were denied their formal roles as protector and provider for their families; and slave women were often subjected to sexual assaults, with impunity, by men on the plantation.[4]

However, such historical accounts of slavery have misled us into thinking that the family as a unit did not exist or was not a viable institution. While it must be conceded that specific tribal languages and culture were extinguished by slaveowners, the African ethos was not. Due to their own instincts for survival, members of separate, and often warring, tribes reorganized as a collective community. They formed a solidified group based on the African principle of contiguity and unity. Within the context of slavery and the limited options open to them, the slaves developed a new sense of family and redefined their roles and the relationships between them.[5]

Although legal marriage between slaves was not permitted, there were varieties of socially approved and sanctioned relationships between slave men and women. These relationships were recognized as a strong emotional bond by other slaves as well as the slaveholders. Some of these slave families lived under one roof and functioned as a single family unit. While men did not have the strong patriarchal authority in the family as existed on the African continent, they were generally accorded a certain respect for the qualities of manliness they exhibited, in the form of heroic deeds, securing extra rations for the family, or making their living quarters more comfortable.

The alleged female matriarchy that existed during this time is described by Genovese as "in fact a closer approximation to a healthy sexual equality than was possible for whites."[6] Moreover, the African family had been based on a much greater equality between men and women than the white family. Women had played strong roles in African society in a working partnership with their spouses.[7]

These relationships may not have paralleled the anti-bellum white family, but they were consistent with the sentiments of the slave community. The notion of sexually promiscuous slaves, according to Rawick, has been greatly exaggerated. For instance, few slave marriages were dissolved because of the immoral conduct of one of the partners. Due to the moral code promulgated by Baptist and Methodist churches that served the slave community, the sexual behavior of the bondsmen might be considered rather moderate if measured by our contemporary standards.[8]

The attempts by slave males to resist the rape of their women attests to the fact that sexual relations were not taken lightly. More importantly, the slave community was reorganized as an extended family structure in which all adults looked after all children. In continuation of the African tradition, children were highly valued and cared for. After an exhausting day of laboring in the fields, slave mothers came home to nurse their children under conditions which required a great deal of physical and psychological courage. As a result of their mothers' tenderness and warmth, the children felt loved, a feeling that is deeply imprinted in slave spirituals and narratives.[9]

After slavery there were numerous attempts by the bondsmen to establish a normal family life. Male-female bonds which existed in a de facto form were legalized. Those couples who had been separated during the slave era went to great lengths to be reunited. The former slaves, nevertheless, still encountered obstacles in their quest for a viable family life. Economic imperatives forced many black men to move around the country to find work, leaving the women to carry on many of the family functions. When families remained together, the wife often worked alongside her husband in order to obtain land and an education for their children. It was out of these economic conditions that the role of the strong black woman was forged. This role flexibility allowed many black families to survive the terrible travail of the post-slavery era. Moreover, the assumptions about the disorganized family life of former bondsmen are counteracted by the historical evidence showing that a large majority of Afro-Americans during the period from 1865-1920 were lodged in nuclear families.[10]

During this period, blacks represented a largely peasant class based in the rural South. The model of the family which developed during that time was one of an extended kinship system representing a number of different roles. This type of family structure also encompassed fictive kinsmen who assumed the rights and obligations of those related by genealogical bonds. As a functional kinship grouping, it provided goods and services that individual families could not have obtained by their efforts alone. In the rural South the entire black community would take on a primary group character. As a group they maintained social control and regulated the behavior of individuals in accord with their own moral code—a code very similar to that found in African societies.[11]

It was this type of family structure that provided support functions for the mental health of individuals located in it. By positing a categorical relationship between the nuclear family

and the achievement of functional prerequisites, many behavioral scientists have labeled the black family as a form of social pathology. Many of the social and economic functions ascribed to nuclear families isolated in separate households were
in reality carried out by broader based units, often related, but
not solely, by biological kinship. The anchor for this unit was a
black folk culture which might be best described as a syncretic
form deriving from African values fused with orientations
evolving out of the slave experience. With the security of this
black kinship network and its support functions, the individual
in the family was buttressed against the harsh effects of racial
oppression. It is primarily the transition from rural areas to
urban ghettos and the formation of new social classes which
undermined the influence of black cultural values and con-
comitantly the functioning of Afro-American families.[12]

At this point it should be emphasized that we are discussing
the processes which have weakened the support functions of
family life among a segment of the black population. A large
number of black people still reside in family constellations
which continue to be conducive to a positive mental equilib-
rium. Many of the characteristics aforementioned still exist in
a modified form. However, the trend is toward the vitiation of
black family support functions, and we need to understand the
forces involved in these social transformations. The basic elements are the economic factors compounded by racial colonialism,
which make the establishment and maintenance of a satisfying
family life a never-ending struggle for poor blacks. As the
Hares have noted, the correlation between family stability and
economic and racial oppression are among the highest known
to social science.[13] Among the black middle class, the acquisi-
tion of colonial society's values and the disavowal of traditional
black values removes the anchor of black family life as a buffer
against the operational effects of domestic colonialism.

In order to understand the current functioning of the black
family, we need to examine its internal structure as it existed
prior to the move from the rural South to the urban North. This
can best be accomplished by dividing the family continuum
into stages known as the family life cycle.

THE FAMILY LIFE CYCLE

Dating and Sexual Behavior. The research literature on black dating and sexual patterns is sparse. Among lower class blacks, particularly in the Southern region, the communal ambience brings male and female children together at an early age. The fluidity of roles accommodates the presence of children in adult fraternizing activities such as parties and other festive occasions. It is in this social context that the complementarity of sex roles is enhanced as the adults present a model to their children of heterosexual relationships and sometimes give explicit instructions in the content of the children's future roles. Formal dating as such is uncommon since male-female interaction is more happenstance than planned. Yet, it occurs in a communal fashion as young black children meet and romance each other through the frequent visiting that takes place between households.[14]

The selection of opposite sex mates was often predicated on the basis of personal qualities possessed by the individual, such as honesty, thoughtfulness and respect. The more elaborate prestige ordering system found among the middle class was rare. Women knew that they could not select men on the basis of economic criteria since few of them were able to obtain well paying or even steady employment in a colonial society. Most women were prepared to assume a partnership in the family that would probably include their employment outside the home during much of their married life.

Sex before marriage occurred often among this group and was not laden with feelings of guilt or anxiety. Reminiscent of African orientations, the Afro-American's attitude toward sex is that it is a natural and pleasurable activity. Although not genetically based, blacks possess a certain sensuality that allows them to experience sex directly in terms of a feeling rather than cerebral experience. Thus, sexuality was more a function of the body than the mind.[15]

It should not be interpreted that sex is an indiscriminate act. Sexual activity prior to marriage is invested with a great deal of meaning for the participants. There are frequent attempts by the female to confine her male partner to exclusive sexual relations and vice versa. Yet, there exists no rigid double standard of sexual conduct where one sex is excluded from marital consideration on the basis of their past sexual history. The measure of the individual is not based on his or her sexual morality as much as other standards such as honesty and respect. Consequently, lower class blacks have a number of sexual options open to them without being subjected to the psychological boundaries of a puritanical moral code.

However, the inclination of blacks toward natural responses to sexual stimuli has become somewhat dysfunctional in the urban setting. Due to the reluctance or inability of many black parents to provide their children with a sound sex education, a number of sexually active black females experience an unwanted pregnancy.[16] In the rural South, the birth of a child was an asset since it could easily be accommodated into the family. In the urban environment, however, the unexpected birth of a child to a teenage mother more often means an increase in high school dropouts, inadequate parenting, a risky early marriage, or welfare dependency.

Some of these problems are avoided by the incorporation of the child into some aspect of the extended family. The options exercised by the middle class are not as easily available to women of the underclass. Instead, women of the underclass are regarded by the colonizer as being subjected to unbridled carnal instincts which will only produce children who will become burdens on the public tax roles or future delinquents. Thus, these poor black mothers are forced to participate in government-prescribed means of population control such as sterilization.

Having internalized the dominant group's values, the black middle class—or aspirants to that group—have adopted dating practices similar to those in the white community. Dating behavior is based on the perspectives of the dominant group which serves as the black middle class' referent, and they subsequently become less responsive to the requisites of their black folk culture. The concrete manifestation of this change in value orientations can be visibly demonstrated in the marked differences in black dating behavior by socio-economic position. Among the black middle class a rating-dating system is emerging that closely approximates that of their white counterparts.

The dating system takes on the character of market relations in which individuals maximize their desirable attributes for bargaining in exchange for a desirable commodity possessed by a potential mate.[17]

Specifically, women seek to use the enticement of sexual relations or the possession of certain physical attributes to obtain material goods or the right kind of marriage, i.e., to a man with a high status and income. Men, in turn, require a kind of exclusivity in their wives or girlfriends based upon their economic hegemony as a form of control. The result, then, is relationships based on material possessions rather than the intrinsic merit of the individual. In operation, it means the meeting of individuals who appraise each other according to their recently adopted standards of wealth and beauty. A future marriage proposal will be forthcoming when the participants size up their relative merits and decide that it would be a fair exchange.[18]

One sees the penetration of the colonizer's values into the criteria applied in the sex role bargaining process. The women, for instance, are ranked by how closely they resemble white women in their physical appearance. One study reports that the wives of middle class black husbands are much lighter in skin complexion that spouses of lower class men. And these same middle class husbands share a more conservative view of race relations than their less well-off brethren.[19] Rather than maintaining the naturalistic, sensual attitudes toward sex, middle class black women use it as a tool in gaining entrance to a prestigious marriage. Since middle class black males have more of a double sexual standard, the women in that class must be parsimonious in their premarital sexual activity, a practice best summed up in the saying, "Men won't buy what they can get free." There is some evidence that many middle class black women are less sexually liberated than their white counterparts.[20]

While adopting the values of the majority group, middle class blacks still must contend with the peculiarities of their colonized status. Due to the past vicissitudes of internal colonialism, the educational system has produced more female college graduates than males. In the past, when individuals were selected as mates on the basis of personal qualities, this posed no serious problem. Once their materialistic values gained ascendancy, status homogeneity became the preferred marriage. This has led to an intense competition for the available high status males. The result has been two categories of women winding up as losers in the battle for middle class spouses. One of them would be the present wives of these men since some women take the position that if there are no single men available, they will go after those presently belonging to somebody else. This practice accounts in large part for the high divorce rate in the black middle class. The other category of women who lose are those who are the furthest distance from majority group women. They are dark skinned women who do not otherwise fit the beauty standards of colonial society.[21]

Even the light-complexioned female is disadvantaged as a number of high status black males turn to women of the master race for dating and marriage. While interracial dating is a function of a complex set of forces, it is also a result of the high status black male's internalization of colonial values and prestige standards. If this was not true, we would expect interracial dating to be randomly practiced among the black population. Instead, we find that most blacks involved in this behavior are high status black males.[22] As one investigator of the subject commented, "Because he has a higher status now than ever before, he becomes more desirable as an object for marriage."[23] Furthermore, for males who accept whiteness per se as the sine qua non of desirability, women of the majority group become free to pick and choose. However sympathetic one may be to the individual's right of free choice in his or her selection of dating partners, there is little doubt that the issue of interracial liaisons has become a divisive one in the middle class black community.[24]

MARITAL STABILITY

In one normative sense, marriage does not appear to be a very viable institution for large numbers of Afro-Americans. The apparent trend is toward fewer blacks joining the conjugal state, and more of them leaving it. In 1930, husband-wife families represented 80 percent of all black households but fewer than 40 percent in 1982. Historically, blacks were more likely than whites to have been once married. Recent trends indicate an increase in marriage among whites and a decline among blacks.[25] The reasons for these changes may vary among segments of the black population. A major factor is the conditions of urban life that make marriage a fragile institution among blacks. The fact that marriage among Euro-Americans has been primarily rooted in property relations while colonized blacks have been largely stripped of their ties to the land is not an inconsequential aspect of this problem.

The black underclass simply is prevented by internal colonialism from achieving success in marriage. Their awareness of this fact of life often prevents them from uniting in matrimony at all. Males, in particular, shy away from the institution because they do not expect to be able to support a wife and children. As incomes rise, so do the number of black men who marry. The divorce statistics confirm the fears of failure among lower class blacks. The proportion of divorced black men tended to decline as the amount of income increased. However, the lowest divorce rate exists among men with median incomes. A probable reason for this anomaly is the greater penetration of colonial values in the marriages of high status black males.[26]

In the period between 1971 and 1981, the black divorce rate increased from 92 to 233 per 1,000 married persons, while it grew from 48 to 100 among whites.[27] This period actually resembled that of an economic depression for blacks and compounded the normal problems they face in a racist society. As Frances Welsing asserts, "Ninety percent of what happens in a black male-black female relationship is not controlled by black people but by the power of the social system."[28]

The system she speaks of works in a variety of ways to disrupt the marriages of black people. It is estimated that the unofficial unemployment rate for blacks in 1982 was 46 percent.[29] With irregular employment—and low wages when employed—many black males fear their authority and esteem in the family is threatened. They begin to experience anxiety over their ability to meet their family responsibilities. A common response is to become hostile or indifferent toward their wife and children when rendered unable to meet family obligations.

Some black couples worked out their economic difficulties by the employment of both spouses. The decline of the nuclear family has eliminated this working partnership for many of these couples. Due to the large increase of white women in the labor force, many black women could not find jobs of any kind. In 1975, 115,000 white women joined the work force, and 34,000 black women joined the ranks of the unemployed.[30] The welfare system, ostensibly designed to assist families, often serves to break them up as intact units. A study of the relief system reported that "the intact family fares substantially than the female-headed family." About a third of these families studied had only pretended to break up in order to receive the higher benefits. Some wives deliberately choose the steady and higher income of the welfare system over a less reliable husband.[31] As one husband put it, "She says she never knows whether I can keep bringing in the food, but the county is always there with whatever she needs."[32]

Lower income blacks in urban areas particularly experience difficulty in making marriage work. In rural middle-sized communities, individuals and marriages were more stable because they lived in an environment where marital roles took priority over the superstud character. In the South, men saw stable relationships as a compliment to them, while the role of hustler and pimp became popular in the urban ghettos of the North. To a large extent hustling was a survival mechanism for some urban males, but it also reflected a change in values for those who migrated north. At any rate it was, and is, antithetical to marital stability. The longer blacks are in the North, the more their values become transformed. Despite the disadvantages of growing up in the South, recent studies show that recent black migrants to the North are more likely to have stable families and earn higher incomes.[33]

As to the specific causes and nature of marital conflict among blacks, drugs, alcohol, sexual infidelity and physical abuse are ranked as the most prevalent reasons. Most studies available show that black wives are less satisfied with their marriages than their white counterparts.[34] As income levels rise, so do the number of blacks who are married and living with their spouses.[35] But a high income does not guarantee a satisfying marriage. The reasons may differ, but high status blacks have their share of marital conflicts. In high income black families, the men complain of the financial demands placed upon them by their wives, demands which colonial society does not allow them to meet. The women protest what they call the insensitivity and sexual infidelity of their husbands.[36] A basic problem with these high status couples is their acceptance of colonial values relating to roles and performance in marriage. A couple of black psychologists claim that blacks who try to emulate whites have the most problems whereas black just living and making do with what they have are the most adjusted.[37]

Herein probably lies the explanation of why median income blacks have the lowest divorce rate. Not as super-oppressed as the underclass, they can surmount the economic hurdles while their lower acculturation of colonial values means they do not come into conflict over such matters as male dominance or female avarice. High status black males often view women as property and impose rigid rules of sexual fidelity for their wives while themselves participating in a number of extramarital affairs. As a result of finding a younger or prettier woman, they may cast their wives aside. Unlike lower income black males, high status black men are more likely to marry and just as inclined to get divorced, but have a higher remarriage rate. As Glick and Mills note, the poor man experiences greater difficulty than the man of greater means in convincing a potential marriage partner to enter into remarriage with him.[38]

As for the women, they are often the unwitting victims of their husband's poverty and the abusive behavior it may produce, or the higher status husband's exploitative values. Hence, it is little surprise that many black women feel that the world is passing them by and that there is little they can do about it. One survey reports that half of the black women feel they rarely get a chance to enjoy themselves, compared to only 20 percent of the white women interviewed.[39] The suicide rate is also increasing faster among black women than any other group. A significant finding in the few studies on black suicides is that they occur more often among married women.[40] Psychiatrists report an increase in the number of women suffering from mental depression, and a major reason for their depression, according to one survey, is concern over heterosexual relationships. As one black woman complains: "It is hell being black and female in this white male dominated society...rejection is our constant companion...all too often by our husbands and lovers..."[41]

THE FEMALE-HEADED HOUSEHOLD

It is rare to find the female-headed household as part of the family life cycle. However, a prevalent pattern among blacks is an early entry into marriage, divorce, and the formation of a household headed by the female partner. This pattern seems to be emerging almost as the modal type of family system for blacks. During the period from 1960-82, this type of family system increased from 21 percent to 47 percent. It only increased from six to 15 percent among whites who have a much higher rate of remarriage than exists among the black population.[42] Some of this racial gap in female-headed households may be narrowed if we ever get an accurate census count of blacks. Since a fourth of the black population, particularly the males, were missed in the census enumeration, the number of black female-headed households may be overstated by the undercount of black men who may be with their families.

The data clearly indicate a close correlation between female-headed households and socio-economic status. As income rises, so do the number of two-parent families. However, other factors are also operative. Historically, blacks living in rural southern areas were intact family units. It is primarily the destructive influence of internal colonialism that is eroding away the base of black family life. This erosion is occurring in precisely those areas where blacks have been stripped of their cultural traditions and para family systems that made the family, in whatever form, a viable unit. To wit, the female-headed household is most often a product of urban conditions, of social forces which are gradually eliminating the pool of available black men for marriage, and producing tension in black marriages which tear them asunder. In the past, the father-absent family was primarily a function of different mortality rates for black men and women, which created a large number of widows at an early age. In addition, the need of many black men to migrate to cities to seek work meant many families would be headed by women.

Under contemporary conditions the largest proportion of families headed by women are predominantly a result of two precipitating factors: the high divorce and separation rate and out-of-wedlock pregnancies. We have to look at other underlying factors to really understand this phenomena. Whites, too, have a high divorce rate but a much lower proportion of female-headed families. The reason why can apparently be attributed to their much higher rate of remarriage. Many black women would also like to remarry but are unable to because of the low pool of available mates. There is a small number of black men due to a number of intersecting forces, most of them directly traceable to the functioning of internal colonialism.

With 46 percent of black men unemployed, it is not surprising to find a disproportionate number of them in prisons, the military or narcotized by drugs. However, the most significant trend is the spiraling mortality rate of black males. While the death rates of whites and black women declined in the sixties, the rate for black men decreased slowly. In the marriageable years of ages 20-30, black males are twice as likely to die as white males. These deaths will usually stem from social causes (i.e., internal colonialism) such as homicide, drug addiction, suicide and stress-producing diseases.[43]

The other major cause of female-headed households, an out-of-wedlock birth, was not a serious problem in the past. In the South, the children were easily incorporated into the extended family structure. Although such a family grouping is still prevalent, even among blacks, it is in rapid decline. And the unwed mother eventually got married. Now there are fewer men available for marriage. Furthermore, the prospects of marital success with a male who cannot find work of any kind are so low as to encourage many black women to remain single. As one government official has noted: "When there's no job in the inner city, with everything against them, with welfare designed primarily for one-parent homes, illegitimacy and welfare are as sound a response for the poor black girl as a shotgun marriage is for a middle class white."[44]

Assumptions about the pathology of the female-headed family have often been erroneous. While not present, the biological or social father and his kin are often supportive of his family by providing services and finances to them. A female-based kin network also exists for the exchange of scarce goods and services in the form of child care, gifts and money.[45] However, we should be cautious lest we glorify what is essentially a pragmatic adaptation to an undesirable situation for many black women. These one-parent families had a median income of $7,802 in 1982, less than one-third of the income of two parent families headed by a white male. An overwhelming majority have incomes below the poverty level while having more children to support than two-parent families. More than one-half of black children are living in one-parent homes, which has reduced 52 percent of all black children to a subsistence standard of living.[46] Such a reality has taken its psychological toll. One psychiatrist reports his observation of numerous black women who attempted or threatened suicide because there was no man around and they believed they were incapable of raising their children alone.[47]

The one-parent family has become the majority family system for blacks. The interaction between the machinations of internal colonialism and a chaotic and exploitative economy will continue to make marriage an impossibility or a fragile arrangement for many black people. There is no inherent pathology in such a family form. Children are probably better off, psychologically, than in conflict-ridden, two-parent families. A major problem for the children is the strong correlation between one-parent families and economic deprivation. However, with the decline of black cultural supports for those living in such families, the years ahead may be ones of hardship for the women and children lodged in such units. Either a renewal of old adaptive forms is needed or new strategies devised to meet the problems which will eventually emerge.

CHILDBEARING AND SOCIALIZATION

Fertility patterns among blacks have undergone considerable modification as a result of their urbanization and differentiation.

One of the most striking changes is simply the decline in their birth rate. While the black population is still growing at a faster rate than the dominant majority group, the black fertility rate actually declined at a faster pace. In the period between 1960-1970, white fertility decreased only by 27 percent in contrast to 37 percent among blacks in urban areas.[48] The nature and process of this decline is significant. Among lower income blacks, abortion, sterilization and contraceptive use contributed to the lower number of children born to black women.

Unquestionably, many black women have voluntarily decided to limit the number of their children as more and more black families fall below the poverty level. However, a number of these women, especially poor ones, are forced to reduce their families in order to get welfare or other government assistance. Despite negative black attitudes toward abortion, the proportion of black women getting abortions is as high or higher than that of white women. A number of cases have recently been reported of black women being sterilized without their knowledge or consent.

The drop in the fertility rate among older and married black women means the proportion of births to young and unmarried black mothers has risen. In 1982, more than one in four blacks was born to a mother under the age of 20.[49] As older and married black women use contraceptives and abortion to lower their birth rates, a larger proportion of black children are born to teenage women who are reaching puberty earlier and emotional maturity later.

In the black middle class, the fertility rate has declined to such a low point that it is no longer reproducing itself. The birth rate in the black middle class is about the lowest in the United States. Many have no children, and a majority have only one child. A large factor in this low birth rate is the long period of the wife's employment, which delays the age at which college-educated black women bear children. More significant is the secondary sex ratio of births to middle class black women. Unlike typical population trends in the United States, the majority of children born to middle class black families are girls. In the one study that intensely investigated this phenomenon, a sex ratio of 83 males to 100 females was found in 249 births to black families with incomes between $13,000-$17,000. The reason for this sex ratio disparity is the advanced age of black men in the middle class when they first become fathers. As the age of the father increases, so does the number of female children they sire.[50] An obvious ramification of this sex ratio at birth is an increase in the number of black women without available marriage partners, a problem which already exists due to the larger percentage of black women who graduate from college.

Despite a host of negative assumptions about the ability of black families to produce children with a healthy identity, we find that traditionally the extended family system has provided a number of parenting figures for the child. This is in contrast to a number of middle class white children who are prisoners of the nuclear family system. Either they receive love and approval from their parents or not at all. In general, black children develop a healthy identity because they grow up in households where they experience love and security from a number of kinsmen and significant others, and are not stifled by the rigidity of age and sex roles which exclude them from family activities. Due to their earlier assumption of physical autonomy, black children demonstrate the greatest early acceleration of psychomotor development of all ethnic and racial groups.[51]

Even a number of counter forces buttress much of the negative effect of the absence of fathers from the black household. Within the extended family there are a number of male role models to transmit the content of masculine role behavior to male children. A number of studies found father absence not to have a particularly negative influence on the self concepts of black children.[52] Moreover, many of these "absent" fathers maintain contact with their children and carry out normal paternal functions. Stack found that a mother generally regards her children's father as a friend of the family whom she can recruit for help rather than as a father failing his parental duties. Men who remain with their families have been shown to have warm, nurturing relationships with their children and concurrently providing for their economic and social development.[53]

Notwithstanding the positive aspects of black socialization practices, they have changed over time and space. In the lower-income black urban ghettos, there is an increasing tendency on the part of black parents to abuse their children. This is a result of the tensions produced by poverty conditions and the lack of community control over the anti-social behavior of blacks in urban settings.[54] Inadequate parenting, especially by teenage and one-parent families, has contributed to the arrogance and negativism emerging among black youth. The formation of youth gangs and the beatings of elders, children and other blacks are manifestations of this problem. This is atypical behavior for black youth and dissimilar to the values of the black community. However, the values these youths are adopting are often taught them by forces outside their community. They are socialized into the values of the colonizer through the mediums of the schools, television, movies and radio. These are values built on materialistic strivings, the use of violence and individualism.

THE FUTURE OF THE FAMILY

In this discussion of black family life, we have painted a mixed picture of its functioning. This should not be seen as another treatise on the pathology of black family life but rather as a balanced and dynamic perspective which reflects the evolution of the black family over time and space. It is not that the family is no longer a strong institution, but a more truncated form has emerged as blacks moved to the cities and differentiated into various socio-economic classes. Many blacks continue to find support for their needs and aspirations within the warm environs of the family. However, an increasing number of them have ceased to find the kind of family life that they are allowed to have very satisfying. The most pronounced trend we see is the tendency of many blacks not to enter marriage at all and to abstain from bringing children into the world.

We have already described the conditions that have shaped the black family into its present form. The operational effects of an internal colonial order were much more destructive once blacks moved into the cities where they could not maintain the cohesiveness and sense of peoplehood they had known in the South. It is probably no coincidence that the rate of marital breakup is significantly greater for blacks born and living in Northern areas than those who migrated from the South.[55] In the case of the middle class black, the role he or she adopts will be determined partially by acceptance and rejection of the values of the majority group. The middle class black is not as susceptible to the destructive influence of economic forces as those consigned to the underclass. The adoption of rules and values consonant with those held by the colonizer inevitably bring middle class blacks into conflict with the cultural traditions of black people.

What, exactly, is the status of the contemporary black family? It would appear that the trend is toward attenuation of its traditional structure. In a period when one-half of black men are out of work and black family income has declined to 56 percent of white family income, a stable, gratifying family life becomes difficult to sustain. Without the cultural supports that have allowed them to transcend those economic forces in the past, the black family has retreated into a variety of other family forms. Among the visible manifestations of these changes are increases in black singlehood, female-headed households, homosexuality and interracial marriages. Underlying many of these transformations are changes in the white family, the emergence and acceptance of women's liberation ideology, and alternative family lifestyles. None of the aforementioned family forms need to be regarded as negative per se. However, they are concomitants of urban poverty, crime, suicide and mental dislocation among blacks.

In sum, the black family is dialectically linked to the functioning of internal colonialism. The relationship between changes in the economic order and black family functioning are quite clear. What is not understood is that culture is a two-edged sword: It can act as a mechanism for survival or as an apparatus of control. To the extent that blacks forsake the family and the role they must play in it, the greater their vulnerability to the destructive forces of racial colonialism. Diffused groups of people who are detached from their cultural roots are powerless to resist the forces of oppression that they must eventually encounter in a society which is based on race and class exploitation. The family represents the basic collectivization of the black community and contains within it the potential for black survival in a world composed of the colonizers and the colonized.

CHAPTER EIGHT

Blacks in Politics:
A Case Study in Neo-Colonialism

The right to vote for a candidate of one's choice in political elections is the one characteristic that allegedly distinguishes the United States from the Soviet Union. Theoretically, any race or class has its interests represented by democratically elected members of the legislative and executive branches of government. As true of many American creeds, the concept of political democracy has never been fully applied to black Americans.

Blacks arrived on U.S. shores in 1619, but they did not get the right to vote until the passage of the 14th Amendment in 1865. That legal right could not be exercised for 70 years after the Reconstruction era due to a series of disenfranchising codes and acts of violence and suppression against blacks by the Ku Klux Klan and other white groups. Only after passage of the Voting Rights Act in 1965 did blacks regain the voting franchise in the South. The effect of the Voting Rights Act can be seen in the increase of black elected officials from 1,160 in 1969 to 6,056 in 1985.[1]

Although blacks are approximately 15 percent of the voting age population in the U.S., they only hold 1.2 percent of all elective offices in the country. Black voting strength is diluted by a number of factors, including reapportionment and gerrymandering practices that favor white voters and the lower percentage of black voter turnout. In 1984, only 56 percent of voting age blacks actually voted, compared to 61 percent of the white voting age population.[2]

This racial differential in voter turnout seems strange in light of the importance of government policies to most black Americans. Aside from their dependence on governmental bodies to insure their civil rights, black people, more than whites, look to the political arena as a source of jobs and services. As Landry has noted, government jobs were the first entry into the middle class for most blacks, beginning in the 1940's when they could obtain positions as clerks in the post office.[3] Increasingly, as the black vote became more important to white politicians, a trade off was made for white collar, decent wage jobs in the public sector. No such leverage was possible or attempted for the most part in the private sector, which continued to hire blacks only for low paying, menial work. As a result, 44 percent of blacks work in the public sector compared to 11 percent of whites. Probably an even higher percentage of the black middle class is employed in government service. And, unlike middle class white government employees, blacks reported that they could earn more in public service than in the private sector–an average of $2,000 more a year.[4]

As blacks have sadly learned, their opportunity for class mobility in the private sector is seriously constrained by discriminatory forces. Those blacks were hired by private businesses often responding to government laws and pressures. As that pressure is lifted and laws enforced, blacks are the first and primary victims of economic recessions. Barry Bosworth, a senior economist at the Brookings Institute, claims that "generally, for every white that is put on the unemployment rolls, two blacks are added. That seems to be holding true in this recession. Black workers tend to have less seniority than white workers." And, he adds, "you can't rule out discrimination. It may not be legal, but it's a fact of life."[5] Under an administration insensitive or hostile to blacks and not needing the black vote, the same pattern is exemplified in the public sector. Among federal government employees in 1981, minorities represented about nine percent of the work force but were 40 percent of the fired employees.[6]

The strength of the black vote is only significant when whites are equally divided between two candidates. In 1980, Reagan only received eight percent of the black vote and still won the Presidency by a decisive margin of over eight million votes. Hence, not only could he dismiss the black vote but it became part of his strategy to engage in symbolic racism to pacify the white voters who voted for him for race related reasons.

While blacks who lose their jobs may have some alternatives to sustain themselves, the hardest hit are those who depend on government programs and benefits. Although the majority of people on welfare are not black and most blacks are not on welfare, as a group they rely more heavily than whites on public assistance programs. Blacks constitute a third of those who receive food stamps and Medicaid, live in public housing and almost half of those getting Aid to Families with Dependent Children. Conversely, they make up only eight percent of those receiving Social Security retirement benefits, nine percent of those on Medicare or entitled to veterans' benefits. Under the Reagan Administration, the government programs in which blacks were over-represented were slashed by as much as 25 percent while the predominately white programs were spared the budget axe.[7]

Hence, it is understandable why Democratic Party politicians consistently receive 90-95 percent of the black vote, since blacks have suffered more under Republican administrations. As much as 80 percent of the black population is dependent on the public sector for jobs, services and benefits. Even blacks working in the private sector are more likely than whites to have children enrolled in public schools, to depend on government contracts for business and receive government subsidized loans. As one black labor union leader lamented, "We have not had the luxury of swinging back and forth in politics, like a lot of whites, who can afford to be liberal today and conservative the next days."[8]

Not only are blacks dependent on white politicians to trade votes for jobs and benefits, to which they are entitled to as citizens, but black politicians heavily rely on them in a number of ways. On the other hand, many white politicians use the anti-black sentiment among white voters for electoral victories. Racist appeals and slogans were long a staple of Southern politics. George Wallace, for example, lost in his first try for the governorship of Alabama in 1958 when his opponent accepted the support of the Ku Klux Klan and Wallace denounced the racist group. After his defeat, Wallace vowed never "to be out-nigguhed again." In subsequent elections he adopted the slogan, "segregation now! segregation tomorrow! segregation forever!" and built his whole political career on racist appeals.[9] As overt racism became politically unfashionable, the slogans developed into code words that had popular appeal to white voters. One of them was law and order. Although blacks are more likely to be the victims of crime, the votes for law-and-order white political candidates come primarily from white voters. Since the popular image of the criminal, in the minds of the white public, is that of the gun toting black male, the message is a subtle racial one.

Concomitant with the law and order theme to attract white votes is the support of capital punishment for certain crimes. Although numerous studies demonstrate that capital punishment is not a deterrent to violent crime, the white electorate continues to support its use. One reason may be found in Bower's survey of how the death penalty is employed. Bower found it to be almost exclusively reserved for blacks who kill or rape whites.[10] According to white columnist Pete Hamil,

> Three young whites, joy riding in a van the other night, grabbed two young black women off the street, beat, raped and sodomized them. There are people who demand the death penalty for blacks when they do such things to white women; they don't shout so wildly when the victims are black. Obviously, there is a strong undertone of racism in the calls for the death penalty.[11]

Opposition to reverse discrimination and busing to achieve school integration are other issues that have strong racist appeal. The most popular current appeal is getting government off our backs and government deregulation. Whites assume this means cutting welfare expenditures and gutting affirmative action laws that they believe only benefit blacks. When the Reagan Administration's policies adversely affected whites, one of Reagan's white supporters lamented, "We thought he was going after the big fat black women on welfare—not us."[12]

Few government programs benefit only blacks. Indeed, according to a National Urban League study, "The problem was that much of the funds went to areas that had little need for them." Most government programs for the disadvantaged had reached only a fraction of those in need. It is estimated that only 10 percent of the government funds allocated to the poor actually reached them. The rest went to the maintenance of huge bureaucracies or were given to businesses, most of whom were staffed by whites. Thus, the largest beneficiaries of these programs were white.[13] Still, the conventional wisdom is that only blacks will be hurt by any reduction in government social programs. One empirical test of this hypothesis was the Wright survey on attitudes toward welfare by white. It was discovered that whites with positive attitudes toward blacks were more likely to favor welfare spending than those with racist attitudes.[14]

Given the aforementioned factors, it seems naive at best and self-serving at worst to argue that American politics is color blind. While politicians are known to engage in practices that are not part of their personal convictions, some are equally as racist as their white supporters. Richard M. Nixon, the former and discredited President of the United States, won electoral office on a law and order campaign that had strong racist appeal. One of his former top aides, John Ehrlichman, revealed that Nixon sincerely believed federal programs like affirmative action and busing simply would never do any good because blacks are genetically inferior to whites.[15] In the last decade, a number of white elected and appointed officials have been forced to resign when their racist attitudes became public. Chances are that the discreet racists in public service are much more numerous. Tony Brown cuts through the facade of a color blind democracy with his pungent declaration, "Let's stop the hypothetical nonsense that race is not a factor when in reality it determines everything."[16]

RACISM CALIFORNIA STYLE

California is a mosaic of geographical, cultural, social and political elements. Its borders house both the radicals of Berkeley and the John Birch Society of Orange County. Not only is California the most populous state, it is one of the most racially diverse. Hispanics, Asians, Native Americans and blacks make up a third of the state's population. Politically, California appears to be a progressive state. Blacks and women are mayors of four of the state's five largest cities. A black male presides over the state assembly, and there are many black county and city officials. Yet, in the last 20 years, California has experienced: (1) the passage of a state proposition to legalize racial discrimination in housing, which was declared un-constitutional by the courts; (2) the uprooting of every black person, by white groups, from their homes in the town of Taft; and (3) the election of a member of the Ku Klux Klan as the Democratic candidate for a U.S. Congressional seat.

With that history in mind, Tom Bradley, black Mayor of Los Angeles, decided to run for Governor of California on the Democratic ticket in 1982. He was armed with the knowledge that around the nation, fewer than a dozen blacks won statewide elections from 1970 to 1980.[17] The list included one senator, two lieutenant governors and one superintendent of public instruction. Two of the four highest statewide offices in California had been won by blacks. Certainly, Bradley was aware that his race could be used against him by his opponents.

When Bradley first ran for Mayor of Los Angeles in 1968, his opponent, Sam Yorty, defeated him with an overt racist campaign that warned whites that blacks would take over everything, including the police department, if a black man was elected mayor.[18] Bradley knew that the heaviest black voter turnout could not elect him since blacks represented only 7.5 percent of California's population even less of the registered voters. The other minority groups would give him most of their votes, an advantage over any white opponent.

Among the reasons cited for Bradley's defeat was the low turnout and percentage of votes (70 percent) he received from Hispanic voters. However, that group did not have the same personal interest in Bradley's election and probably voted more in response to his political record. That record included his courtship of farmers who were exploiting Hispanics, his weak support of the Farm-Labor Relations Act, designed to protect farm workers, and a rather permissive attitude toward sweatshops employing cheap Hispanic labor and police brutality toward them. Hispanics' lukewarm attitude toward Bradley might have accounted for his low margin of victory in his home county of Los Angeles (56 percent).

Still, Bradley would need to attract about 40 percent of the white vote in order to win. Six weeks before the election, he declared, "I don't think there is a significant number of people who will vote on racial considerations."[19] On November 2, 1982, Tom Bradley was defeated by 50,000 votes (.007 percent) in his attempt to become the nation's first elected black governor in California's closest and most confusing election in the 20th century.

Before examining what happened and the lessons to be learned, let's look at Tom Bradley, the man. His rise to political fame is the quintessential Horatio Alger story. Born the son of a Texas sharecropper and a domestic servant, he won a sports scholarship to the University of California-Los Angeles, where he was a star athlete. After graduation, he joined the then segregated Los Angeles Police Department and rose to the rank of lieutenant, simultaneously earning a law degree by attending night school. After being elected to the Los Angeles City Council, Bradley was elected Mayor of Los Angeles, which had only a 17 percent black population. His political style has been alternately described as conciliatory and Uncle Tomish. During his 10 years as mayor, he rarely took strong stands on issues that were racial, projecting himself as a mayor of "all the people."[20] Those who knew Bradley were convinced that he was committed to basic goals of blacks. However, as one white columnist noted, "He's the kind of black that people (i.e. whites) feel comfortable with."[21]

With all of those factors combined, Bradley appeared a cinch to become the nation's first elected black governor. So many things seemed to be working in his favor. According to pre-election polls, he had one of the highest name recognitions and the *highest* popularity rating in the state. He was the perfect candidate for a conservative era. By all accounts, his own included, he was more conservative or moderate than his Democratic predecessor, Jerry Brown. Despite his reputation as an opportunist and a flake, Brown appointed a record number of women and minorities to state and judicial offices, was supportive of environmental restrictions on business development and generally refused to operate in the political mainstream. Conversely, when Bradley walked into a room full of white businessman, it was "Bradley country."[22]

Everything a white Democratic candidate receives, Bradley received: endorsements from labor unions, fundraising events, contributions from special interest groups, even the endorsements of California's major newspapers. Less than a month before the election, he held a 13 point lead in the polls. Only four percent of the white voters claimed they would vote against him solely because he was black. Bradley's opponent, George Deukmejian said, "Tom Bradley and I agree. Race is not an issue."[23] Compared to Bradley's former opponents, Deukmejian's racial messages were subtle. He stressed his tough stand on law enforcement. Bradley was opposed to a tough stand, but said he would enforce the law. Deukmejian stressed that he would be a Governor of all Californians, implying to some that Bradley would favor minority groups. Bradley's ads emphasized how California was stronger when it worked together, weaker when it was divided.

Given the positive factors that favored Bradley, why did he lose and how much of a factor was race in the final outcome? Interestingly enough, Deukmejian's two largest political victories occurred because he had the good fortune to be pitted against black opponents. Four years earlier he won the race for state attorney general against a black woman, former Congresswoman Yvonne Burke. Ms. Burke believes her race and sex contributed to her defeat. According to her, "It (racism) cannot be used in a personal way. It has to be used in a mass media way. It also must be veiled. The things they used against me were such issues as the death penalty, which I opposed. It has to be indirect."[24] The fact that two blacks had won statewide offices in the past was misleading. One, Mervyn Dymally, was elected lieutenant governor because many white (and black) voters did not realize he was black. Four years later he was defeated. When Dymally was defeated in 1978, the Democratic candidate for governor won by a large margin. It is interesting to note that only the black Democrats lost in the statewide races. Moreover, the only time in recent years when a split ticket for the top two seats has been elected was when a black was running for one of the seats. The other black candidate who won a statewide race, Wilson Riles Sr., ran against a right-wing Republican who had alienated most Democratic and many Republican voters.

Certainly, Deukmejian's campaign manager was aware of the advantage of being white in winning a statewide race. Or, so he told reporters in his comment that hidden anti-black sentiment among California voters would swing a close election to Deukmejian. To wit, he said, "If we are down five points or less in the polls by election time, we're going to win, due to this anti-black feeling. It's just a fact of life. If people are going to vote that way, they certainly are not going to announce it for a survey taker."[25] For being so honest about Deukmejian's strategy, the campaign manager was fired.

THE NEO-COLONIAL STRATEGY

Race was the definitive variable in Tom Bradley's campaign. Some 100 years after slavery ended, only two decades after the end of official racial apartheid in the U.S., it is simplistic to consider a black man's ascendancy to the most powerful position, in the country's most important state, a race-free issue. Nevertheless, we need to understand that not all the race-related factors worked against Bradley. In fact, the power structure wanted Tom Bradley in the governor's role *because* he is black. And, his occupancy of that position might not have served the interests of blacks. Those who knew Bradley's political history realized he was not a threat to white hegemony. As one of Bradley's advisers put it: "He is not really a black politician. He is an establishment politician."[26] Bradley reinforced that view by his pro-business approach, his financial support from wealthy whites and his assiduous avoidance of any race related issues. His courtship of business assumes there is a harmony of interests between working class minorities and the corporate world. This seems a slight variation of Reaganomics, which has resulted in the wealthy being enriched at the expense of the working masses. If blacks and Hispanics did not turn out in large numbers for Bradley, his record as Mayor of Los Angeles and his conservative orientation seem a sufficient explanation.

Had Bradley been elected governor, he would have taken over the reins of a state with an estimated one billion dollar deficit at the time. Either he would have been forced to raise state taxes or slash social programs. States do not have a lot of fat to cut since they mainly fund health, welfare and educational services. Since Bradley painted himself as a fiscal conservative, we can only guess as to his course of action. His election would have been a victory for the opponents of affirmative action and special programs for minorities.

A constant theme in his campaign ads was how, through hard work, Bradley made the most of his opportunities and succeeded in life. The obvious implication is that he made it without affirmative action or other special programs therefore so can other minorities. Bradley's election would have been a reaffirmation of the prevalent belief among whites that race does not matter. It's only a person's willingness to work hard and take advantage of opportunities that are equally available to all groups.

While whites could revel in the election of a black to the governorship, thus affirming their commitment to equal opportunity for all, the minority unemployment rate exceeded 15 percent in the state at the time. Minority enrollment in state colleges was on the decline, social services were being cut and racist actions against minorities were on the rise. It is also instructive to note that Bradley would have presided over a state which is projected to have a 45 percent minority population by the year 2,000.[27] Given the typical census undercount of minority populations, that could indicate minorities will be the majority in California in less than 18 years. What would be better for whites than an establishment politician, genetically black, and ostensibly in control of allocating dwindling resources resources among the competing interest groups?

Bradley's advisers gave testimony to his proposed role in describing the racial message in one of his ads. The ad showed Bradley talking about how many who benefit from welfare shouldn't and how others who should be helped get trapped in a welfare cycle that saps individual initiative. As governor, he could fight welfare fraud. The message was, a Bradley adviser said, that a black governor could deal with welfare. It would also be easier for him to deal with cuts in health and educational services that disproportionately benefit racial minorities. The hope, of course, was that Bradley could defuse any protests and social movements by minorities over their continued unequal share of the state's resources.

It was a classical neo-colonial strategy that failed for one simple reason: the deep seated racism in U.S. society. Once they exploited racism to divide the working class, the U.S. ruling elite could not turn it off at will. Despite all the subtle, and not so subtle, messages that Bradley was a safe black candidate, white racism prevailed. Bradley's first mistake was in believing the polls that once showed him with a lead of 22 points over Deukmejian. Two days before the election, Bradley had a lead of seven points. Even after the polls had closed, Mervyn Field, one of the most respected pollsters, predicted a Bradley victory by 10 percentage points. Rarely have the polls been so far off. Surely, they took racial bias into account. Two months before the election, Field was quoted as saying, "I think that anybody who says there is no residual resentment toward a minority group member running for public office is a fool. It exists." Another leading pollster anonymously explained, "The smart money boys have isolated his (Bradley's) race as 'the factor.' It's uppermost in their minds."[28]

The pollsters figured in a four to five percent racial bias factor in their predictions. In a close election, that would be enough to defeat Bradley. He lost by less than one percent. However, the negative racial bias was much larger. The pollsters might have used the model of Dr. Alfred Kinsey, the sex researcher. His finding that 50 percent of U.S. women had engaged in premarital sex in the 1940's is widely quoted. What is not generally realized is that only 35 percent of the women in Kinsey's sample admitted to premarital sexual activity. Kinsey added the other 15 percent as "the lie factor," that is, the tendency of people to lie when there is a discrepancy between their behavior and societal norms.

It is the fact that the anti-black vote was as large as 25 percent that made the polls so wrong in Bradley's case. Other factors cannot explain his loss when everything else was controlled. Democrats received 58 percent of the total vote cast in California's state senate races in the same election. Bradley received 48 percent of the total state vote for governor. With a Republican administration in Washington presiding over the nation's highest unemployment rate since the Depression era, it is extremely difficult to imagine anything other than the racial factor contributing to Bradley's defeat. Although ex-post facto explanations attributed the "blame" for Bradley's loss on a low turnout of black voters, the exit polls showed that blacks were nine percent of those who voted, although only making up seven percent of the voting age population. With one exception, Democrats made dramatic gains throughout California, adding seven Congressional seats and winning all other statewide offices. The only incumbent constitutional officer who lost was another black man, Wilson Riles Sr., the state Superintendent of Public Instruction. Given Bradley's lead in the polls, his high popularity ratings, endorsement by the state's major newspaper and other Democrats who won, what other factor, besides race, can account for his defeat?

One post-election comment was, "When you lose by 50,000 votes of more than 7.5 million cast, there are a lot of reasons. The margin is so minuscule."[29] An analysis of the vote totals by county does not provide much of a clue. Ironically, Bradley carried mostly the counties along the coast and counties in the northern part of the state, although his base was in southern California. A cursory look at the geopolitical areas shows he won the majority of the vote only in liberal northern California counties, in those where minorities are prevalent, unemployment rates were high and his home county of Los Angeles. With the comparatively high voter turnout, Democrats had an edge with the 2-1 ratio of Democratic registered voters. None of that worked for Bradley.

Election post mortem explanations did begin to deal with the racial factor. One political columnist surmised, "The much-rumored hidden vote of bigotry against the black Los Angeles Mayor obviously was bigger than expected. Many voters may have unconsciously wondered whether the black candidate would 'really' be tough on crime."[30] Mervyn Field explained his post-election prediction of a Bradley victory by the distortion in his exit polls, caused by the unusually high number of voters, presumably conservatives (i.e. whites) who refused to participate in Field's survey.[31] It is in the findings of the polls of Public Response Associates, Bradley's pollsters, that we uncover the depth of the anti-black vote. Ten percent of the whites surveyed consistently said they thought Bradley would do too much for blacks. Another 10-15 percent said they didn't know. The pollster's assumption was that part of that second group chose not to answer because they didn't want to admit to prejudice.[32]

In another separate poll, nine percent of those who described their political orientation was liberal voted for Deukmejian out of a personal dislike for Bradley.[33] Considering Bradley's colorless, bland personality, it was hard for anyone to dislike him for other than ideological or racial reasons. Although the anti-black vote may have been as high as 25 percent of the white vote, it was cancelled out by some other factors. Minorities, comprising 20 percent of the voters, gave Bradley 80 percent of their votes. White women, for a number of reasons, gave Bradley a slim majority (51 percent) of their votes. The predominantly white Republican Marin County voted for Bradley because many thought it was time for a black governor. White radicals who generally vote for a third party candidate voted for Bradley because he is black. The Communist Party went on record with an endorsement of Bradley's candidacy, claiming it was a forum on racism. Still, the radical Peace and Freedom Party drew almost 70,000 votes for its gubernatorial candidate, enough to have supplied Bradley with a small margin of victory. The question remains whether Bradley's taking a more radical stance on the issues would have attracted enough radical votes to balance the conservative white voters that might have shifted to his opponent. In the end, he lost, and it may be the masses of black people who were the real winners in this whole scenario.

SUMMARY

The implications of the California gubernatorial race are manifold. Bradley's loss demonstrates that race is still decisive in determining a black person's life chances, regardless of any meritorious attributes he or she may possess. Apparently, it is a fact of life that must be repeated over and over again before it is engrained in the black consciousness. While that "fact of life" should not dissuade blacks from aspiring to the highest levels of life in the U.S., the lesson must be implanted that the successes of individuals who happen to be black are not inextricably linked to the fate of blacks as a group. Whereas black individuals may be measured by the racist and invidious evaluations of their racial group, the image of the group is not altered by the individual successes of its members. The successes of individual blacks are simply seen as exceptions to the generally inferior ability and status of the collective. Few individuals will be successful since most blacks will continue to be subjected to white stereotypes of blacks as intellectually inferior, indolent and morally flawed.

However, white society will continue to permit a few blacks to attain positions heretofore reserved for whites. As the socio-economic conditions of the black masses worsen, black success symbols will increase in number. This dichotomy preserves the myth that success in America is based on merit, not racial membership. If this myth of a meritocracy is not accepted by the black masses, the hope is that whites will find it a viable explanation for the inequality between the races that prevails. It is a self-serving ideology because whites are allowed to retain their racial privileges while believing that racial inequality is a function of genetic deficits and character flaws in those who remain at the bottom of the social strata.

Ultimately, whites are the real victims in this neo-colonial scheme. They forfeit their long term class interests for short term racial gains. As they are belatedly discovering with the effects of Reaganomics, for every "big, fat" black woman who loses her welfare benefits, four white workers lose their jobs and other whites are denied access to government benefits—benefits that their tax dollars paid for. Only wealthy whites will prosper under political leaders such as Reagan and Deukmejian. They do not represent racial interests as much as they represent class interests. The class reality of both blacks and whites must overtake the racial reality if the U.S. is ever to be a true political democracy.

BRADLEY'S POST MORTEM

Some years after Bradley's 1982 gubernatorial campaign, debate continues over how he managed to snatch defeat from the jaws of victory. Willie Brown, the black Speaker of the California Assembly, was blunt in his appraisal of Bradley's campaign strategy. According to Brown, Bradley narrowly lost the governor's seat because of race and because he should have made more of an effort to get out the black vote. Brown said, "His (Bradley's) deliberate strategy was not to campaign to blacks. It was a terrible strategy. A five percent higher turnout in the black community would have turned the election. His skin color cost him the election. There is no doubt in my mind of that."[34] In one informal poll of blacks in Los Angeles, 10 percent said Bradley defeated himself by his low key approach to the problems and issues of the black community. Those polled stated that "he (Bradley) never publicly expressed concern about the mass of police killings that took place during his tenure as mayor, and he never came to the black areas of the city except at times for his re-election."[35]

While it was true that 250,000 registered black voters stayed away from the polls, blacks did vote in proportion to their population ratio in the state. Obviously, Bradley's strategy of ignoring black voters did not inspire a larger than normal turnout. However, other forces were operative in his loss. A lower than expected turnout among Hispanics, Asians and other minority groups also hurt him. These groups represent almost 35 percent of the state's population but only 15 percent of those who actually voted.[36] It goes without saying that Bradley made no attempt to encourage minorities to vote for him. But, he needed their votes because his narrow loss was caused by a substantial shift of white voters in the last days of the campaign. On election day, Bradley received 43 percent of the white vote to his opponent's 55 percent. Even Bradley had to admit that racism was a factor in his defeat, when he remarked, "I always said I did not think there would be a significant racial element in the election. I wasn't saying there would be no degree of racial motivation.[37]

In the ensuing years, Bradley prepared for another run for the governor's seat, this time against an incumbent governor. Despite Bradley's advanced age (69) and previous loss, he was assured of the Democratic nomination. His stewardship of the successful and ultra-patriotic 1984 Olympic games had increased his standing in the polls, as well as his overwhelming re-election victory as Mayor of Los Angeles. A poll taken one year before the 1986 election showed Bradley leading Governor Deukmejian by 50 percent to 44 percent.[38] Of course, Bradley had huge leads in the polls prior to his last defeat in 1982. This time he decided to use a different campaign strategy. He claimed he had hoped for a more enthusiastic response from minorities in his last campaign and didn't get it because he spent 95 percent of his time fundraising. Contrary to his past neutral stand on racial and liberal issues, Bradley advocated pay equity for women, removal of investments in South Africa from Los Angeles' portfolio and a city ordinance to protect AIDS victims from discrimination. He helped to bring some chain stores to a low income neighobrhood and campaigned for a charter amendment that would create two seats on the City Council in heavily Hispanic and Asian-American neighborhoods.[39]

Nevertheless, Bradley attempted a delicate balancing act between minority and majority communities, business and workers. While trying to reach out to progressive voters, he offended them with a decision to allow a oil company to drill for oil in a scenic coastal community. Bradley may have alienated minority voters by his position against capital punishment to one favoring the death penalty. In 1986 he ran against an incumbent governor with a favorable job rating despite his lack of visibility and unconditional support of Reaganomics. However, the normal course of political events do not apply in Bradley's case. Despite his carefully cultivated image as a "safe" black, according to Bercy, "he (Bradley) is black and for some folks that's a big problem."[40] As the head of a campaign management company put it, "When you come down to it, a lot of people can support a black mayor of their city but can't go for a black as governor of their state."[41] Whether a black candidate who denies the significance of race can overcome all the racial forces against him to achieve the governorship of the largest state in the United States is a story worth watching.

THE JESSE JACKSON CAMPAIGN

The Jesse Jackson campaign for the 1984 Democratic Presidential nomination provided a vivid contrast to the campaign of Tom Bradley. Whereas Bradley rose from a police officer up through the normal political channels to run for Governor of

California, Jackson's roots were in the civil rights movement, and he had been a political activist working against the system for 25 years. Bradley felt he would get the black vote merely by his genetic kinship with that group while Jackson believed he deserved black support because he had paid his dues. Bradley hoped to minimize the negative effects of racism by avoiding any discussion of racial issues and public association with racial minorities. Jackson built a black political base and tried to expand it to other disenfranchised groups such as women, gays, the disabled, Asians, Hispanics and Native Americans.

A central difference between the two men was that Bradley was a colorless, loyal Democrat with no program to aid racial minorities but with the party machine behind him. Jackson had more charisma than any of his Democratic opponents, a program to deal with the ills and inequities of U.S. society but no party machinery to back up his efforts. In the end, both men lost due to their blackness, Jackson by a larger margin than Bradley. There is a lesson to be learned from both campaigns.

Jesse Jackson cut his political teeth on the campaign of Harold Washington for Mayor of Chicago in 1982. That was a grassroots effort that was buffeted by a hostile white community, adversarial press and party machinery. The political lines were drawn so strongly along racial lines that the black community was mobilized to vote in record numbers. With the defection of a small percentage of whites, the blacks of Chicago managed to elect Harold Washington. Jackson was part of that effort and realized the untapped potential of the black vote. In black leadership forums he raised the idea of a black candidate for the Democratic nomination for President. Although blacks represented only 12 percent of the voting age population, they were 25 percent of the registered Democrats. The black leadership group was reluctant to endorse the idea because they believed a black candidate could not win, and most were entrenched in the tradition of bartering black votes to a white candidate who promised patronage or specific legislation to assist blacks. While the black leadership was debating whether anyone should run, Jackson declared himself a candidate.[42]

Jackson's circumvention of other black leaders in declaring his candidacy meant blacks would not have a united front in their first "serious" national campaign. It is questionable whether unanimity among blacks was possible. In 1972, Shirley Chisholm, then a Congresswoman from New York, ran for the Democratic nomination with even less support than Jackson. Her campaign was noticeably ignored by the media and the black leadership because of her gender.[43] However, Chisholm did not have the national recognition, charisma, background or the backing of black religious leaders, all of which Jackson possessed. Had the black leadership decided to run a candidate, it probably would not have been Jesse Jackson. One charge against him was that he was an ego tripper who was more interested in attention than results. Moreover, he had never held any public office, and his position as a Baptist minister did not set well with people who believed in the separation of church and state. The white leadership of the Democratic Party was silently opposed to Jackson because of their fear that he would siphon off black votes from white candidates. Their opposition was largely unarticulated since they did not want to alienate Jackson's black supporters.

Whatever Jackson's personal shortcomings, he lent a certain dynamism to the Democratic campaign that attracted the attention of the mass media. With very little money, lacking the backing of established black political leaders, and a hastily assembled and inexperienced campaign staff, Jackson made use of his fiery oratory, photogenic appeal and novice status to attract more attention than his white rivals for the Democratic nomination. The Democratic primaries officially began in New Hampshire, where blacks are less than one percent of the population. Jackson eventually received seven percent of the vote in that state, aided by television debates which showed him the most articulate, compassionate and relevant of the Democratic candidates. Many whites confessed that Jackson was the best qualified candidate but would not vote for him because the racism of other whites meant he could not win. As one white male voter lamented, "It's just a shame Jackson isn't white. We've got to face up to this. There are white people in this country who don't see the man, they just see the color."[44]

Although Jackson addressed issues that cut across racial lines, he did not receive much of the white vote. Moreover, his heaviest white support came in states where the percentage of blacks was lowest. That may be explained by his tendency to reach out to white constituencies where black voters were low in number. There's an old axiom that whites are more liberal on racial matters where there's little chance of black competition for jobs, housing, education and other programs. At any rate, Jackson received about five percent of the votes cast by whites in the primaries.[45] Voter behavior studies revealed that whites gave Jackson high marks on his ability to inspire and command respect but displayed negative attitudes toward him because of his race.[46] The potency of race is so strong that Jackson received a lower percentage of white votes than such offbeat white candidates as Sister Boom Boom (a transsexual nun), a dead candidate, one under indictment and a man who changed his name to Eager Beaver. Stating his reason for not endorsing Jackson, Atlanta Mayor Andrew Young said, "I know Jesse. I like Jesse. But he scares the hell out of white folks."[47]

There were charges that Jackson's appeal to black voters convinced whites that he would favor blacks over them. Black voters were accused of bloc voting. In reality, whites expect blacks to vote for white candidates but rarely vote for black candidates. Whites, on the other hand, engage in racial bloc voting without having it interpreted that way. In contrast, Jackson received 61 percent or better of black votes in only 13 states, with a high of 87 percent in New York and a low of 45 percent in Alabama. His greatest support from whites was nine percent in the California primary. In other words, whites voted far more as a racial bloc than did blacks, who gave about 40 percent of their vote to white candidates.[48]

In some regions of the country, white males gave Reagan as high as 90 percent of their votes.[49] White males are the same group that has lost its exclusive monopoly on the society's positive values in the last 20 years. The increased conservatism of white males is certainly linked to the fact that they are no longer a majority of the American workforce. Women and minority groups are simply taking a larger share of new jobs. Thus, white males vote overwhelmingly for a candidate like Ronald Reagan who implicitly a return to the days of white males' unchallenged superiority over other groups, or even the stabilization of the status quo. Surveys report that 48 percent of whites, but only 14 percent of blacks, are satisfied with the way things are going in the U.S. Only six percent of whites surveyed thought civil rights was an important issue in the 1984 Presidential campaign compared to 38 percent of blacks. The national unemployment rate of eight percent became a non-issue to white candidates but remains strong to a black underclass whose unemployment stays in the range of 30 percent and as high as 50 percent among black youth.[50]

The racism of the white electorate extended into the press coverage of Jackson's campaign. Jackson was always referred to by his race while white candidates were not. The criticism of his "Hymie" remark about U.S. Jews seemed to carry the message that it was not wrong to be a white racist since blacks are just as bigoted as whites are. After his virtual crucifixion by the white press, Jackson commented, "Those of us who are black are projected in the media as less intelligent than we are, less hardworking, less patriotic, more suspect." He went on to say that "to refer to me as the black candidate is racist because my blackness is self-evident. So when somebody refers to me as black, they are not describing me, they are defining me to confine me."[51] Cherylle Greene, the Executive Editor of *Essence* magazine, noted that the biased coverage by the white press of Jackson's Presidential bid demonstrated that "freedom of the press belongs to those who own it." She added that "such coverage reflects the general hostility that society holds towards blacks and poor people in this country."[52]

Jackson's campaign was more successful than anyone imagined prior to its beginning. Neither he nor his supporters ever thought he would win either the Democratic nomination or the Presidency of the United States. In the past the black vote had been considered loyal support more a neutral balancer of power for white candidates who set the agenda with their white constituencies as the target audience. Not only did Jackson's candidacy mobilize black voters to use the ballot to challenge institutional racism and economic inequality, but Jackson raised issues and suggested solutions that the white ruling class and its minions did not want addressed in a national forum. Even whites expressed admiration for Jackson's adherence to principles as reflected in his stands on the economy, foreign policy and dispossessed groups. Thus, he heightened the consciousness of millions of Americans through the quality of the issues he raised.

Although the Rainbow Coalition never went far beyond Jackson's initial black support, partly due to some organizational problems which prevented an effective communication to non-black groups, Jackson did tap the strong disaffection among other racial minorities. Had his campaign been more effectively organized and financed, it is possible that he would have received the majority of votes cast by other third world groups. Jackson received limited support from some white blue collar workers who responded to his program for full employment, major reductions in military spending and increased housing and health care programs. Jackson's program for women's rights was largely responsible for a white woman, for the first time in U.S. history, being selected as the Vice Presidential candidate of a major political party in the United States.

In all the debate over Jackson's race and alliance with black voters, what was ignored was the fact that he represented the most progressive program within a major political party in U.S. history. A white candidate such as George McGovern actually captured the Democratic nomination in 1972 with a less liberal program. Jackson's race prevented the congealing of progressive forces. As Chrisman has noted,

> Because of racism, the white left and working classes and middle classes could not rally sufficiently behind Jackson, still believing that black politics is only the politics of either accommodation or disruption, not a response to the total social and economic conditions of the society. The bourgeoisie opposed Jackson precisely because it comprehended the class context of his candidacy.[53]

Ultimately, Jackson's campaign took on the character of a social movement. It raised consciousness and spurred black voter registration efforts. Unlike Bradley's campaign, Jackson's broke with the ruling class' doctrine that the interests of capitalism and workers are the same. Bradley's embrace of the system gave him the support of the corporate oligarchy, which felt it served their interests to have a black at the helm of what will be the first industrialized state to have a non-white majority. Still, the ruling class found that even the safest black would be unacceptable to large numbers of whites. Jackson's campaign was more relevant because it involved large masses in a movement that expressed their objective interests. Such a movement can ultimately result in meaningful social change while the attainment of a position such as governor or President is more symbolic than substantive. It gives the illusion of power, but the fact of impotence remains. Only a social movement based on class and racial consciousness can break the chains of oppression that link us to an exploitative system.

CHAPTER NINE

The Urban Plantation

Some years ago, the city was proclaimed the black man's land. Due to concentration in large urban centers and the power of numbers in achieving political power, it was predicted that blacks could obtain through a geopolitical strategy what centuries of protest and petition could not do. Such a dream has become a nightmare as America's cities have increasingly become cesspools of crime, unemployment, family breakdown and physical blight.

The prediction of cities as the black man's Mecca ignored the fundamental relationship of neo-colonialism between the black and white communities and the institutionalized, unequal distribution of political and economic power. A most dramatic sign of the future of cities is the rapid increase of black middle class flight to the suburbs. Across the the country the number of blacks in suburbs increased 19.5 percent in the early 1970's, in contrast to only 7.3 percent for whites. Between 1981 and 1982 the suburbs received a net black migration of 318,000. However, this migration does not mean that racial segregation in residential housing has ended. In many cases black suburbanization is simply the result of central city black neighborhoods expanding across city boundaries and into the inner suburbs—often older suburbs vacated by whites that have begun to deteriorate.[1]

Originally, blacks were a peasant group who made their living on the land. Around the beginning of the 20th century certain events precipitated a massive black migration to the cities of the North and South. Between 1910 and 1920, a complex of push-and-pull factors propelled over a million blacks out of the countryside into the nation's cities. Among these factors were natural disasters, the mechanization of agriculture and World War I, which created a demand for labor and industrial expansion in the North. There have been additional waves of black migration. Between the end of World War II and 1980, over four million blacks moved out of the South. As a result, the proportion of the black population residing in cities increased from 44 percent to 85 percent. Although the census count is inaccurate, at minimum the figures[2] show that the majority of the U.S.'s 25 largest cities are non-white.

However, the decline of black faith in the urban dream is symbolized by black people's return to the South. Between 1970 and 1980, there was an average net migration each year of 39,000 blacks to the South.[3] Most of the blacks who moved to the South were natives of the area. Strangely, they returned to the South for the same reasons they originally went North, career opportunities, less discrimination and a better quality of life. Before romanticizing the virtues of Southern life, it would behoove us to look more carefully at black existence in the South. Most of the returnees are middle class blacks who are moving into skilled and professional jobs. They, too, are concentrated in large cities which may be only 10 or 20 years behind the problems of Detroit, Chicago and other large cities. Working class blacks, on the other hand, have a different set of problems.

In a very real sense the black culture in the South was a positive one. Because Southern blacks were a cohesive group with a strong sense of family and a hard work ethic, they produced most of the black leaders and members of the middle class in the U.S. Despite, or perhaps because of, the hard lines of racial segregation, Southern blacks have exceeded the progress of their Northern brethren. Studies indicate that black migrants to the North are more likely to have stable families and earn higher incomes than blacks born there.[4]

The South, nevertheless, is changing, and not all for the better. Desegregation, urbanization and acculturation are bringing Southern black life in line with its Northern counterpart. Witness, for example, the desegregation of black public schools. Heretofore, these schools had served as the secular focus of much black community life and provided an occupational base for the black elite. Various studies show that black children in the dual school system of the South had far more motivation to achieve than they are receiving under the integrated system today and more political consciousness.[5] As a result of school integration in 17 states, the number of black teachers in the U.S. fell 13 percent from 1975-1978, costing the black community an estimated 240 million dollars.[6] Since the 1954 school desegregation decision, Southern school systems have dismissed, demoted, dispatched and discriminated against a large number of black teachers. These important role models for black youth have large disappeared.

The economic resurgence of the South is largely a myth for black workers. In order to take advantage of low corporate tax levels and cheap labor, large numbers of foreign and Northern industries have relocated in the South in recent years. Concomitant with this industrial expansion has been the decline in agricultural employment and a significant decrease in black farm operations. In 1920 there were over one million black farmers, and in 1978 less than 57,000 remained. The farm population of the South is becoming increasingly white due to a difference in the rates of population decline of the races. Between 1970 and 1980 the number of blacks on farms decreased by 57 percent, or two and a half times the rate for white-operated farms.[7] Much of this disparate decline in farm tenancy must be attributed to the economic purge of black farmers from their land. The ascendancy of Northern and foreign capitalists has pushed thousands of black tenant farmers off their lands. Government support for these farmers has been largely non-existent.[8]

Many of these black farmers and their families have been oppressed into service in the new factories and industries arriving from the North. One example is the textile industry. Almost 75 percent of the nation's textile workers are employed in the South. The textile union reported that blacks in the industry increased from less than one percent in 1964 to 18 percent in 1975. Due to the availability of unemployed blacks in the South, many of them former farmers, the Southern percentage of black textile workers is estimated to be 25 percent, and many plants in the Carolinas are predominantly black.

Textile workers in the South are ranked at the bottom of all industrial workers nationwide, earning an average of $3.46 per hour compared to $6.43 per hour in the automobile industry.[9] The Northern industrialists have capitalized on the existence of right-to-work laws, which allow all workers to refuse to become union members in the South. Furthermore, the political conservatism of the region has prevented the formation of a radical political organization. Instead, the traditional racism of whites has made them captives of reactionary conservatives, like Ronald Reagan and Jerry Falwell.

The "new South" is modeling itself after the old North. Racism is taking a very subtle form in comparison to the blatant racism and segregation of the past. Racially segregated public schools have been supplanted by segregated academies, private, often church run schools with all white students. One of the highest rates of suburbanization can be found outside Southern cities where whites flee from the increasingly black inner cities. Mississippi, probably the most racist Southern state, has changed the least. Race has become the all important issue in the state's politics. More than 94 percent of white males in Mississippi voted for Reagan for President in 1984. Their votes reflected a desire to maintain the racial status quo, a situation in which 91 percent of managerial jobs are held by whites in a state that is 36 percent black.[10] Even more enlightened cities like Atlanta have witnessed a dramatic change in the racial compositions of their public schools. In 1970, 35 percent of Atlanta's schools were white compared to six percent in 1985.[11]

PROBLEMS OF THE CITY

One can see in bold relief the receptacle of despair that cities have become for many blacks. The key factor is economic. There has been a discernible decrease in manufacturing jobs located in the inner city. As businesses relocate to the predominantly white suburbs and the South, racial minorities are left to scramble for fewer, and poorer, jobs. While the number of jobs across the country increased at twice the rate of the population between 1970-1975, the reverse was true in urban centers. In cities, the population increased at a faster rate than the number of jobs. Many of the new jobs available to black residents in cities have been in the area of government service. In a number of larger U.S. cities there are actually fewer manufacturing jobs than government and service jobs.[12] As the taxpayer's revolt gathered steam, city governments have reversed the increase in local government jobs that once made up for part of the loss of manufacturing jobs.[13]

We have already mentioned the heavy concentration of blacks in cities, but other non-white minorities also compose a large segment of the urban population. Unlike the earlier European immigrants of some years ago, the new arrivals to the city are almost all non-white, from Mexico, Central America, the Caribbean and Asia. Corresponding with the immigrants' entry on the urban scene has been the flight of both white residents and businesses. Between 1960 and 1980, the number of whites living in central cities declined by five million, or six percent, while the number of blacks rose by 4.8 million, or 38 percent.[14] The flight of whites who are relatively affluent and the invasion of poor third world groups have weakened the tax base of cities and crippled their ability to provide social services for the new residents.

One can easily see the plight of urban blacks in the bare statistics. Rather than cite all the bleak economic facts, it is sufficient to quote the U.S. Civil Rights Commission's findings on the progress that minority groups have made in the last 16 years: "Majority males have continued to enjoy broader opportunities and to reap disproportionate benefits while women and minority males have in many instances fallen even farther behind."[15]

One might wonder how this conclusion fits with the prevalent view among white Americans that blacks have overcome most of the obstacles to racial equality. A primary reason for this confusion has been the tendency of researchers and federal agencies to compare a minority group's progress only with its past performance. In an absolute sense, blacks have improved their status in U.S. society. However, when you compare their progress with that of the dominant group, white males, it is clear that blacks have not made any inroads into the racial gap in education, jobs or income. Indeed, they have actually fallen behind.[16]

Besides economic inequalities, inner city blacks face a whole array of problems. By almost universal consensus it is admitted that the urban school system is in poor shape. In fact, it is almost an admission of poverty to enroll one's child in a public school. While the decline in quality of the public schools may be attributed to a combination of factors, it is probably no coincidence that the deterioration of those schools corresponded with their changing composition to a majority non-white student body in most large cities. Hence, we find large numbers of students being graduated from public schools without obtaining the fundamental ability to read and write well. Most of these functionally illiterate graduates are third world people, particularly Latino and black males.

Educational institutions represent one of the most important instruments of colonial rule and lie at the heart of the colonial process. Ever since blacks arrived on these shores, education has been an important issue in the black/white confrontation. For the majority of Americans, education has always been regarded as the major means to upward mobility in the class structure. Hence, to limit the access of blacks to educational systems is to maintain the racial privileges of the white majority. It is rarely stated in that way but rather is widely regarded as a result of black inability to take advantage of educational opportunities due to their inherent intellectual deficiencies.

During the days of slavery, black access to education was rare, and since then it has been inadequate in the racially segregated schools of the South. It is believed that blacks did not receive any formal education until the 18th century in colonial America. Informal education was little more available as many slaveholders were opposed to slaves learning to read. The quest for a decent education has been a long, bitter struggle for blacks. Free blacks did receive some instruction from free schools set up by religious societies in the 18th and 19th centuries, but as the Southern racial system of Jim Crow grew harsher, the education of blacks was increasingly restricted.[17] Up to the present time, the standards of education for blacks remain low because of the belief that they are incapable of profiting from an education.

The statistical evidence seems to bear this out when it is revealed that blacks score lower on every index of school performance than whites. There are differences of opinion on why these racial gaps in educational achievement exist. One school of thought is that the deprived family and socioeconomic background of black children means they enter the school setting with certain deficits that make it difficult for them to compete equally with white children.[18] Others believe that the primary effects of poverty and race are the attitudes they create in white or middle class teachers. When the teacher is led to expect a poorer performance from a child because he is poor and black, that attitude is what determines a child's performance. A black child enters school with a real zest for learning but soon discovers that the teacher expects little of him or her and subsequently also begins to expect little.

Other educators note that the belief that black children are culturally deprived only serves as a rationalization for the educational neglect of those children. Such theories perpetuate the inferior education blacks receive at every level and maintain their colonial status. These theories only entrench racial differences in class positions and make the schools an instrument in fostering class inequalities based on race in the larger society.[19]

That is precisely the role educational institutions play in colonial societies. In addition to maintaining the inferior status of its subjects, education acts as a formidable instrument of political power in its role as a transmitter of goals, values and attitudes of the colonial order. The educational system selects those values and attitudes favored by the ruling class and teaches them as universal truths. School remains one of the major institutions for socializing colonial subjects into the values of the colonizer. According to Cleaver, "They teach the exploited and the oppressed people to virtually love the system that is exploiting and oppressing them. The oligarchy has an interest in seeing to it that the curriculum is to its liking and that it does not expose the true nature of the decadent and racist society we live in."[20]

On the urban plantation, schools have become holding grounds for the youth of the underclass. Although a skilled workforce is essential to the needs of mature capitalism, it can afford to neglect the educational needs of black youth because they represent only the reserve labor pool of modern industry. It is instructive to note that federal and state government aid to public schools declined from a peak of just under nine percent in fiscal 1980 to 6.6 percent in 1983.[21] The society is rapidly developing a two-tier educational system, with those who can afford it sending their children to private schools and the poor being educated in inferior public schools. Private schools now educate 5.7 million of the 45.2 million U.S. students at the elementary and secondary levels. Although black children are more than 15 percent of the nation's school age children, they represent only 7.2 percent of the private school households in the U.S.[22]

Even the public school systems in large cities are racially segregated. One report revealed that enrollment in the nation's 10 largest urban school districts was more than two-thirds minority in 1980 and growing fast. In the populous Northeast, the percentage of predominantly minority schools increased from 67 percent to 80 percent.[23] Within the same school system, the education offered black students is substantially different from that offered to white students. Black students are more likely to be enrolled in special education programs and less likely to be enrolled in programs for the gifted and talented. They are overrepresented in vocational education programs and underrepresented in academic programs.[24] The view of an increasing number of educators is that if you are the child of low income parents, the chances are good that you will receive limited and often careless attention from adults in your high school. If you are the child of upper middle class parents, the chances are good that you will receive substantial and careful attention.[25] Little wonder, then, that about 44 percent of black teenagers suffer from illiteracy, a fact that Kozol estimates costs U.S. society 15 billion dollars each year—in costs of prisons, industrial accidents caused by a failure to read and in welfare payments to those who cannot adequately read or write.[26]

WELFARE CAPITALISM

Welfare, a favorite whipping boy of the politicians, is another racist code word for voters and one of the most effective instruments of colonial control ever devised. This system has managed to make many blacks into wards of the political state, dehumanize them and tear families apart. Welfare serves primarily to maintain the industrial reserve army of capitalism at the mere subsistence level and enforce social control of the black population by colonial intermediaries euphemistically known as social workers. As in colonial societies, welfare fosters a dependency in the native population and erodes ambition and the work ethic. Welfare recipients are subjected to the most dehumanizing practices, such as invasion of privacy, sterilization, bureaucratic intrusion into their sex lives, control over their children and various facts of economic exploitation caused by their subject status.

While these conditions may not have been the intentions of those who originally designed the welfare system, they have now become the objective results. Piven and Cloward list two chief functions of the welfare program: to restore order when mass unemployment leads to outbreaks of turmoil and to regulate labor. These regulative functions of welfare, Piven and Cloward assert, are required by the chaotic nature of a capitalist economy. The first function serves to maintain the existing political-economic order. When families are dislocated by mass unemployment, they may ultimately come to question the social order itself. To re-establish the system's legitimacy and authority, a substitute system of social control must replace it, at least temporarily.[27]

In the process of regulating labor, the welfare system gains control over its client population by distributing the resources men and women depend upon for survival. By giving vitally needed assistance, welfare enforces the work doctrine itself by the conditions it applies to the aid it gives. Usually the employable poor are redirected into the work force by one of two means. They may work in the public sector, such as parks or the sewage collection system. Or they may be contracted out to private employers who hire the poor and racial minorities. In the former instance, the welfare system incorporates surplus labor deriving from a declining state of the economy, and in the latter case, its policies are designed to overcome the poor correlation between the labor market requirements and the characteristics of the labor force. The purposes these policies serve are chiefly economic: to maintain the stability of capitalism. However, they are couched in the moral terms of the Protestant ethic of work as marking the value of the individual.[28]

There is a clear cut link between the relief system and black oppression. On a national level almost half the families receiving Aid to Families with Dependent Children (AFDC) are black. Life on the whole is a constant ordeal for those in need of AFDC. Most welfare recipients live at the bare subsistence level. Moreover, more than half of the poorest black families receive no assistance whatsoever. The majority of black families receiving welfare are headed by women. Remedies suggested by the government to restructure welfare into "workfare" are only subtle attempts to force several million black welfare mothers to work—most at wretchedly paid, menial jobs no better than domestic servants.[29]

It has become fashionable, even among blacks, to attack the welfare system as eroding the work ethic and disrupting the black family. Such attacks blithely ignore the fact that real cumulative benefits for both the elderly poor and for families enrolled in the AFDC program declined substantially during the 1970's. During the Reagan Administration's five years in office, the percentage of blacks with incomes below the poverty level rose from 35 to 38 percent. The anti-welfare ideology gained ascendancy during a five-year period when the income of the wealthiest one-fifth of U.S. families rose by nearly nine percent, and the real income of the poorest one-fifth of families— a disproportionate number of whom are black—has declined by almost eight percent.[30] A survey on the outcome of such disparities revealed that a majority of blacks did not have enough money in 1984 to provide clothing, food or medical care for their families.[31]

The diatribes against welfare for the poor take on racial dimensions because the operation of mature capitalism causes a disproportionate number of blacks to receive government subsidies. However, whites receive sizeable government benefits that are not income tested. As one writer observed,

> Isn't it droll that the same people who complain about poor folks getting Medicaid don't complain at all getting tax free employer contributions to their health insurance plans? This is middle class Medicaid. Those who gripe about public housing for the poor don't gripe about deducting their mortgage interest payments from their taxable income. Worse of all are the farmers and Westerners. They talk a good game about government meddling and rugged individualism, but they thrive because of the government. Farmers who complain about welfare are on it. The West was a WPA (Workers Public Administration) project long before Franklin Roosevelt was born.[32]

More than one third of U.S. households receive some form of federal non-cash aid and almost one-half receive some sort of government benefits. Most of these recipients are white. For example, 63 percent of the four million food and utility recipients are white; 62 percent or 3.1 million of the households receiving free or reduced school lunches are white; 59 percent or 1.5 million of the households living in subsidized housing are white; and 89 percent of the 16.5 Medicare recipients are white.[33]

In the controversial book by Charles Murray, *Losing Ground*, Murray alleges that the increase in black female-headed households is due to the anti-poverty programs of the 1960's because the government started providing an alternative lifestyle that abdicated personal responsibility and thereby reduced incentives to work and get married.[34] This contention defies reality by insisting that black women would forfeit the benefits of family life for the meager stipends offered by the welfare system. A more likely explanation is that teenage pregnancies (most out of wedlock) and female-headed households have increased dramatically because of the shortage of employed black men available for marriage. The declining employment participation of black males from 75 percent in 1960 to 54 percent in 1982 was matched by an increase in female-headed households from 21 percent in 1960 to 42 percent in 1982.[35]

As for why black males experienced such a decline of participation in the nation's labor force, it can largely be traced to structural economic changes in the last two decades. Most of the largest cities lost manufacturing jobs in the 1970's and were transformed into centers of administration, information exchange and service provision. Thus, brain power replaced muscle power as the requisite of most city jobs. These changes were occurring while the deteriorating public school systems were failing to transmit functional literacy skills to young black males. Many of them have not mastered the necessary basic skills in written and verbal communication and computational proficiency to permit employment in the types of jobs currently available in the marketplace.[36] The problem is compounded by the fact that a majority of black teenagers obtain no work experience in their adolescent years. The proportion of black teenage males who have never held a job increased from 32.7 percent to 52.8 percent between 1966 and 1977. For black males under age 24, the percentage grew from 9.9 to 23.3 during the same period.[37]

There are other factors that contribute to high rates of black unemployment. Some of them are due to the decline in labor intensive industries and the displacement of unskilled and semi-skilled black workers as a consequence of automation and robotization. Being confined to the central cities reduces black employment opportunities as more businesses move out of the inner cities into suburban areas. In 1982 one half of all black youth and 60 percent of unemployed blacks lived in the central cities.[38] Racism certainly plays its part. Black youth often depend on formal networks (i.e. employment agencies, placement offices) while white youth may have the informal connections of parents, friends and neighbors available to them. Thus, we find white high school graduates have an unemployment rate only one half that of black high school graduates. Employers often inflate skill and educational requirements for jobs as a way of controlling the intake of black applicants.[39] A major factor has been the fact that the largest increase in new jobs has been in small businesses with fewer than 25 employees. It is generally easier to reduce racial discrimination in huge bureaucratically organized, strongly led organizations than in small ones.

A combination of the above forces has pushed almost a majority of black males out of the labor force. Black males were hit most severely during the economic recession of 1980-1982 when their official unemployment rate peaked at 22 percent for adults and 53 percent for teenagers. Also, about 10 percent of blacks were employed part-time in 1984 compared to seven percent of white workers. During the alleged economic recovery of 1984, 75 percent of the families who escaped poverty that year were white families headed by men. In 1985 one out of every seven new job seekers was black, and it was projected that one in five will be black by 1990.[40] Despite claims of progress, the situation of blacks in cities has continued to deteriorate. The observation by Claude Brown of conditions in Harlem in 1984 are most poignant. According to him,

Today's manchild has fewer choices than my generation and those choices are more depressing than ours. As a final recourse, we could always enlist in the armed services. Manchild 1984, unable to even pass the exams for the services, can go into crime or become a drug addict (both of which almost invariably involve spending a significant portion of one's life in jail), go to an early grave (which occurs with alarming frequency) or be extremely fortunate and evade all the foregoing eventualities.[41]

THE GHETTO

Blacks are concentrated in cities because they often cannot move elsewhere. According to a study commissioned by the Department of Housing and Urban Development, blacks trying to rent houses or apartments encounter discrimination by rental agents three out of four times.[42] This discrimination still happens in the face of a 1968 Fair Housing Act which forbids discrimination in the sale or rental of housing units.

To further compound the problem of securing decent housing, blacks now find themselves plagued by white relocation in the inner city. This relocation is occurring throughout the U.S. and often at the expense of blacks. As young, middle class whites tire of certain problems of suburban living, they are resettling in the city. As a result, thousands of the black poor, who are renters, find themselves displaced to other poor areas, often to be evicted time and time again. One finds that blacks represented 20 percent of all those who moved in 1982, mostly to meet housing needs.[43] The practice of "redlining" by financial institutions also complicates the poor housing situation of blacks. Loans are denied for housing purchases or improvements in certain minority neighborhoods.

The gentrification of ghetto housing has caused a decline in the black populations of such cities as Washington, D.C. and San Francisco and has eroded the cultural and political bases of blacks. While the mere presence of whites has increased property values in black residential areas, it also results in higher property taxes, which poor people cannot afford.[44] Gentrification does not particularly enhance social relationships between the races. The whites who move into black areas still associate with members of their own race in mono-racial social outlets. As Wilkins has noted, "I sense a substantially decreased interest on the part of whites in seeking out blacks for social contacts as compared to the 1960's."[45] Blacks often resent whites who move in with them physically but exclude them socially. A black lawyer commented, "I've seen whites move into the city and they imagine that they're being pioneers. But before long, the bars go up on the windows and the big dogs come out. I found it downright unneighborly and offensive."[46]

A greater problem, however, is the continued segregation of blacks in urban ghettos. One study reported that 75 percent of urban residents live in highly segregated blocks. The study concludes that black poverty is the root of this ghettoization because poor people cannot afford to move from the inner city.[47] Yet, the pattern of housing segregation indicates that only racial discrimination, operating through market practices, is sufficient to explain the persistent pattern of black central city enclaves surrounded by outlying white areas with interaction generally occurring only at the perimeters. This housing segregation is accomplished by the confluence of real estate, banking and government practices. Real estate agents typically steer potential black purchasers to houses in areas that are predominantly black or in transition to such a state. Blacks are denied bank loans for housing purchases in certain neighborhoods.[48] Not only do the mortgage lending policies of government agencies such as the Federal Housing Authority confine black demand for housing to specific geographical areas, but most of the nearly 10 million residents of federally financed housing are segregated by race, with whites faring much better than blacks. An investigation by a Dallas newspaper uncovered no locality where federally subsidized housing was fully integrated or where conditions were equal for whites and blacks living in separate projects. The newspaper's conclusion was that "the Federal Government was deeply involved in the creation of the ghetto system and it has never committed itself to any remedial action."[49]

These patterns of housing segregation are not just matters of individual choice. The potency of race is such that a house in a predominantly black neighborhood is devalued by thousands of dollars in its appraisal on the housing market. This partly explains why blacks, who represent 12 percent of the U.S. population, receive only seven percent of its income. A major reason for this disparity is that blacks receive 1.2 percent of their income from property, compared with seven percent for whites.[50] And, the confinement of black home purchases to predominantly black neighborhoods inflates the prices blacks must pay by restricting the available supply. The outcome of such racist practices is a restriction of the ability of blacks to accumulate home equity and thus wealth. On the other hand, 44 percent of the homeless in the U.S.—those people living in the streets rather than in shelters—are black men in their late 20's to mid-30's, and 16 percent are women.[51] As the former Mayor of Philadelphia, William Green, has observed, "Cities have become the Indian Reservations of the 20th century. We've turned our backs on them, allowed the poor to gather there."[52]

The aforementioned problems often take their toll on urban blacks. Mobility and migration have caused a dramatic increase in the black suicide rate. One sociologist reported a strong correlation between black suicide and migration from one state to another. Between 1970 and 1975 the suicide rate among blacks rose to the point where it was nearly as high as that of their white peers. But whereas suicide increases for whites with advancing age, it reaches its peak in the young years for blacks.[53]

Other blacks are killing themselves more slowly with drugs and alcohol. The drug and alcoholism rate is about four times higher for blacks than whites. Obtaining medical attention for these or other health problems is difficult. While blacks suffer higher rates of diabetes, strokes and a variety of chronic illnesses, they are at the mercy of public hospitals, and therefore, are the first victims of government cutbacks. When blacks go to a hospital, they are more likely to receive inadequate treatment. One study revealed that for two routine types of surgery, blacks were two to four times more likely than whites to get a less experienced surgeon.[54]

Living in cities has become a hazard to black health. In a report by Congressman John Conyers, he cited figures which show a doubling of cancer among blacks vis-a-vis whites. Fatal bouts of hypertension are 15 times higher for blacks, and they have a 37 percent higher risk of occupationally induced diseases and a 20 percent higher mortality rate from occupationally related diseases. Black children suffer from lead poisoning at a rate three times higher than that of white children. These mortality rates have their roots in the structure of racial inequality. Over 75 percent of hazardous waste cites studies were located in predominantly black communities. The higher cancer rates are often a result of job patterns. About 89 percent of black workers labor at coke ovens—the most dangerous part of the industry—compared to 32 percent of white workers. Along with disparate exposure to toxic substances in their living and work environment, blacks have a significantly lower survival rate from cancer, a result of the generally inferior health care available to them.[54]

ECONOMICS OF THE URBAN PLANTATION

Economic institutions have never played a significant role in black life although the myth of a black business empire has existed for a number of years. Unlike other ethnic groups, blacks never developed a strong merchant class that could supply its members with jobs, capital and philanthropic donations to schools and charities. Ofari attributes this, in part, to the tradition of African communal practices where goods, services and land were collectively shared. The idea of buying and selling or employing labor for the purpose of exploitation was alien to people of African descent.[55] Consequently, after slavery ended and blacks were theoretically free to engage in private enterprise, not only did they lack a strong capitalist ethic but they did not possess any knowledge of business techniques or practices.

Some blacks have engaged in commercial ventures since they arrived on these shores. Free blacks owned property, a few owned slaves, and others engaged in such enterprises as tailoring and clothing, newspapers, cooking and livery stables. After emancipation, the freedmen established themselves in banks, insurance companies, large farms, real estate, cosmetics and small businesses that were service-oriented such as hairdressing and barbershops. Many of the larger businesses failed because of black ignorance of business methods and poor management. The smaller commercial enterprises have always been marginal operations that seldom supported more than the proprietor and his family.

A number of reasons account for black business people's failure to gain a strong toehold in the capitalist world. Foremost among them are the obstacles put in their way by white racism. They have generally been restricted to serving the impoverished black market and rarely allowed to compete in the general market. White banks have refused to grant them credit and capital to start or expand any commercial enterprises. Thus, black business people have never been allowed to maintain anything but marginal enterprises. Being confined to a clientele characterized by low incomes, high levels of unemployment, comparatively large debts and few financial assets, they are forced to operate in an extremely bad business environment. The enterprises that survived have been those that whites would not open to blacks, such as insurance companies, mortuaries, barbershops and restaurants. When white entrepreneurs realized a profit could be made by catering to this part of the black market, they began to monopolize them too. Today, there are fewer black-owned life insurance companies, banks and hotels than there were in 1929.[56]

One common reason for black business failure is poor management. A major factor here is that many blacks who go into business do so simply because they cannot find decent employment, and they start an enterprise with very little capital and a limited inventory. They tend to be the less capable blacks because those who are poorly educated but bright will enter the underworld of the hustler and pimp. Others who have obtained a higher education go into the professions instead of business because they expect a higher rate of return.[57]

The lack of black businesses appears strange considering the strength of the black market. As a group, blacks have an income higher than all but eight nations throughout the world, with a yearly earned income of 202 billion dollars. Yet in 1982, 239,239 black-owned businesses had total receipts of 12.4 billion dollars and 166,000 employees.[58] This is best explained by economic colonialism, as Roy Innis points out:

> There is a striking similarity between so-called black communities and underdeveloped countries. Both have always been oppressed. Almost always there is an unfavorable balance of trade with the oppressor or exploiter. Both suffer from high unemployment, low income, scarce capital, and we can point to a series of other similarities.[59]

One other similarity to the colonial countries is the lack of trust and confidence between black merchants and their customers. Most black businesses are owned by a single person because of the lack of confidence blacks have in one another. The customers complain of discourteous treatment, inflated prices and the low quality of goods and services. Some of the black merchants respond that blacks expect more of them than white merchants, that they demand social services and credit but fail to pay their bills on time. And, some black merchants charge that many blacks prefer to trade with whites than with their own kind.[60] A fairly accurate assessment of this situation is that internal colonialism has created a tiny class of black capitalists who tend to be inept and who engage in shoddy business practices that are noticeable because they do not have the capital or expertise to refine their unethical business procedures in the same way as more wealthy white capitalists.

Despite the fantasy of black capitalism as a solution to black poverty, it has been an abject failure. Although there was an increase of 47 percent in the number of black-owned firms between 1977 and 1982, the average annual receipts of black-owned firms decreased from $37,392 in 1977 to $36,685 in 1982. When inflation is accounted for, the decline is actually from $37,000 to $23,000 in constant 1977 dollars. As a source of jobs, black businesses are negligible. Only 11.4 percent of black firms had paid employees in 1982. Nearly one in every 11 black businesses was either a barber or beauty shop. If the sales of all the 100 largest black businesses were combined, they would not rank with one white-owned company in the top 100 of the Fortune 500 roster.[61] At the present rate of progress, it will not be until the year 2,334 that blacks will equal their white capitalist counterparts. Cross sums up the myth of black capitalism well: "Black people in the United States function essentially as appendages to the body of American capitalism. The machines, the plants, the oil wells and the stock certificates which represent capital value…are owned and controlled entirely by whites."[62]

In terms of overall sales, whites, and increasingly Asians, dominate the businesses in black ghettos. Rarely do white and Asian merchants ever live in the areas of their business operations, which means that the profits from their exploitative economic practices are spirited out of the black community at night. The economics of the ghetto are very similar to that of classical colonial societies. Inhabitants of the ghetto are primarily workers who earn low wages and are dependent on the small stores in their community for goods and services. Lacking transportation and awareness of prices elsewhere for comparable merchandise, ghetto dwellers are particularly vulnerable to the sales pitch of the merchant who sells them inferior merchandise at higher prices.[63]

Among the many practices typical of the ghetto merchant is the sale of goods on credit installments with very high interest rates. Knowing that he is dealing with an uneducated, powerless native, the ghetto merchant often uses deceptive advertising and misrepresentative sales contracts, refuses to return deposits and employs coercive efforts to collect nonexistent debts. These techniques are much more prevalent in the ghetto because blacks are powerless to stop them. When they refuse to pay, or are unable to, the legal system allows the ghetto merchant to attach the native's meager wages to recover the merchant's costs while providing the native with no redress against these unethical business practices.[64]

THE POLITICAL SOLUTION

Promises of the urban dream were often located in the electoral process. The black majorities in the cities would elect one of their own to political posts—the most visible, and sometimes most powerful, being that of mayor. Perhaps the die was cast when blacks elected Carl Stokes as mayor of Cleveland in 1967. The first 10 appointments Stokes made were 80 percent white. After he served three years as mayor, 70 percent of black housing was still classified as substandard, and only 20 of the city's

180 schools passed health and safety inspection in one year. Despite the need for social services, more than 60 percent of the city's budget was allocated to the police.[65] After Stokes' election, a succession of blacks gained access to the office of mayor in the U.S.'s largest cities. The effect of black political power has been largely the same: blacks are no better off than under white mayors.

Sometimes it has been more a function of black political strategy than a lack of will in improving the lot of black citizens. Although few, if any, big city black mayors have received a majority of white votes in their quest for office, most have catered to the "sensitivities" of the white community by assuming a moderate position on racial issues. Often, black mayors in big cities have gone overboard to assure whites they were not black militants by maintaining a large white presence in city hall. Former Cleveland Mayor Carl Stokes has lamented,

> Wherever you have an aggressive black mayor, there's always one accusation after the other, one charge after another, confrontations every day you're in office, demands that you won't show any favoritism to black people and won't retaliate for all the favoritism that white people have enjoyed over the years. All that drains you and grinds you down and makes you a little frustrated.[66]

There are some black mayors who have found the position carries little authority with it. Sometimes it is the form of city government which they inherit, with a city manager or commissions having the real control over policy and jobs. Otherwise, they are subject to shrinking revenues. More than one half of the cities surveyed said they would have to reduce services in the 1984 fiscal year, and more than one third expected to cut the city work force.[67]

Elected black officials who reply to the needs of the black community often find themselves under attack by the shite-controlled media and government agencies. A two-year study by the National Association of Human RIghts Workers documented what seems to be a systematic and nationwide harassment of black elected officials. The study found that more than 100 of these officeholders had been victims of various forms of harassment. The conclusion was: "The higher the level of office, or the ore outspoken the official, or the greater the influence and power, the higher the incidence of harassment."[68]

However, a number of black politicians have been nothing but neo-colonial pawns, whose primary allegiances have been to white institutions and values. Few of these black politicians have developed or implemented a single new program or policy of any benefit to urban blacks. Moreover, black mayors have carried out cutbacks in social services, opposed school desegregation, participated in strike-breaking attacks on government employees, ordered police attacks on black communities, tolerated police brutality and done little about high rates of black unemployment. For example, when Atlanta's garbage collectors—most of them black—struck for a 50 cents-an-hour raise in 1977, the black mayor fired all of them. One observer noted that "he has employed every tactic in union busting that has come along since the robber barons."[69]

It is probably no coincidence that the increase of black mayors corresponds with the changing color composition of the cities. Black mayors increased from 135 in 1975 to 255 in 1984.[70] This increase reflects a conscious decision by the Democratic Party to run more black candidates in order to contain the move toward more independent black political motion. As the Joint Center for Political Studies has concluded, the vast majority of blacks have benefited little from the election of blacks to political office. For instance, after 16 years in office, Kenneth Gibson not only failed to improve the social and economic conditions of Newark's non-white population, but the conditions became worse. One result of the black disillusionment with the electoral process is a decline in black voter participation. Until the Jesse Jackson campaign ignited black voter interest in 1984, only 36 percent of the voting age black population was registered to vote. In the 1984 election, the black turnout increased to 56 percent.[71]

On a national level, black political strategy has been equally ineffective. Black leaders and organizations have encouraged the traditional black loyalty to the Democratic Party. On occasion, blacks have subordinated demonstrations and protests to their greater goal of electing Democrats to office. Most of the mainstream black organizations such as the NAACP and the National Urban League joined in the "elect Democrats" strategy. Meanwhile, both the Republican and Democratic candidates are owned and controlled by the wealthy banks and corporations who profit from the exploitation and oppression of blacks.

Unfortunately, black voters are still voting on purely racial grounds and ignoring the class factor. In part, that is necessary because white politicians have demeaned them after securing their votes. Time after time, white politicians have campaigned for the black vote and betrayed blacks afterwards. A classical case was that of Jane Byrne, the white former mayor of Chicago. After blacks provided the margin of victory in her first mayoral campaign, she appointed whites to the school board and public housing authority. When she ran for re-election in the Democratic primary, black Congressman Harold Washington pulled off an upset when Byrne and a white opponent split the white vote and Washington rolled up 84 percent of black voters and six percent of white voters. In a city where 90 percent of the registered voters were Democrats, a primary victory was generally tantamount to election. The general election provided the most vivid example of racism in politics since the 1960's. An obscure white Republican, with a history of treatment for mental illness, won the support of white Democratic politicians and eventually received about 82 percent of the white votes in an overwhelmingly Democratic city.[72] As white columnist Mike Royko noted, "It's a racial struggle, and that's all it has been since the last of the votes for mayor were counted."[73] Another white columnist, David Broder, observed, "This is a city where anything you want depends on who you know in City Hall. When whites say that Washington's election would mean the blacks will 'get it all,' they are in effect acknowledging their guilty understanding that, in the past, blacks got next to nothing. They cannot believe that the dispossessed will be more generous than their long time masters."[74]

Washington won the mayoral contest by a slim majority. About 18 percent of the white vote provided his margin of victory, a vote he received because that segment of the white population decided the issue of racial tranquility exceeded any political issue involved in the election. In the ensuing years, Washington's tenure was marked by budget crises, school strikes and the ongoing conflict between him and the city council majority bloc of white aldermen. Faced with a shortage of revenues, Washington was forced to make cuts in the city work force and dropped mostly blacks from the payroll.[75] Even in electoral victory, the blacks of Chicago lost. At least the Washington campaign exploded the myth of a color blind electorate. One political analyst claims the key to a black candidate's victory is to win a greater share of the white than the white candidate receives of the black vote.[76] A contrary opinion is that black candidates should concentrate only on black areas and not waste time trying to woo white voters.[77] Some 20 years after the first election of a big city black mayor, it is still rare to find a black candidate who can draw more than 15 to 20 percent of the white vote.

The election of black mayors only fosters the illusion of black political power. The advantages are negligible. One study reported that although most cities with black mayors have high unemployment rates and declining populations, more blacks were added to city payrolls than in other cities. In black-run cities, the black percentage of the municipal work force increased by an average of 16 percent in comparison to an increase of 6.9 percent in cities without black mayors.[78] These minor gains, most of which accrue to the black middle class, are offset by the ability of black mayors to use reactionary methods and escape criticism from members of the black community. Not one large city black mayor has been defeated in a re-election effort. That makes it easier for the National Conference of Black Mayors to endorse the Reagan Administration's proposal to adopt a sub-minimum wage on the pretext of reducing teenage unemployment. A leading economist's response was that "a sub-minimum wage is bad economic policy and abominable social policy."[79] Current minimum wage jobs go begging because they provide little or no useful training and experience and are characterized by poor working conditions and no opportunities for advancement.

Probably the most grotesque example of a counterproductive

black mayor is that of Wilson Goode, the mayor of Philadelphia. He won office when blacks gave him 98 percent of their votes. Almost two years after his election, he approved a police action that killed 11 blacks and burned two square blocks of homes in order to move against a black political group accused of health code violations. Goode took full responsibility for the outcome and drew support for his actions from white conservatives and law and order advocates. Because he is black, few black leaders criticized him, and local polls showed two thirds of the city's black population approved his handling of the situation.[80] Among those who dared to speak out against Goode was a group of political activists who placed an ad in the local newspapers entitled "Draw the Line." It read,

> When black elected officials use their positions of power to attack black people, or to cover up for or excuse such attacks, they are no friends of ours and don't speak for or represent the interests of black people. In the past, lines were clearly drawn on this question. Those who attacked black people were counted among our enemies. This line must be firmly drawn again. Murder is murder, no matter whether those responsible are black or white."[81]

THE CHANGING FACE OF RACISM

We may or may not have seen the last of racial lynchings, segregation of public facilities, exclusion from the voting booth and the like. These acts of racism have largely disappeared as aspects of U.S. life at this point in time. The racism that remains is much more covert and, therefore, harder to resist. It is clear that many white Americans believe that continuing inequality between the races, if they acknowledge any, is due to moral failings of individuals rather than racial discrimination. Every major poll taken in recent years shows a wide gap in black and white perceptions of race relations. One poll revealed that 53 percent of whites believed blacks had an advantage over white in opportunities, due to reverse racism.[82] Joel Dreyfuss calls this the new racism: "It denies the existence of racism and accepts no responsibility for inequality. The effect of such an attitude places black demands in the position of being outrageous, irrational, even oppressive."[83]

These changes in white attitudes did not occur in a vacuum.

With the increasing competition for jobs and changing social values, whites have chosen to hold on to their racial privileges. Blacks may have assumed that they made their gains through an outpouring of white good will and feelings of guilt. Yet, when one sociologist tested the theory of white guilt, he found that white guilt regarding black inequality was virtually nonexistent.[84] Black gains that were achieved came about through independent group struggle. Much of this struggle was in concert with traditional allies who have since deserted blacks. Labor unions have encouraged racism by their support of the seniority rule, which works against newly hired minority workers. A number of Jewish organizations are on record as being against affirmative action programs designed to help minorities.

The Bakke case was most representative of the new racism. In a society where white males monopolize almost 90 percent of the top positions and whites in general hold 98 percent of the most prestigious jobs, it seems absurd to speak of "reverse discrimination" against white males. Yet, it is that same concept that was given legitimacy the U.S. Supreme Court on June 28, 1978. The court's decision only symbolized a trend that had already been set into motion. Black enrollment in college and professional schools had been declining for several years before Bakke. Black enrollment in medical schools peaked at 7.5 percent in 1974 but declined to a low of 6.8 percent in 1983. While the number of black high school graduates increased by 29 percent between 1975 and 1981, their college enrollment rate declined by 11 percent.[85] The trend was summed up well by a University of California vice president: "I have this nightmare that it's 2150 and California is like South Africa. The state and its institutions are run by white folks while the populace is minorities."[86]

While polls show that whites, by an overwhelming majority, are opposed to affirmative action, that opposition is based on the myth that ability is the only factor that determines admission to college or obtaining a job. In all the debate over the fairness of affirmative action, few people mention the standards by which qualifications are determined. For admission to college the major criterion is often scores on standardized tests. These tests usually contain a cultural bias in favor of whites. Witness what happened when blacks were admitted with lower test scores. The majority managed to perform well and graduated along with their higher scoring white peers. It was not black students' abilities to do college work that prevented their admission to college in the past, but the barriers set up by those standardized tests.

There are other informal elements that are more important than merit in achieving certain goals in this country. Money, politics and nepotism influence college admissions throughout the nation. That was true in the Bakke case although Bakke chose to focus on the powerless minorities, who were admitted to medical school ahead of him, rather than on the whites who had lower scores. While whites seek to dismantle affirmative action programs in order to make merit the only consideration, Granovetter has found that the majority of his sample reported that having the right contacts assured whites their initial job placement.[87] The use of social networks and kinship ties for success in the work world is a basic element of social organization. Affirmative action was only a mechanism, and a weak one at that, for bettering the odds for minorities.

A more serious issue, one of greater impact on urban blacks, was the so-called taxpayers' revolt. When California voters approved Proposition 13 in 1978 by a two thirds vote, it was quite clear that there was a racial difference in the perception of the issue. Over 90 percent of the blacks voted against it while 75 percent of the whites voted for it. The measure, which reduced local government revenues by seven billion dollars, most of which redounded to large corporations, was supposedly a revolt against waste in government spending and high taxes. David Broder came closer to the point when he wrote: "It is not anti-government. That mislabels it. It is a mood which is perfectly willing to use government for goals that appeal to the personal interests of the majority (i.e. whites) while denying its assistance to the minority who may be victims. That is how it is in Reagan's America in 1984. The middle class majority wants government looking out for middle class interests."[88]

Few politicians in recent history have exploited the cultural narcissism and latent racism of whites better than Ronald

Reagan. Despite a widespread perception that his policies favor the wealthy, he achieved a landslide Presidential victory in 1984. The key to his victory was the vote of white males. Reagan won every category of white male votes except white Jewish males. Even white male union members gave him 54 percent of their votes. As a local Democratic Party chairman commented, "We are losing them...A lot of whites who started working in the factories, now they are more affluent. They've got a home, two cars, tuition to pay. They are saying 'well Jesus, the Democratic Party is getting more and more liberal. How is that going to benefit me?'"[89] Among white, Protestant males in the South, Reagan's total vote exceeded 90 percent. A post-election analysis reported that many white males may support women's rights out of economic necessity since in most cases both husband and wife work, but resent the jobs they think they have lost to minorities. White males rely heavily on middle class spending and tax code policies that they will not lightly give up. Jesse Jackson aptly summarized the Reagan political strategy:

> Reagan's whole thing has been to play upon the endangered species complex that white males have. White males represent the most threatened species in American politics. Twenty-five years ago, white males didn't have to compete. Blacks did not have civil rights. (White males) didn't have to compete with Hispanics. They didn't have to compete with women.[90]

To placate his major constituency, Reagan pledged his administration would not discriminate against white males. Although they represent less than one third of the U.S. population, white males compose 90 percent of the judges appointed to the federal district courts. About 75 percent of the household that moved out of poverty in 1983 were headed by white males. The Reagan Administration proposed to spend 1.3 trillion dollars on the Defense Department over a five-year period. The typical defense worker at the time was a 48-year-old white male with an advanced degree or high technical skills.[91] While increasing military expenditures that benefited mostly white males, Reagan administered cutbacks in food stamps, public housing, AFDC, family planning and child nutrition programs and others that were needed by blacks and women.

Reagan's policies hurt a cross section of the black population. A report issued three years after Reagan had been in office concluded that in terms of income, poverty status and unemployment levels, blacks were worse off in 1984 than they were in 1980 and that the economic gap between blacks and whites had widened since 1980. The author of the report suggested that for the first time the U.S. government was pursuing policies that actually make black Americans worse off economically and divide them further from white Americans. While an additional 1.3 million blacks were thrown into poverty by Reagan's policies, even the black middle class was negatively impacted by Reaganomics. Some 60 percent of all black college graduates have historically depended on the government for employment, compared to 17 percent of whites. Blacks experienced a loss of an average of $2,000 in disposable income from 1980 to 1984.[92]

Both black and white commentators assailed Reagan's racist policies. CBS newsman, Bill Moyers, claimed, "We are a racist society and racial prejudice under the Reagan regime has become politically palatable again."[93] Despite his claim that he did not have a racist bone in his body, Reagan engaged in a variety of actions that would be deemed racist. Besides the obvious official efforts to weaken affirmative action, truncate the Voting Rights Act and provide tax-exempt status to racially segregated schools, he has pandered to racism by going to the South and proclaiming that it shall rise again and invoking the name of Jefferson Davis.[94] Those and numerous other deeds led one newspaper columnist to assert:

> Ronald Reagan is the most dangerous U.S. President of the 20th century. Possibly only Woodrow Wilson, the openly bigoted son of a Virginia cleric who had obvious Ku Klux Klan leanings and silent Calvin Coolidge who stood idly by and watched the Ku Klux Klan murder hundreds of blacks during the 1920's came close to being as dangerous to the race as Reagan.[95]

The 1980's have born witness to the polarization of races and classes. Racial polarization is a volatile issue which can take the form of violent conflict. In fact, a Department of Justice report predicted the eruption of racial and ethnic conflict in some U.S.

cities. White supremacist groups have escalated their violence against blacks and other minorities.[96] The increase of racial minorities in the cities has heightened white anxieties and altered relationships of power in many urban areas. Despite the belief that cities are in a state of decay, Jacobs claims that almost all wealth derives from the output of cities. While whites may have relinquished political control of cities, they still control the economic life of cities. And, only a productive city base leads to sustained wealth. Life in a country without strong or any cities, she says, will cause civilization to collapse.[97] Thus, cities may remain the stronghold of U.S. capitalism, but for blacks they remain an urban plantation.

SUMMARY

In predicting the future development of blacks in cities, it is necessary to look at two parallel trends. One is the continued movement of some blacks into the middle class and the division of this group into two different sub-strata: those who align themselves with the black masses and identify with their struggle for liberation, and the neocolonial elites who will accept the values of the ruling class and serve their interests by acting as intermediaries between them and the bulk of oppressed blacks. The other trend is the growth of the lumpen proletariat, perpetuating a pyramidal class structure which may encourage class antagonisms in the black community. Somewhere in the middle will be the bulk of black working people who may identify with the struggle of either group—one for neocolonial control in the form of black dominance in community businesses and politics, and the other working to destroy the structure of class and racial exploitation. Unlike the past, the latter group may take on important leadership roles in this struggle.

The most inevitable trend in black class patterns is the growth of the lumpen proletariat class. In a society undergoing its greatest growth in service areas that require professional and technical skills, the largely unskilled black underclass may become an army of the permanently unemployed. The ascendancy of automation and cybernation, where machines do the work of men, reduces the need for labor in all sectors but the fringe areas. Yet the movement of black peasants from the rural South will continue to bring in large numbers of unskilled people to whom the only jobs available will be as cooks, servants or waitresses for affluent whites.

Even in these menial jobs, blacks may face serious competition from unskilled whites who will become surplus labor as a result of automation and cybernation. History shows that whites are content to leave low-status jobs to blacks in relative periods of economic prosperity but when in great need of work, invoke their racial privilege to enter those black employment areas.[98] Already, the unemployment rate for black youth is more than 50 percent in certain inner city areas. Additional blacks continue to drop out of the work force because of their inability to find jobs.

The neighborhoods of the underclass remain a repository of all the problems, crime, violence, drugs, which internal colonialism has created and maintained. It has become a no-man's land where no one wants to go for any legitimate purpose and has been abandoned to whatever uses the dispossessed may want to put them. The black middle class exists in a very fragile world and guards its hard fought gains jealously, thus erecting a defense against the erosion of their achievements. Moreover, since the black middle class exists on the fringe of the white middle class, the former doesn't have the resources to solve the problems of the blacks below them.

There are suggestions about what efforts the black middle class can make to expedite black liberation. Lerone Bennett lists them as: (1) to define and maintain a community-wide policy leading to black control of the resources and culture of the black community (2) seize control of the structures which define and control black people and (3) assume responsibility for the financial support of black institutions and movements.[99] Others have demanded that the black bourgeoisie commit suicide as a class. This act of class suicide means that they must be willing to set aside personal gain and join with the black poor, unemployed and workers around their common priorities.[100]

The question must be asked whether blacks can develop an egalitarian subsystem in a society so overwhelmingly structured on class inequality. Most likely the answer is negative. A more probable development is the emergence of a class of black petty bourgeoisie who will undertake the exploitation of the black masses that is now done directly by the white colonial power structure. Hence, we shall witness larger numbers of blacks being elected to public office, programs created to develop a black capitalist class and black functionaries replacing whites in the roles of colonial mediating positions such as teachers, social workers, policemen, etc.

One of the solutions left for us to address is the possible unity of working class whites and blacks. At this point in time it is difficult to foresee this unity taking place. It would require the white workers to give up their racial privileges for a united class struggle, and there is no indication that they are currently willing to make that sacrifice. Because blacks are increasingly becoming the lumpen proletariat, whites are rapidly being assimilated into the middle class. Whites have experienced a much larger entry into white collar jobs than the total increase in the total work force. As we have already noted, the number of whites in poverty is declining sharply while blacks increased their numbers in this category. Given these factors and alternatives, we will continue to live in a class and race divided society until the contradictions of monopoly capitalism make themselves felt.

Notes

FOOTNOTES FROM CHAPTER ONE:

1. Robert Staples, *Introduction to Black Sociology*, Chapter One, (New York: McGraw-Hill, 1976).
2. Bill Strickland, "Black Intellectuals and the American Social Scene," *Black World*, 25, (November 1975):7.
3. E. Franklin Frazier, *Race and Culture Contacts in the Modern World*, (New York: Knopf, 1957), pp. 177-188.
4. While I agree that those groups fit more perfectly into the colonial model, almost all my examples refer to the black community. Most of the literature focuses on black-white relations with the possible exception of Blauner's work and a few others. I use the internal colonialism model exclusively for the North American situation although it has also been applied to ethnic and religious conflicts in Latin America and European nations.
5. Theodore Draper, *The Rediscovery of Black Nationalism*, (New York: The Viking Press, 1969), pp. 3-13.
6. Frantz Fanon, *Black Skin, White Masks*, (New York: Grove Press, 1952).
7. Frantz Fanon, *The Wretched of the Earth*, (New York: Grove Press, 1963).
8. V.I. Lenin, *The Development of Capitalism in Russia*, (Moscow: Progress, 1956).
9. Harold Cruse, *Rebellion or Revolution*, (New York: William Morrow and Company, 1968), pp. 76-77 (reprinted in this book but originally published in 1962).
10. Kenneth Clark, *Dark Ghetto*, (New York: Harper and Row, 1965), pp. 11.
11. Robert Blauner, "Internal Colonialism and Ghetto Revolts," *Social Problems* 16, (Spring 1969), pp. 393-408. This article and his other works will hereafter be referred to in the book composed of his internal colonialism essays, *Racial Oppression in America*, (New York: Harper and Row, 1972).
12. c.f. Joyce Ladner, (ed.), *The Death of White Sociology*, (New York: Random House, 1973).
13. Blauner, *Racial Oppression in America*, op. cit., pp. 102-113.
14. Robert L. Allen, *Black Awakening in Capitalist America*, (New York: Double-day Anchor Books, 1970). Also see, Stokely Carmichael and Charles V. Hamilton, *Black Power*, (New York: Random House, 1967).
15. c.f. Fanon, *The Wretched of the Earth*, pp. 167-189. Blauner, op. cit., pp. 124-162.
16. Staples, op. cit., Chapter Nine, "Majority Groups."
17. Robert Blauner and David Wellman, "Towards the Decolonization of Social Research" in Ladner, op. cit., pp. 310-330.
18. c.f. Dennis Forsythe (ed.), *Black Alienation, Black Rebellion*, (Washington, D.C.: College and University Press, 1975).
19. William K. Tabb, *The Political Economy of the Black Ghetto*, (New York: Norton, 1970).
20. Dominique O. Mannoni, *Prospero and Caliban, The Psychology of Colonization*, (New York: Praeger, 1964).
21. Earl Ofari, *The Myth of Black Capitalism*, (New York: Monthly Review Press, 1970).
22. Albert Memmi, *Dominated Man*, (Boston: Beacon Press, 1968), p. 46.
23. Blauner, op. cit., p. 22.
24. Henry Kamm, "Whites in Rhodesia: To Keep What We Have," *San Francisco Chronicle*, April 4, 1976, p. 16-17.

25. Blauner, op. cit., pp. 9-10.

26. Memmi, op. cit., pp. 193-194.

27. Albert Memmi, *The Colonizer and the Colonized*, (Boston: Beacon Press, 1965).

28. Ibid.

29. Robert Chrisman, "Aspects of Pan-Africanism," *The Black Scholar*, 12 (July-August 1973), pp. 2-8.

30. Earl Anthony, "Pan African Socialism," *The Black Scholar*, 3 (October 1971), pp. 40-45.

31. Franklin Alexander, "A Critique of Neo-Pan-Africanism," *The Black Scholar*, 12 (July-August 1973), pp. 9-15.

32. Blauner, op. cit., pp. 124-161. Also see Diane K. Lewis, "The Black Family, Socialization and Sex Roles," *Phylon*, 36 (Fall 1975), pp. 221-237.

33. Fanon, loc. cit., pp. 165-200.

34. Henry Winston, *Strategy for a Black Agenda*, (New York: New Outlook Publishers, 1972), p. 13.

35. Among them, Kenneth Clark, Floyd McKissick, Roy Innis and Charles Hamilton.

36. This group would include Robert Allen, Robert Blauner, Stokely Carmichael, Huey Newton and James Boggs.

37. Fanon, op. cit., p. 38.

38. Robert C. Smith, "Beyond Marx: Fanon and the Concept of Colonial Violence," *Black World*, 22 (May 1973), pp. 23-33.

39. c.f. Dennis Forsythe, "Radical Sociology and Blacks" in Ladner, op. cit., pp. 213-233.

40. Winston, op. cit., p. 27.

41. *Leon Trotsky on Black Nationalism and Self-Determination*, (New York: Merit Publishers, 1967), p. 8.

42. "A Transitional Program for Black Liberation," *International Socialist Review*, (November-December 1969), pp. 56-57.

43. Smith,. op. cit.

44. Blauner, p. 13.

45. James M. Jones, *Prejudice and Racism*, (Reading, Massachusetts: Addison-Wesley, 1972), p. 116.

46. John Walton, *Internal Colonialism: Problems of Definition and Measurement*, unpublished paper, Northwestern University, 1975.

47. Douglas Davidson, "The Furious Passage of the Black Graduate Student" in Ladner, op. cit., pp. 23-51; George Napper, *Blacker Than Thou*, (Grand Rapids, Michigan: Eerdmans Publishing Company, 1973).

48. Robert Staples, "White Racism, Black Crime and American Justice: An Application of the Colonial Model to Explain Crime and Race," *Phylon*, 36 (March 1975), pp. 14-22; Staples, "Internal Colonialism and Black Violence," *Black World*, 23 (May 1974), pp. 16-34; George T. Mitchell et. al., "Police Conduct and the Black Community: The Case of Jackson, Mississippi," *Journal on Political Repression*, Volume 1, No. 1 (1975), pp. 92-110.

49. Two exceptions are, J.H. Howard, "Toward A Social Psychology of Colonialism" in *Black Psychology*, R. Jones, ed., (New York: Harper and Row, 1972), pp. 326-334 and Jerome Bennett, "Colonial System," *Ebony* (April 1972), pp. 33-41.

50. Donald J. Harris, "The Black Ghetto as Internal Colony: A Theoretical Critique and Alternative Formulation," *The Review of Black Political Economy*, (Summer 1972), pp. 3-33.
51. Walton, op. cit.; Blauner, op. cit.
52. Nathan Glazer, "Blacks and Ethnic Groups: The Difference and the Political Difference It Makes" in *Key Issues in the Afro-American Experience*, N. Huggins et.al., eds., (New York: Harcourt, Brace and Jovanovich, 1971), pp. 200-211.
53. Winston, op. cit., p. 16.
54. William K. Tabb, "Marxian Exploitation and Domestic Colonialism: A Reply to Donald J. Harris," *The Review of Black Political Economy*, (Summer 1974), pp. 85-86.
55. Rodolfo Stavenhagen, "Decolonizing Applied Social Sciences," *Human Organization*, 30 (Winter 1971), p. 336.
56. Quoted in Allen, op. cit., p. 8.
57. Lenwood G. Davis and Winston Van Horne, "The City Renewed: White Dream–Black Nightmare," *The Black Scholar*, 7 (November 1975), p. 5.
58. *Report of the National Advisory Commission on Civil Disorder*, (New York: Bantam Books, 1968), p. 22.
59. Henry J. Aaron, *Shelters and Subsidies*, (Washington, D.C.: The Brookings Institute, 1972), pp. 32-34, 74-123.

FOOTNOTES FROM CHAPTER TWO

1. Gary T. Marx, *Racial Conflict*, (Boston: Little, Brown and Company, 1971), p. 173.
2. Dennis Forsythe, *The Sociology of Black Separatism*, a paper presented at the Annual Meeting of the American Sociological Association, New York, 1973.
3. Lerone Bennett Jr., "Liberation," *Ebony*, 25 (August 1970), pp. 42-43.
4. Robert Chrisman, "Aspects of Pan-Africanism," *The Black Scholar*, 4 (July-August 1973), p. 2.
5. Clarence G. Contee, "Afro-Americans and Early Pan-Africanism," *Negro Digest*, 19 (February 1970), p. 24-30.
6. Edmund Cronon, *Black Masses: The Story of Marcus Garvey and the Universal Negro Improvement Association*, (Madison: University of Wisconsin Press, 1955).
7. W.E.B. DuBois, *The World and Africa*, (New York: International Publishers, 1965).
8. W.E.B. DuBois, Speech at the Fourth Afro-Asian Solidarity Conference at Winneba, May 10, 1965.
9. Adolph L. Reed Jr., "Pan-Africanism—Ideology for Liberation?" *The Black Scholar*, 3 (September 1971), pp. 2-13.
10. Stokely Carmichael, "Pan-Africanism—Land and Power," *The Black Scholar*, (November 1969).
11. Bill Mandel, "Disappearing Act," *San Francisco Sunday Examiner and Chronicle*, California Living, April 14, 1985, p. 8.
12. Melville Herskovits, *The Myth of the Negro Past*, (New York: Harper, 1941).
13. John Blassingame, *The Slave Community*, (New York: Oxford University Press, 1972), p. 18.
14. Blassingame, op. cit., pp. 41-76.
15. Carol B. Stack, *All Our Kin: Strategies for Survival in a Black Community*, (New York: Harper and Row, 1974), pp. 90-107.
16. Hylan Lewis, *Blackways of Kent*, (Chapel Hill: University of North Carolina Press, 1955), pp. 140-145.
17. Lawrence W. Levine, "The Concept of the New Negro and the Realities of Black Culture," in Nathan Huggins et. al., eds., *Key Issues in the Afro-American Experience*, (New York: Harcourt Brace Jovanovich, 1971), pp. 134-135.
18. Ralph H. Metcalfe Jr., "The Western African Roots of Afro-American Music," *The Black Scholar*, 1 (June 1970), pp. 16-25.
19. Charles Keil, *Urban Blues*, (Chicago: University of Chicago Press, 1966), p. 27.
20. Donald Byrd, "The Meaning of Black Music," *The Black Scholar*, 3 (Summer 1972), p. 30.
21. Katherine Dunham, "The Negro Dance," in Sterling Brown et. al., eds., *The Negro Caravan*, (New York: The Dryden Press, 1941), pp. 991-1000.
22. Esi Sylvia Kinney, "Africanisms in Music and Dance of the Americas," in Rhoda L. Goldstein, ed., *Black Life and Culture in the United States*, (New York: Thomas Y. Crowell Company, 1971), p. 55.
23. Albert Murray, *The Omni-Americans*, (New York: Outerbridge and Dienstfrey, 1970), pp. 49-53.
24. Frantz Fanon, *Black Skin, White Masks*, (New York: Grove Press, 1967).

25. R. McDavid, "American Social Dialects," *College English*, 26 (January 1965), pp. 254-260.
26. J.L. Dillard, *Black English: Its History and Usage in the United States*, (New York: Random House, 1972).
27. Dorothy Z. Seymour, "Black Children, Black Language," *The Washington Post*, June 25, 1972, p. B5.
28. Marianne LaFrance and Clara Ma Yo, *Gaze Direction in Interracial Dyadic Communication, a paper presented at the Eastern Sociological Association, Washington, D.C., 1972, p. 32.*
29. Ivan Van Sertima, "African Linguistic and Mythological Structures in the New World," in R. Goldstein, ed., *Black Life and Culture in the United States*, (New York: Crowell, 1971), p. 55.
30. Blassingame, op. cit., pp. 20-21.
31. Ulf Hannerz, *Soulside: Inquiries into Ghetto Culture and Community*, (New York: Columbia University Press, 1969), pp. 115-117.
32. Lewis, op. cit., pp. 74-78.
33. "Poor Nations Get Poorer as Recession Eases," *The National Leader*, October 13, 1983, p. 2.
34. "The Rise of a New Class of Black Africans," *San Francisco Chronicle, Briefing*, January 11, 1978, p. A-5.
35. David Lamb, "Black Africa," *San Francisco Chronicle, Briefing*, June 25, 1980, p. A-1.
36. U.S. Bureau of the Census, *Demographic Estimates for Countries with a Population of 10 Million or More: 1981*, (Washington, D.C.: Superintendent of Documents, U.S. Government Printing Office, 1981).
37. "Africa's Economic Progress Is Called Poor," *The National Leader*, June 9, 1983, p. 5.
38. "Dealing with Apartheid," *Newsweek*, March 11, 1985, pp. 28-40.
39. "Poor Nations Get Poorer as Recession Eases," loc. cit.
40. Glenn Frankel, "How Europeans Cut Up Africa," *San Francisco Chronicle, Briefing*, February 20, 1985, p. A-2.
41. Courtland Cox, "Sixth Pan African Congress," *The Black Scholar*, 5 (April 1974), p. 32.
42. Haki R. Madhubuti, "The Latest Purge," *The Black Scholar*, 5 (September 1974), p. 54.
43. Imamu Baraka, "Some Questions About the Sixth Pan African Congress," *The Black Scholar*, 6 (October 1974), p. 45.
44. Theodore Draper, *The Rediscovery of Black Nationalism*, (New York: Viking Press, 1970).

FOOTNOTES FROM CHAPTER THREE

1. J.E. Goldthorpe, *The Sociology of the Third World*, (Cambridge, London: Cambridge University Press, 1975).

2. Irving Louis Horowitz, *Three Worlds of Development*, (New York: Oxford University Press, 1966).

3. George Manuel, *The Fourth World*, (New York: MacMillan, 1974).

4. "The Fourth World: A Geography of Indigenous Struggles," *Antipode: A Radical Journal of Geography*, vol. 16, no. 2 (1984).

5. Ibid., pp. 3-4.

6. David Stea and Ben Wisner, "Introduction," *Antipode*, loc. cit.

7. Laverne K. Mitchell, "Lost Black Queens," *Black Male/Female Relationships*, 7 (Autumn 1982), pp. 41-46.

8. Hazel M. McFerson, "Part-Black Americans in the South Pacific," *Phylon*, 53 (June 1982), pp. 177-180.

9. Personal Correspondence, Bobbi Sykes, October, 1982.

10. Department of Aboriginal Affairs, *Aboriginals in Australia Today*, (Canberra, Australia: Australian Government Publishing Service, 1981).

11. A.C. Walsh, *More and More Maoris: An Illustrated Statistical Survey of the Maori Today*, (New Zealand: Whitcombe and Tombs, Ltd., 1971).

12. G. Antony Wood, "Race and Politics in New Zealand" in *Politics in New Zealand*, Stephen Levine, editor (New Zealand: Allen and Unwin, 1978), pp. 333-342.

13. Frank Stevens, *Racism: The Australian Experience*, (Sydney: Australia and New Zealand Book Company, 1978).

14. Jim Brumby, "Wealth Is Passing Australia By," *The Age*, June 14, 1982, p. 3.

15. "Report of the World Council of Churches," *Justice for Aboriginal Australians*, (Sydney: Australian Council of Churches, 1981).

16. Stevens, loc. cit.

17. Melbourne is a city of three million people, the second largest city in Australia. There are only 15,000 Aborigines in Melbourne.

18. "Going for the $889 Billion Market," *Ebony*, (August 1985), p. 38.

19. Ibid.

20. *The Toorak Times*, July 18, 1982, p. 11.

21. Robert Staples, "Black on Black: An Afro-American's Visit to Aborigineland," *Identity*, 4 (June 1982), pp. 15-33.

22. Department of Statistics, *1981 Census of Population and Dwellings, New Zealand, Maori Population*, (Wellington, New Zealand: March 1983); Bureau of the Census, *America's Black Population: 1970 to 1982*, (Washington, D.C.: U.S. Government Printing Office, August 1982). Unless otherwise noted, all statistical information comes from these two sources.

23. Donna Awatere, "Women Speak Out: The First National Black Women's Hui," *Broadsheet*, (November 1980), pp. 10-14.

24. Department of Statistics, New Zealand, loc. cit.

25. U.S. Bureau of the Census, loc. cit.

26. Ibid.

27. George M. Frederickson, *White Supremacy*, (New York: Oxford University Press, 1981).

28. New Zealand Department of Statistics, loc. cit.; U.S. Bureau of the Census, loc. cit.

29. Ibid.

30. Department of Statistics, *District Court Tables, 1982*, (Wellington, New Zealand, 1983); *Crime in the United States: 1982*, Federal Bureau of Investigation Crime Report, (Washington, D.C.: 1983).

31. New Zealand Department of Statistics, loc. cit.; U.S. Bureau of the Census, loc. cit.

32. Manuel, op. cit. *The Fourth World: Victims of Group Oppression*, (London: Sedgwick and Jackson, 1972).

33. Robert Blauner, *Racial Oppression in America*, (New York: Harper and Row, 1972).

FOOTNOTES FROM CHAPTER FOUR

1. National Center for Education Statistics, *Participation of Black Students in Higher Education: A Statistical Profile from 1970-71 to 1980-81*, (Washington, D.C.: U.S. Department of Education, 1983). The proportion of black undergraduate students has remained stagnant in the last five years.
2. Ibid. The percentage of black undergraduate students has remained stable for the last five years, comprising 9.4 percent of the total with no movement toward the 15 percent required for parity.
3. Ibid. Black students enrolled at black colleges in 1982 were only 16.5 percent of all black students.
4. "Students Lives Affected by Attending Black Schools," *Jet*, January 15, 1981, p. 8.
5. Solveig Torvik, "The Decline of Black Enrollment in Universities," *San Francisco Chronicle*, May 30, 1979, p. 4.
6. "Why They Choose Separate Tables," *Newsweek on Campus*, (March 1983), p. 14.
7. Jamie Robinson, "Discrimination in Health Care Persists," *Synapse*, February 23, 1978, p. 1.
8. "Freshmen Motivated by Money," *San Francisco Chronicle*, January 21, 1983, p. 26.
9. "Why They Choose Separate Tables," *Newsweek on Campus*, op. cit., p. 6.
10. That view of the U.S. economy declining in productivity due to the poor work of unqualified minorities has apparently been communicated to foreigners. At least one sociologist has pointed out that Japanese auto manufacturers have established all their U.S. auto plants in areas that are lily white. The Japanese response was "we go where the most productive workers are." "Toyota-UAW: A Happy Union?" *San Francisco Sunday Examiner and Chronicle*, March 13, 1978, p. A-11.
11. Stanley Robertson, "L.A. Confidential," *Los Angeles Sentinel*, July 29, 1982, p. A-6.
12. Max Weber, *The Theory of Social and Economic Organization*, (New York: Oxford, 1941), pp. 329-336.
13. Joel Dreyfuss, "The New Racism," *Black Enterprise*, 10 (January 1978), p. 42.
14. "Words of the Week," *Jet*, August 18, 1978, p. 32.
15. "Blacks Still Trail Whites in Job Market," *Jet*, December 20, 1982, p. 12. In 1978, white high school dropouts had a lower unemployment rate than black college graduates.
16. "Blacks See Renaissance of Job Discrimination," *Sun Reporter*, January 24, 1980, p. 2.
17. Gary Becker, *The Economics of Discrimination*, 2nd edition, (Chicago: University of Chicago Press, 1971).
18. Stephen Jay Gould, *The Mismeasure of Man*, (New York: Norton, 1981).
19. Mark S. Granovetter, *Getting A Job: A Study of Contacts and Careers*, (Cambridge, Massachusetts: Harvard University Press, 1974).
20. Mary Claire Blakeman, "The Key to Getting a Job Is Still a Matter of Who You Know," *Co-op News*, December 20, 1982, p. 3.
21. Kenneth B. Clark, "No, No, Race, Not Class, Is Still at the Wheel," *The New York Times*, March 22, 1978, p. A-28.
22. "The Dollar Payoff in College Degrees," *San Francisco Chronicle*, March 4, 1983, p. 5.

23. "Freshmen Motivated by Money," *San Francisco Chronicle*, loc. cit.

24. Mitchell Lynch, "Hard-Nosing in Academe," *American Way*, (March 1983), p. 64.

25. Edward B. Fiske, "After Steady Rise, the Number of Black Doctoral Students Falls," *The New York Times*, July 21, 1981, p. C-1. At some of the more elitist universities, black graduate student enrollment has decreased by nearly 50 percent.

26. Kent G. Mommsen, *Black Ph.D.s in the Academic Marketplace: Supply, Demand and Price*, a paper presented at the American Sociological Association meeting, New York, August 1973.

27. Edgar G. Epps and G.R. Howze, *Survey of Black Social Scientists*, (New York: Russell Sage Foundation, 1971).

28. Theodore Caplow and R. McGee, *The Academic Marketplace*, (New York: Basic Books, 1958), p. 16.

29. Paul Burstein, *Equal Employment Opportunity: What We Believe, What We Know, What Research Can Show*, a paper presented at the American Sociological Association meeting, San Francisco, September 1982.

30. Eva C. Galambos, *Racial Composition of Faculties in Public Colleges and Universities of the South*, (Atlanta: Southern Regional Education Board, 1979), p. 1. It is safe to assume that blacks represent fewer than two percent of the faculty at predominantly white universities.

31. Paul R. Williams, "Minorities and Women in Sociology: An Update," *ASA Footnotes*, (December 1982), p. 6.

32. Congressman Gus Hawkins, "Minorities Just Hired in University System," *Los Angeles Sentinel*, November 23, 1978, p. A-7.

33. *Report to the California Legislature on the Status of Affirmative Action Personnel Programs*, (University of California: Office of the President, December 1977), p. 37.

34. Peter Dworkin, "A Minority Population Boom in State," *San Francisco Chronicle*, 1982, p. 1. If present migration and fertility trends continue, it is predicted that non-whites will be the majority in the United States by the year 2080.

35. Susan Stern, "UC Faces Enrollment, Funding Decline, Report Says," *Synapse*, October 25, 1979, p. 1.

36. Galambos, loc. cit.

37. Grace Lichtenstein, "Affirmative Action Has Little Effect at Colleges," *The New York Times*, December 6, 1977, p. 1.

38. Susan Stern, "Minority Faculty Criticize UC," *Synapse*, April 18, 1980, p. 1.

39. Betty D. Maxwell, *Employment of Minority Ph.D.s: Changes Over Time*, (Washington, D.C.: Commission on Human Resources of the National Research Council, 1981).

40. Burstein, p. 12.

41. Harry Edwards, *The Struggle That Must Be*, (New York: MacMillan, 1980), p. 292.

42. cf. Edward Fiske, "Social Science Data—An Easily Misused Weapon," *San Francisco Chronicle*, January 23, 1980, p. A-5.

43. "The Publishing Game: Getting More for Less," *Science*, 211 (March 1981), pp. 1137-1139.

44. Duncan Lindsey, *The Scientific Public System in Social Science*, (San Francisco: Jossey-Bass, 1978), pp. 120-124.

45. Williams, op. cit., pp. 7-8.
46. cf. Jonathan Kaufman, "The Pressures on a Black Executive," *The Boston Globe*, February 8, 1983, pp. 1, 16.
47. "Why They Choose Separate Tables," *Newsweek on Campus*, op. cit., p. 7.
48. Williams, loc. cit. Whether a black obtains tenure or not is often contingent on when, and at what level, he or she entered the university. Those who arrived during the time of student protests are more likely to be tenured while the more recent entrants are increasingly being denied tenure.
49. Galambos, op. cit., pp. 14-17.
50. Congressman Gus Hawkins, loc. cit.
51. John Wideman, "Publish and Still Perish: The Dilemma of Black Educators on White Campuses," *Black Enterprise*, 10 (September 1978), pp. 44-49.
52. Lichtenstein, loc. cit.
53. Burstein, loc. cit.
54. Pierre Van den Berghe, *Academic Gamesmanship: How To Make a Ph.D. Pay*, (New York: Abelard-Schuman, 1970), pp. 67-68. The comments about blacks are this author's paraphrase of Van den Berghe's description of female faculty members.
55. Kim Jane Scheppele, *When Secrets Become Lies: Privacy and the Social Control of Deception*, a paper presented at the American Sociological Association meeting, San Francisco, September 1982, p. 6.
56. Burstein, loc. cit.
57. Alvin W. Gouldner, *The Future of Intellectuals and the Rise of the New Class*, (New York: The Seabury Press, 1979).
58. Eric Hofer, *The Ordeal of Change*, (New York: Harper and Row, 1963).
59. Joe Reichwein, "Whites on Blacks: Opportunities Plentiful," *The National Leader*, February 17, 1983, p. 12.
60. U.S. Civil Rights Commission, *Unemployment and Underemployment Among Blacks, Hispanics and Women*, (Washington, D.C.: U.S. Government Printing Office, 1982).
61. William J. Goode, "Why Men Resist," in *Family in Transition*, Arlene Skolnick and Jerome Skolnick, editors (Boston: Little, Brown and Company, 1983), p. 207.

FOOTNOTES FROM CHAPTER FIVE

1. George M. Frederickson, *White Supremacy*, (New York: Oxford University Press, 1981).
2. William J. Wilson, *The Declining Significance of Race*, (Chicago: University of Chicago Press, 1978).
3. *Money Income and Poverty Status of Families and Persons in the United States: 1982*, (Washington, D.C.: U.S. Government Printing Office, 1983).
4. Henry E. Felder, *The Changing Patterns of Black Family Income, 1960-1982*, (Washington, D.C.: The Joint Center for Political Studies, 1984).
5. U.S. Department of Justice, Law Enforcement Administration, *Census of Jails and Survey of Jail Inmates 1978. Preliminary Report*, (Washington, D.C.: U.S. Government Printing Office, 1979), p. 2, Table 1.
6. "One-Third Steal on Job, Study Finds," *San Francisco Chronicle*, June 11, 1983, p. 2.
7. Jane Carroll, "Why It's so Tough for Cops to Catch These New Crooks," *San Francisco Examiner*, July 26, 1983, p. B-6.
8. Sandra Gregg, "Professor Gets Prison Term in Kickback Scheme," *The Washington Post*, April 16, 1983, p. D-1.
9. Alfred Blumstein, "On the Racial Disproportionality of United States Prison Populations," *The Journal of Criminal Law and Criminology*, 12 (Fall 1982), pp. 109-118.
10. Robert Staples, *Racism and the Decline of Civilization*, unpublished paper, 1982.
11. "Apartheid's Harsh Grip," *Newsweek*, March 28, 1983, p. 31.
12. David P. Calleo, "An International Look at Taxation," *San Francisco Chronicle*, June 15, 1983, p. A-3.
13. Gerald C. Wright Jr., "Racism and Welfare Policy in America," *Social Science Quarterly*, 57 (March 1977), pp. 718-730.
14. Pete Hamill, "A Big City Weekend of Death," *San Francisco Sunday Examiner and Chronicle, This World*, September 19, 1982, p. 7.
15. Dan Dorfman, "10 Billion To Stay Alive," *San Francisco Examiner*, April 15, 1981, p. D-1.
16. "1 of Every 375 Americans Is a Lawyer: More Coming," *San Francisco Sunday Examiner and Chronicle*, July 31, 1983, p. A-2.
17. *Bureau of Justice Statistics Bulletin*, (Washington, D.C.: United States Department of Justice, April 1982).
18. *Crime in the United States: 1980*, Federal Bureau of Investigation Uniform Crime Report, (Washington, D.C.: Federal Bureau of Investigation, 1981).
19. "America Is Still the Promised Land," *San Francisco Sunday Examiner and Chronicle, This World*, July 15, 1979, p. 26.
20. U.S. Department of Justice, Bureau of Justice Statistics, *Capital Punishment 1984*, (Washington, D.C.: U.S. Department of Justice, August 1985), p. 9.
21. Charles Silberman, *Criminal Violence, Criminal Justice*, (New York: Random House, 1977).
22. Law Enforcement Assistance Administration, *Criminal Victimization in the United States: January-June 1973*, (Washington, D.C.: U.S. Government Printing Office, November 1974), Vol. 1, p. 3.
23. Bureau of Labor Statistics cited in *The National Leader*, August 25, 1983, p. 4.

24. A. Leon Higginbotham, *In the Matter of Color: Race and the American Legal Process, The Colonial Period,* (New York: Oxford University Press, 1978).

25. The National Minority Advisory Council on Criminal Justice to the Law Enforcement Assistance Agency, *The Inequality of Justice. A Report on Crime and the Administration of Justice in the Minority Community,* (Rockville, Maryland: National Criminal Justice Reference Service, 1982).

26. Scott Christianson, *Disproportionate Imprisonment of Blacks in the United States: Policy, Practice, Impact and Change,* unpublished paper prepared for the National Association of Blacks in Criminal Justice, March 1982.

27. Blumstein, op. cit.

28. William G. Nagel, Statement before the Subcommitee on Penitentiaries and Corrections, United States Senate, October 6, 1977.

29. *The Inequality of Justice,* op. cit.

30. Thomas C. Fleming, "Weekly Report," *Sun Reporter,* June 9, 1983, p. 14.

31. "Crime's Link to Hard Times," *San Francisco Chronicle,* August 9, 1981, p. 7.

32. "Blacks' Environment More Stressful than White," *Jet,* September 5, 1983, p. 7.

33. "Black Feel Powerless in American Society: Poll," *Jet,* August 24, 1983, p. 12.

34. "Urban Crime—'A Kind of Guerilla Warfare'," *San Francisco Chronicle, This World,* September 27, 1981, p. 17.

35. P.O. Montaga, *Occupations and Society: Toward a Sociology of the Labor Market,* (New York: John Wiley and Sons, 1977).

36. Phillip J. Bowman, "Toward a Dual Labor-Market Approach to Black-on-Black Homicide," *Public Health Reports,* 95 (November-December 1980), pp. 555-556.

37. *America's Black Population: 1970 to 1982. A Statistical View,* (Washington, D.C.: U.S. Government Printing Office, 1983).

38. Ruth M. Glick and Virginia V. Neto, *National Study of Women's Correctional Programs,* (Washington, D.C.: U.S. Government Printing Office, June 1977).

39. Cassia Spohn, Susan Welch and John Gruhl, "Women Defendants in Court: The Interaction Between Sex and Race in Convicting and Sentencing," a paper presented at the American Sociological Association meeting, San Francisco, 1982.

40. "Those American Kids Who Kill and Rob," *San Francisco Chronicle,* May 4, 1977, p. 17.

41. "Urban Crime—'A Kind of Guerilla Warfare'," loc. cit.

42. Ibid.

43. Frantz Fanon, *The Wretched of the Earth,* (New York: Grove Press, 1966), p. 31.

44. Albert J. Reiss Jr., "Police Brutality—Answers to Key Questions," *Transaction,* (July-August 1968), pp. 10-19.

45. *The New York Times,* November 5, 1980, p. 1.

46. *San Francisco Examiner,* June 20, 1983, p. A-9.

47. "New Questions Arise on Policing Police," *The New York Times,* April 4, 1983, p. E-4.

48. Louis Lomax, *The Negro Revolt,* (New York: New American Library, 1962), p. 59.

49. Patrick Osten, "Find Black Men Most Likely To Be Shot by Cops," *Chicago Sun Times,* May 16, 1977, p. 4.

50. "Black Police Face Racism, Hostility," *The National Leader,* May 17, 1982, p. 6.

51. "N.Y.'s Black Cops Quite Police Union," *San Francisco Chronicle,* December 9, 1976, p. 38.

52. John A. Williams, "One More Time: Cops!" *The National Leader*, August 25, 1983, p. 15.
53. The Rand Corporation, *Racial Disparities in the Criminal Justice System*, (Santa Monica, California: The Rand Corporation, July 1983).
54. Richard P. McGlynn, James C. Megas and Daniel Benson, "Sex and Race in Factors Affecting the Attribution of Insanity in a Murder Trial," *Journal of Psychology*, 93 (April 1976), pp. 93-99.
55. "Law Suppresses Minorities, Panel Says," *San Francisco Chronicle*, October 18, 1980, p. 6.
56. "Blacks on Death Rows in U.S. Prisons," *Ebony*, (September 1983), p. 34.
57. William Bowers, *Executions in America*, (Lexington, Massachusetts: Lexington Books, 1974), p. 78.
58. "The Record Number on Death Rows in the U.S.," *San Francisco Chronicle*, July 5, 1983, p.36.
59. Neal Pierce, "Rx for Penal Sanity: Fewer Prisons," *San Francisco Sunday Examiner and Chronicle*, June 19, 1983, p. B-9.
60. United States Department of Justice, *Prisoners in State and Federal Institutions*, (Washington, D.C.: 1980).
61. "Judge Says Jail Unsafe for Prisoner," *San Francisco Chronicle*, April 10, 1981, p. 3.

FOOTNOTES FROM CHAPTER SIX

1. Karl Marx, *Selected Writings in Sociology and Social Philosophy*, (London: McGraw Hill, 1964).
2. Sterling Brown, "Negro Characters as Seen by White Authors," *Journal of Negro Education*, 2 (April 1933), pp. 179-203.
3. Thomas R. Cripps, "The Death of Rastus: Negroes in American Films Since 1945, *Phylon*, 28 (Fall 1967), pp. 267-275.
4. Alvin Poussaint, "Blaxploitation Movies–Cheap Thrills That Degrade Blacks," *Psychology Today*, 7 (February 1974), pp. 22-33.
5. Charles Allen, "In Defense of Bad Black Movies," *The Black Scholar*, 4 (December 1972), pp. 62-63.
6. Takashi Bufford, "Casting Call: Only Morons or Villains Need Apply," *The National Leader*, May 5, 1983, p. 19.
7. Ibid., p. 18.
8. Ernie Hudson, quoted in "A Hit Movie Payoff. There's More to Life than Ghostbusting," *San Francisco Chronicle*, August 14, 1984, p. 36.
9. Bufford, op. cit., p. 19.
10. Robert Chrisman, "Subjective Factors in the Reelection of Ronald Reagan," *The Black Scholar*, 16 (January/February 1985), p. 15.
11. David Sterritt, "Movies Revert to the Old Stereotypes," *San Francisco Examiner*, August 10, 1984, p. E-10.
12. "Fighting Back in Hollywood," *Black Enterprise*, September 1982, p. 28-35.
13. "Fewer Female TV Writers–Bias Blamed," *San Francisco Chronicle*, December 28, 1982, p. 31.
14. Joel Selvin, "Safe Reggae From Ten Guys Who Decided to Form a Band," *San Francisco Chronicle*, February 24, 1984, p. 66.
15. John Rockwell, "In Pop Music, The Races Remain Far Apart," *The New York Times*, March 18, 1984, p. 4-1.
16. "Black Music Association Launches Campaign to Get Blacks in Music Mainstream," *Jet*, June 11, 1984, p. 18.
17. Rockwell, loc. cit.
18. Betty Pleasant, "Is MTV Racist?," *Los Angeles Sentinel*, December 8, 1983, p. A-3.
19. "More Whites Buying Music by Black Artists: Survey," *Jet*, July 16, 1984, p. 19.
20. "Herbie Hancock said 'No' to Blacks in Rocket Video," *Jet*, January 9, 1984, p. 15.
21. "Roberta Flack Says Black Music Stars Not Equal," *Jet*, June 18, 1981, p. 55.
22. Peter Stack, "Women Pull Music Pursestrings," *San Francisco Chronicle*, July 25, 1984, p. 52.
23. Peabo Bryson quoted in "Black Balladeer on a Crossover Mission," *San Francisco Chronicle*, August 20, 1984, p. 43.
24. "BMA Confab Charges Whites Shortchange Black Music," *Jet*, June 18, 1981, p. 59.
25. Pleasant, op. cit., p. 18.
26. Stack, loc. cit.
27. Pamela Douglas, "Minority Groups Push Olympic ABC-TV Hirings," *The National Leader*, December 29, 1984, p. 5.
28. J. Fred MacDonald, *Blacks and White TV, Afro-Americans in Television Since 1948*, (Chicago: Nelson Hall Publishers, 1983), p. xv.

29. Ibid., p. 21.
30. Ibid.
31. W. Agustus Law and Virgil A. Clift, editors, *Encyclopedia of Black America*, (New York: DeCaper Press, 1981), p. 723.
32. MacDonald, op. cit., pp. 3, 4, 12.
33. Leonard Maltin and Richard Bann, *Our Gang, The Life and Times of the Little Rascals*, (New York: Crown Publishers, Inc., 1977), p. 1.
34. Ibid., p. 259.
35. Ibid., p. 258.
36. Law and Clift, op. cit., p. 723.
37. MacDonald, op. cit., p. 27.
38. Ibid., p. 29.
39. Law and Clift, op. cit., p. 724.
40. Tim Bracks and Earl March, *The Complete Directory to Prime Time Network TV*, (New York: Ballantine Books, 1979), pp. 439-440.
41. Law and Clift, op. cit., p. 724.
42. Lynn Norment, "The Bill Cosby Show, The Real Life Drama Behind the TV Show About a Black Family," *Ebony*, 40 (April 1985), p. 28.
43. Emory Bogardus, *Immigration and Race Attitudes*, (New York: Heath, 1928).
44. Kark Mannheim, *Ideology and Utopia*, (New York: Harcourt, Brace and World, 1930), p. 36.
45. Harold Cruse, *The Crisis of the Negro Intellectual*, (New York: Morrow, 1967), p. 166.
46. Ralph Ellison, "A Very Stern Discipline," *Harpers*, (March 1967), pp. 76-95.
47. Douglas, loc. cit.
48. "Big Media, Big Money," *Newsweek*, April 1, 1985, pp. 52-59.
49. MacDonald, op. cit., p. 8.
50. Pamela Douglas, "Fighting MAAD About Hollywood Film Discrimination," *The National Leader*, October 7, 1982, p. 21.
51. W.I. Thomas and Dorothy Thomas, *The Child in America: Behavior Problems and Programs*, (New York: Knopf, 1928), p. 572.
52. Tony Brown, "How to Watch White TV," *Sun Reporter*, November 25, 1982, p. 6.
53. Richard L. Allen, "TV Research and Blacks," *Sun Reporter*, October 14, 1982, p. 6.
54. Tom Joe and Peter Yu, *The Flipside of Black Families Headed by Women: The Economic Status of Black Men*, (Washington, D.C.: Center for the Study of Social Policy, April 1984).
55. Jonathan Kozol, *Illiterate America*, (New York: Doubleday, 1985).
56. Norment, op. cit., p. 30.
57. Charles Fuller quoted inn "Blues for Black Actors," *Time*, October 1, 1984, p. 76.
58. Ibid., p. 75.

FOOTNOTES FROM CHAPTER SEVEN

1. Wade Nobles, "Toward An Empirical and Theoretical Framework for Defining Black Families," *Journal of Marriage and the Family*, 40 (November 1978), pp. 679-690.
2. Arthur Mathis, "Contrasting Approaches to the Study of Black Families," *Journal of Marriage and the Family*, 40 (November 1978), pp. 667-678.
3. Leonard Lieberman, "The Emerging Model of the Black Family," *International Journal of Sociology of the Family*, 3 (March 1973), pp. 10-22.
4. E. Franklin Frazier, *The Negro Family in the United States*, (Chicago: University of Chicago Press, 1939).
5. Nobles, op. cit.
6. Eugene Genovese, *Roll, Jordan, Roll: The World the Slaves Made*, (New York: Random House, 1974).
7. Denise Paulme, editor, *Women of Tropical Africa*, (Berkeley: University of California Press, 1963).
8. George P. Ranier, *The American Slave: From Sundown to Sunup*, (Westport, Connecticut: Greenwood Press, 1972).
9. John Blassingame, *The Slave Community*, (New York: Oxford, 1972).
10. Herbert Gutman, *The Black Family in Slavery and Freedom, 1750-1925*, (New York: Pantheon Books, 1976).
11. Virginia Young, "Family and Childhood in a Southern Negro Community," *American Anthropologist*, LXXII (April 1970), pp. 269-288.
12. Niara Sudarkasa, "Interpreting the African Heritage in Afro-American Family Organization," *Black Families*, Harriette McAdoo, editor, (Beverly Hills: Sage Publications, 1981), pp. 37-53.
13. Nathan Hare and Julia Hare, *The Endangered Black Family*, (San Francisco: Black Think Tank, 1984).
14. Florence Halpern, *Survival Black/White*, (Elmsford, New York: Pergamon Press, 1972).
15. Alyce Gullattee, "Black Sensuality," *Essence*, 2 (November 1971), pp. 28-31.
16. Melvin Zelnik, John Kanther and Kathleen Ford, *Sex and Pregnancy in Adolescence*, (Beverly Hills: Sage Publications, 1981).
17. Robert Staples, *The World of Black Singles: Changing Patterns of Male-Female Relations*, (Westport, Connecticut: Greenwood Press, 1981).
18. Ibid.
19. Thomas Pettigrew et. al., "Color Gradations and Attitudes Among Middle Income Negroes," *American Sociological Review*, 31 (June 1966), pp. 365-374.
20. Staples, loc. cit.
21. Robert Staples, "The Role and Importance of Beauty in the Black Community," *Black Male/Female Relationships*, 3 (Autumn 1982), pp. 32-40.
22. David Heer, "The Prevalence of Black-White Marriage in the United States, 1960 and 1970," *Journal of Marriage and the Family*, 36 (May 1974), pp. 246-259.
23. Ernest Porterfied, "Mixed Marriage," *Psychology Today*, 6 (January 1973), pp. 71-78.
24. Nathan Hare and Julia Hare, loc. cit.
25. U.S. Bureau of the Census, *America's Black Population 1970 to 1982: A Statistical Review*, (Washington, D.C.: U.S. Government Printing Office, 1983).

26. Paul Glick and Karen Mills, *Black Families: Marriage Patterns and Living Arrangements*, (Atlanta, Georgia: Atlanta University, 1974).

27. U.S. Bureau of the Census, *America's Black Population 1970 to 1982*, op. cit.

28. Carol Morton, "Mistakes Black Men Make in Relating to Black Women," *Ebony, 30*, (December 1975), p. 171.

29. Tom Joe and Peter Yu, *The Flip Side of Black Families Headed by Women: The Economic Status of Black Men*, (Washington, D.C.: Center for the Study of Social Policy, 1984).

30. National Urban League Research Department, *Quarterly Economic Report on the Black Worker*, 2 (Spring 1975), pp. 1-8.

31. P. Kihss, "New Study Says Relief System Penalizes Intact Families Here," *The New York Times*, June 15, 1975, p. 1.

32. J. Jones, "Father's Side Can't Compete with Welfare," *Los Angeles Times*, March 26, 1971, p. 22.

33. L. Long and R. Lynne, *"Migration and Income Differences Between Black and White Men in the North,"* American Journal of Sociology, 80 (March 1975), pp. 1391-1409.

34. Karen Renne, "Correlates of Dissatisfaction in Marriage," *Journal of Marriage and the Family*, 32 (February 1970), pp. 54-67.

35. U.S. Bureau of the Census, *America's Black Population 1970 to 1982,* op. cit.

36. Morton, loc. cit.

37. J. Ford, "Black Men and Women: Deteriorating Relationships," *Los Angeles Sentinel*, March 1, 1973, p. C-13.

38. Glick and Mills, op. cit., p. 10.

39. J. Slevin, "Money Woes Felt by Black Women," *The Washington Post*, April 3, 1972, p. D-12.

40. Jesus Velasco-Rice and Lizbeth Mynko, "Suicide and Marital Status: A Changing Relationship," *Journal of Marriage and the Family,* 35 (May 1973), pp. 239-244.

41. Black Women's Community Development Foundation, *Mental and Physical Health Problems of Black Women*, (Washington, D.C.: Black Women's Community Development Foundation, 1975), pp. 27, 40.

42. U.S. Bureau of the Census, *America's Black Population 1970 to 1982*, loc. cit.

43. Robert Staples, *Black Masculinity: The Black Male's Role in American Society*, (San Francisco: The Black Scholar Press, 1982).

44. Michael Malloy, "The Black Kid's Burden," *The National Observer*, November 15, 1975, p. 18.

45. Carol B. Stack, *All Our Kin*, (New York: Harper and Row, 1974).

46. U.S. Bureau of the Census, *America's Black Population 1970 to 1982,* loc. cit.

47. F. Willis, personal communication, 1983.

48. U.S. Bureau of the Census, *Fertility of American Women: June 1983*, (Washington, D.C.: U.S. Government Printing Office, 1984).

49. Naomi Gray, "Sterilization and the Black Female: An Historical Perspective," *Mental and Physical Health Problems of Black Women*, op. cit., pp. 80-90.

50. U.S. Bureau of the Census, *Fertility of American Women: June 1983*, op. cit.

51. Ruth McKay, "One-Child Families and Atypical Sex Ratios in an Elite Black Community," *The Black Family: Essays and Studies*, 2nd edition (Belmont, California: Wadsworth, 1978), pp. 177-181.

52. Diane K. Lewis, "The Black Family: Socialization and Sex Roles," *Phylon*, 36 (Fall 1975), pp. 221-237.
53. Roger H. Rubin, "Adult Male Absence and the Self Attitudes of Black Children," *Child Study Journal*, 4 (Spring 1974), pp. 33-45.
54. Stack, loc. cit.
55. Noel Cazanave and Murray Straus, "Race, Class Network Embeddedness and Family Violence: A Search for Potent Support Systems," *Journal of Comparative Family Studies*, 10 (Fall 1979), pp. 281-300.
56. U.S. Bureau of the Census, *State and Metropolitan Area Data Book*, (Washington, D.C.: U.S. Government Printing Office, 1982).

FOOTNOTES FROM CHAPTER EIGHT

1. Manning Marable, "Black Political Power: Illusion and Reality," *Los Angeles Sentinel*, June 13, 1984, p. A-7.
2. U.S. Bureau of the Census, *Voting and Registration in the Election of November 1984*, (Washington, D.C.: U.S. Government Printing Office, 1985).
3. Bart Landry quoted in "Economy, Bias Bog Blacks," *The Prince George's Journal*, April 27, 1982, p. A-7.
4. Ibid.
5. Laura McGinley, "Blue-Collar Workers, Blacks, Teens Hit Hardest by Slump's Joblessness," *The Wall Street Journal*, May 5, 1982, p. 1.
6. "Federal Firings Come Faster," *San Francisco Chronicle*, Sepember 4, 1982, p. 9.
7. David Rosenbaum, "Blacks Would Feel Extra Impact From Cuts Proposed by President," *The New York Times*, June 14, 1981, p. 1.
8. Saul Friedman, "Blacks Say They're Getting Wrong Number at White House," *San Francisco Examiner*, September 3, 1981, p. A-13.
9. Manning Marable, "George Wallace Returns: Never Again," *Sun Reporter*, November 4, 1982, p. 8.
10. William J. Bowers, *Executions in America*, (Lexington, Massachusetts: Lexington Books, 1975).
11. Pete Hamill, "A Simple Solution," *San Francisco Chronicle*, August 3, 1982, p. 35.
12. Quoted in *Newsweek*, November 1, 1982, p. 36.
13. "Block Grants Don't Help Poor, Study Says," *San Francisco Chronicle*, July 22, 1981, p. 11.
14. Gerald C. Wright Jr., "Racism and Welfare Policy in America," *Social Science Quarterly*, 57 (March 1977), pp. 718-730.
15. John Ehrlichman, *Witness To Power*, (New York: Simon & Schuster, 1982).
16. Tony Brown's Comments, "Race Decides Political Outcome," *Sun Reporter*, September 2, 1982, p. 6.
17. Adam C. Lymer, "Black Political Influence is Lowest in Two Decades," *The New York Times*, June 3, 1981, p. B-1.
18. Wallace Turner, "Bradley Tests Prospects for Gubernatorial Run," *The New York Times*, July 26, 1982, p. 1.
19. Wallace Turner, "Coast Rivals Fight for Middle of the Road," *The New York Times*, October 17, 1982, p. 16.
20. Larry Liebert, "Race No Issue for L.A. Mayor–Not Yet," *San Francisco Chronicle*, April 10, 1981, p. 12.
21. Herb Caen, "I Choose Freedom," *San Francisco Chronicle*, November 1, 1982, p. 27.
22. Wallace Turner, "Coast Rivals Fight for Middle of the Road," loc. cit.
23. Ibid.
24. Wallace Turner, "Bradley Tests Prospects for Gubernatorial Run," loc. cit.
25. John Balzar, "Deukmejian's Denials," *San Francisco Chronicle*, October 9, 1982, p. 1.
26. Liebert, loc. cit.
27. Peter Dworkin, "A Minority Population Boom in State," *San Francisco Chronicle*, October 21, 1982, p. 1.
28. Tony Brown's Comments, "Race Decides Political Outcome," loc. cit.

29. John Jacobs, "Bradley's Aides Find A Few Harsh Reasons for Unexpected Loss," *San Francisco Sunday Examiner and Chronicle*, November 7, 1982, p. A-14.

30. Larry Liebert, "Post Mortems," *San Francisco Chronicle*, November 4, 1982, p. 57.

31. John Balzar, "Why Pollsters Goofed," *San Francisco Chronicle*, November 4, 1982, p. 1.

32. W.E. Barnes, "Exit Polls Show Hidden Racism Hurt Bradley," *San Francisco Examiner*, November 3, 1982, p. A-12.

33. Ibid.

34. Willie Brown's Views on Bradley, *San Francisco Chronicle*, March 18, 1983, p. 12.

35. Reverend B.A. Meshack, "Preacher Questions Church's Role in Bradley's Defeat," *Los Angeles Sentinel*, November 18, 1982, p. A-2.

36. Mervin Field, "The Four Keys to Bradley's Election Defeat," *San Francisco Chronicle*, February 2, 1983, p. 9.

37. "Bradley Already Looking Toward The 1986 Race," *San Francisco Sunday Examiner and Chronicle*, November 21, 1982, p. B-3.

38. Larry Liebert, "Bradley Leads Deukmejian in New Poll," *San Francisco Chronicle*, August 19, 1985, p. 1.

39. Judith Cummings, "Like Los Angeles, Bradley Stands Tall," *The New York Times*, April 7, l985, p. 4-E.

40. Judith Cummings, "Coast Mayor Seems To Be Preparing to Run Again," *The New York Times*, September 30, 1984, p. 12.

41. Ibid.

42. c.f. Manning Marable, *Black American Politics*, (London: Verso, 1985), Chapter 5.

43. Shirley Chisholm, *The Good Fight*, (New York: Harper and Row, 1973).

44. Lance Williams, "How Our Experts Rated Debate," *San Francisco Examiner*, June 4, 1984, p. A-2.

45. E.R. Shipp, "Jackson to Put Energies into Political Coalition," *The New York Times*, November 10, 1984, p. 7.

46. "Voter Study Shows Jackson Was Weak Among Whites," *Los Angeles Sentinel*, September 19, 1985, p. A-1.

47. "Andrew Young Belittles Mondale Aides," *San Francisco Chronicle*, August 18, 1984, p. 6.

48. c.f. Charles Hamilton, "The Phenomenon of the Jesse Jackson Candidacy and the 1984 Presidential Election," *The State of Black America*, (New York: The National Urban League, 1985), pp. 21-36.

49. Ronald Smothers, "Election Results Troubling Blacks," *The New York Times*, November 9,1984, p. 12.

50. "White Males No Longer Majority of Workforce," *San Francisco Chronicle*, July 31, 1981, p. 1.

51. "Jesse Jackson: Press Downgrades Blacks," *San Francisco Examiner*, September 18, 1985, p. A-8.

52. Quoted in Derrick Martin, "Symposium Analyzes Jackson's Coalition," *Sun Reporter*, July 25, 1985, p. 1.

53. Robert Chrisman, "Subjective Factors in the Re-election of Ronald Reagan," *The Black Scholar*, 16 (January/February 1985), p. 19.

FOOTNOTES FROM CHAPTER NINE

1. U.S. Bureau of the Census, *Current Population Reports*, Series P-20, (Washington, D.C.: U.S. Government Printing Office, 1983).
2. "Where Minorities Are Majority," *San Francisco Chronicle*, October 17, 1984, p. 8.
3. William O'Hare, "Blacks on the Move," *Focus*, May 1984, p. 7. However, between 1981 and 1982 that pattern was reversed and there was a small net out-migration of blacks from the South and a small net migration of blacks into the North.
4. L. Long and L. Heltman, "Migration and Income Differences Between Black and White Men in the North," *American Journal of Sociology*, 80 (May, 1975), pp. 1391-1409.
5. Alvis V. Adair, *Desegregation: The Illusion of Black Progress*, (Lanham, Maryland: University Press of America, 1984).
6. "Educators Worried Over Loss of Black Teachers," *Jet*, April 4, 1983, p. 22.
7. U.S. Bureau of the Census, *Farm Population of the United States 1982*, (Washington, D.C.: U.S. Government Printing Office, 1983). Only 3.2 percent of the farm population in the U.S. is black.
8. Thad Martin, "The Disappearing Black Farmer," *Ebony*, (June 1985), pp. 145-148.
9. Elliot Currie and Paul Rosenstiel, "The Bleak Statistics of Urban Life Carter Must Try to Change," *San Francisco Examiner*, March 22, 1978, p. 9.
10. E.C. Foster and Tekie Fessehatzion, "Blacks and Economic Conditions: The Case of Mississippi Since 1965," *Western Journal of Black Studies*, 8 (Fall 1984), pp. 122-130. The percentage of Southern Blacks in poverty in 1982 was 39 percent, the same proportion as existed there in 1970.
11. William E. Schmidt, "Atlanta's Years of Progress Temper New Racial Disputes," *The New York Times*, May 6, 1985, p. 1.
12. John Jacobs, "Dramatic Changes in Workforce Coming," *San Francisco Examiner*, October 15, 1985, p. C-8.
13. Andrew Brimmer, "The Future of Blacks in the Public Sector," *Black Enterprise*, (November 1985), p. 39.
14. "Trends in Urban Black Population," *San Francisco Chronicle*, August 20, 1981, p. 26.
15. Vera Glaser, "Report: Minorities Made Progress but Less than White Men," *San Francisco Examiner*, August 3, 1978, p. 9.
16. Alphonso Pinkney, *The Myth of Black Progress*, (New York: Cambridge University Press, 1985).
17. Henry Allen Bullock, *A History of Negro Education in the South*, (New York: Praeger, 1970), pp. 1-35.
18. Faustine C. Jones-Wilson, "The State of Urban Education," *The State of Black America 1984*, (New York: The National Urban League, 1985), pp. 95-118.
19. "Study Shows How Schools Victimize Poor," *San Francisco Examiner*, January 25, 1985, p. A-6.
20. Eldridge Cleaver, "Education and Revolution," *The Black Scholar*, 1 (November 1969), pp. 44-53.
21. U.S. Bureau of the Census, *Finances of the Public School Systems in 1982-83*, (Washington, D.C.: U.S. Government Printing Office, 1985).

22. National Center for Education Statistics, *Characteristics of Households with Children Enrolled in Elementary and Secondary Schools*, (Washington, D.C.: U.S. Department of Education, September 1984).

23. Thomas Ferraro, "Civil Rights Pendulum Swinging Back," *San Francisco Sunday Examiner and Chronicle*, May 13, 1984, p. A-8.

24. "Educational Opportunity Has Lessened For Blacks," *Big Red News*, May 25, 1985, p. 10.

25. Walter Karp, "Why Johnny Can't Think: The Politics of Bad Schooling," *This World*, July 12, 1985, p. 13.

26. Jonathan Kozol, *Illiteracy in America*, (New York: Doubleday, 1985).

27. Frances Fox Piven and Richard A. Cloward, *Regulating the Poor: The Functions of Public Welfare*, (New York: Vintage, 1971).

28. Ibid.

29. Pinkney, loc. cit.

30. Bayard Rustin, "The Poor Get Poorer," *Los Angeles Sentinel*, September 20, 1984, p. A-6.

31. George Gallup, "One of Every 5 Adults in U.S. Can't Always Afford Food," *San Francisco Chronicle*, March 19, 1984, p. 7.

32. Jon Margolis, "Just Desserts," *San Francisco Examiner*, February 2, 1984, p. B-3.

33. U.S. Bureau of the Census, "Third of U.S. Households Receive Noncash Aid," *Data User News*, Volume 16, (Washington, D.C.: U.S. Department of Commerce, May 1981), p. 2.

34. Ellen Hume, "A Book Attacking Welfare System Stirs Furor in Washington," *The Wall Street Journal*, September 17, 1985, p. 1.

35. Tom Joe and Peter Yu, *The Flip Side of Families Headed by Women: The Economic Status of Black Men*, (Washington, D.C.: Center for the Study of Social Policy, 1984).

36. Veronica G. Thomas, "Black Youth Unemployment: Issues, Concerns and Strategies for Change," *Urban Research Review*, Volume 9, No. 3 (1984), pp. 1-3.

37. William J. Wilson, "Industrial Policy and the Concerns of Minorities," *Focus*, 12 (March 1984), pp. 5-6.

38. Ibid.

39. Thomas, loc. cit.

40. U.S. Department of Labor, *Employent in Perspective: Minority Workers*, (Washington, D.C.: Bureau of Labor Statistics, Second Quarter, 1985).

41. Claude Brown, "Manchild 1984," *This World*, September 23, 1984, pp. 7-8.

42. "Anti-Black Bias in Housing—New Survey," *San Francisco Chronicle*, April 17, 1978, p. 1.

43. O'Hare, loc. cit.

44. Frank White III, "The Yuppies Are Coming, Young, Affluent Whites Are Taking Over Urban Ghettos," *Ebony*, (April 1985), pp. 155-160.

45. Quoted in Ken Noble, "The Black and White Washington," *The New York Times*, March 21, 1984, p. B-12.

46. Ibid.

47. Peter Grier, "The Springs of Racial Poison Are Not Dry Yet," *San Francisco Examiner*, July 2, 1984, p. C-3.

48. Robert E. Suggs, "A New Weapon Against Housing Bias," *Focus*, 12 (March 1984), pp. 3-4.

49. "Discrimination Is Reported in Federal Housing Projects," *The New York Times*, February 11, 1985, p. 11.
50. Andrew Brimmer, "Sources of Income for Blacks vs. Whites," *Black Enterprise*, (August 1983), p. 33.
51. "More Young Blacks, Women Among Homeless in Nation," *Jet*, July 2, 1984, p. 28.
52. Neal Pierce, "Tough Talk From A Lame Duck Mayor," *San Francisco Sunday Examiner and Chronicle*, December 18, 1983, p. B-11.
53. Robert Davis, *Black Suicide in the Seventies: Current Trends and Perspectives*, Institute for Research on Poverty, (Madison: University of Wisconsin-Madison, March 1978).
54. "Operating Room Racism Studies," *San Francisco Chronicle*, November 24, 1977, p. 75.
55. John Conyers, Jr., "Black Health Problems—Symptom of Social Ills," *Synapse*, February 23, 1984, p. 3.
56. Earl Ofari, *The Myth of Black Capitalism*, (New York: Monthly Review Press, 1970), p. 10.
57. Tony Brown, "Blacks Produce Unemployment and White Wealth," *Sun Reporter*, May 29, 1985, p. 6.
58. Marvin E. Perry, "The Colonial Analogy and Economic Development," *The Black Scholar*, 5 (February 1974), pp. 37-42.
59. U.S. Bureau of the Census, *Minority-Owned Businesses – Black*, (Washington, D.C.: U.S. Government Printing Office, 1985).
60. Quoted in "The American Assembly," *Black Economic Development*, (Englewood Cliffs, New Jersey: Prentice-Hall, 1969), p. 53.
61. Brown, loc. cit.
62. *Recent Changes in Black Owned Businesses*, (Washington, D.C.: Joint Center for Political Studies, 1985).
63. Milton Moskowitz, "Black Businesses Far Behind," *San Francisco Chronicle*, May 31, 1985, p. 41.
64. Perry, loc. cit.
65. David Caplivitz, *The Poor Pay More*, (New York: The Free Press, 1963).
66. Duncan Williams, "Why Democrats Can't Solve Problems Facing Cleveland," *The Militant*, August 3, 1973, p. 18.
67. Carl B. Stokes, "From Legislator to Mayor, and Now A Judge," *Ebony*, (August 1984), pp. 136-138.
68. "Some Cities Caught in Financial Bind," *San Francisco Chronicle*, December 29, 1983, p. 8.
69. Quoted in *Sun Reporter*, June 8, 1978, p. 6.
70. "The Strikebreaker," *Newsweek*, April 25, 1977, p. 29.
71. Robert Pear, "Total of Black U.S. Mayors Up Sharply in Year," *The New York Times*, March 22, 1985, p. 1.
72. U.S. Bureau of the Census, *Voting and Registration in the Election of November 1984*, (Washington, D.C.: U.S. Government Printing Office, 1985).
73. c.f. Manning Marable, *Black American Politics*, (London: Verso, 1985).
74. Mike Royko, "Black and White," *San Francisco Chronicle*, September 14, 1984, p. B-2.
75. David Broder, "The Unraveling of a City," *San Francisco Chronicle*, April 4, 1983, p. 32.

76. Brian Kelly, "Chicago Is Stalled," *Cleveland Plain Dealer*, April 22, 1985, p. 7-B.

77. "Black Mayoral Bids Hinge on White Votes," *The National Leader*, November 10,1983, p. 7.

78. Simeon Booker, "Ticker Tape U.S.A.," *Jet*, December 31, 1984, p. 9.

79. Peter Eisinger, *Black Employment in City Government*, (Washington, D.C.: Joint Center for Political Studies), 1983.

80. Bernard Anderson, "The Folly of the Subminimum Wage," *Focus*, (June 1984), p. 12.

81. "Philadelphians Back Mayor's Actions, Polls Show," *San Francisco Chronicle*, May 16, 1985, p. 4.

82. "Draw The Line," *The Philadelphia Inquirer*, September 25, 1985.

83. Joe Reichwein, "Whites on Blacks: Opportunities Plentiful," *The National Leader*, February 17, 1983, p. 12.

84. Joel Dreyfuss, "The New Racism," *Black Enterprise*, (January 1978), p. 42.

85. Panos Bardis, "Negro Social Inequality and White Guilt in the U.S.A.," *Separata De La Revista Del Instituto De Ciencias Sociales*, (1972), pp. 353-375.

86. "Dramatic Drops for Minorities," *Time*, November 11, 1985, p. 84.

87. University of California System Vice President William Baker quoted in "Tough Questions for UC As It Heads Toward Prosperity," *San Francisco Examiner*, January 31, 1984, p. A-3.

88. Mark Granovetter, *Getting A Job: A Study of Contacts and Careers*, (Cambridge, Massachusetts: Harvard University Press, 1974).

89. David Broder, "Looking Out for the Middle Class," *San Francisco Chronicle*, October 8, 1984, p. 40.

90. Thomas Edsall and Haynes Johnson, "Voter Registration Cuts Both Ways," *San Francisco Chronicle*, July 18, 1984, p. A-5.

91. Quoted in "The Limelight Shifts, but Jesse Jackson Fights On," *San Francisco Chronicle*, August 8, 1985, p. 11.

92. Manning Marable, "Ronald Reagan's Racial Appointments," *Los Angeles Sentinel*, July 20, 1985, p. A-7.

93. "Study Says Blacks Have Lost Ground," *The New York Times*, October 6, 1984, p. 1.

94. Bill Moyers, CBS News Telecast, November 6, 1984.

95. Roger Wilkins, "Turning Away From America's Most Vulnerable People," *San Francisco Chronicle*, November 28, 1984, p. A-2.

96. Stanley Robertson, "What We Gotta Do," *Los Angeles Sentinel*, November 1, 1984, p. A-6.

97. "U.S. Report Sees More Race Tension," *San Francisco Examiner*, May 6, 1985.

98. Jane Jacobs, *Cities and the Wealth of Nations*, (New York: Random House, 1984).

99. Roxanne Mitchell and Frank Weiss, *A House Divided: Labor and White Supremacy*, (New York: United Labor Press, 1981).

100. Lerone Bennett Jr., "Black Bourgeoisie Revisited," *Ebony*, (August 1973), p. 55.

101. Huey Newton, *Revolutionary Suicide*, (New York: Harcourt Brace Jovanovich, 1973).